AF212097

ONE NATION UNDER LAW

This groundbreaking volume shatters many long-standing myths about the Declaration of Independence. Although states-rights advocates have long claimed that the Declaration created thirteen independent nations, Carlton F.W. Larson shows that the Declaration announced the birth of a new nation: the United States of America, a nation governed by an unwritten constitution in which the states were confederated and subject to national authority from the very beginning. Larson counters libertarian claims that the Declaration views government as a necessary evil, demonstrating instead how it embraces constitutionalism, active government, and the rule of law as positive goods. Along the way, Larson debunks other myths, such as the notion that the Declaration is the parchment text enshrined in the National Archives and that it was authored by Thomas Jefferson. By exploring the true meaning of the Declaration of Independence, *One Nation Under Law* helps us better understand America itself.

Carlton F.W. Larson is a Martin Luther King, Jr. Professor at UC Davis School of Law, where he teaches constitutional law and legal history. He is the author of the books *The Trials of Allegiance: Treason, Juries, and the American Revolution* and *On Treason: A Citizen's Guide to the Law*.

One Nation Under Law

THE MEANING OF
THE DECLARATION
OF INDEPENDENCE

Carlton F.W. Larson

University of California, Davis, School of Law

CAMBRIDGE
UNIVERSITY PRESS

Shaftesbury Road, Cambridge CB2 8EA, United Kingdom

One Liberty Plaza, 20th Floor, New York, NY 10006, USA

477 Williamstown Road, Port Melbourne, VIC 3207, Australia

314–321, 3rd Floor, Plot 3, Splendor Forum, Jasola District Centre, New Delhi – 110025, India

Cambridge University Press is part of Cambridge University Press & Assessment, a department of the University of Cambridge.

We share the University's mission to contribute to society through the pursuit of education, learning and research at the highest international levels of excellence.

www.cambridge.org
Information on this title: www.cambridge.org/9781009789028
DOI: 10.1017/9781009789073

© Carlton F.W. Larson 2026

This publication is in copyright. Subject to statutory exception and to the provisions of relevant collective licensing agreements, no reproduction of any part may take place without the written permission of Cambridge University Press & Assessment.

When citing this work, please include a reference to the
DOI 10.1017/9781009789073

First published 2026

Cover image: A Declaration by the representatives of the United States of America in General Congress, July 4, 1776. Image: mikroman6 / Moment / Getty Images

Vintage paper texture background, Katsumi Murouchi / Moment / Getty Images

A catalogue record for this publication is available from the British Library

A Cataloging-in-Publication data record for this book is available from the Library of Congress

ISBN 978-1-009-78903-5 Hardback
ISBN 978-1-009-78902-8 Paperback

Cambridge University Press & Assessment has no responsibility for the persistence or accuracy of URLs for external or third-party internet websites referred to in this publication and does not guarantee that any content on such websites is, or will remain, accurate or appropriate.

For EU product safety concerns, contact us at Calle de José Abascal, 56, 1°, 28003 Madrid, Spain, or email eugpsr@cambridge.org.

To the memory of my grandparents,
Elmer and Elvera Larson and Clarence and Anne Hagen

CONTENTS

ACKNOWLEDGMENTS

This book has been incubating for many years, and I am pleased to acknowledge the assistance of those who have aided me along the way. In some ways, I began this project at the age of six, when I decided to compile a book of America's founding documents. My parents were too kind to tell me that such books already existed and humored me as I banged out the Declaration of Independence on my mother's typewriter. I still have these yellowing sheets, the predecessors to the Appendix of this book. They are ample evidence of William Wordsworth's observation, not long after the Declaration's adoption, that "the Child is father of the Man."

I was inspired to return to the Declaration after taking Akhil Reed Amar's course on the Bill of Rights while a student at Yale Law School. I greatly admired Professor Amar's rigorous textual, historical, and structural approach to the Constitution and thought that those same techniques could be profitably applied to the Declaration of Independence. Professor Amar generously agreed to supervise the paper, and he provided valuable advice and encouragement. I was delighted when the paper was awarded the Benjamin Scharps Prize for the best paper by a third-year law student. Professor Amar and I do not agree on every aspect of the Declaration, but we share a commitment to a historically informed understanding of the nation's founding. (I am also delighted that his brother Vik is now my colleague at UC Davis School of Law, where we have many spirited conversations about constitutional law.)

While I was preparing my law school paper for publication, I had the temerity to mail a draft to Pauline Maier, the country's most eminent scholar of the Declaration. To my surprise and delight, she responded with enthusiasm, and our subsequent conversations about the Declaration over email were some of the most rewarding of my professional life. She graciously treated me (a complete obscurity) as someone worthy of engagement, and I think of her often as a model of academic courtesy and civility.

The *Washington Law Review* was willing to take a chance on the work of a law clerk, and they published the paper in 2001 under the title, "The Declaration of Independence: A 225th Anniversary Re-Interpretation" (a ghastly and uninformative title for which I bear sole responsibility and infinite regret). Although I have written this book from the ground up, the major themes were initially sketched in that piece, and occasional stray sentences from that earlier work have survived here. I am grateful to the *Washington Law Review* for permission to reprint those passages.

The librarians at the Mabie Law Library of the UC Davis School of Law have patiently responded to my endless interlibrary loan requests. In their hands, accessing obscure materials seems a sort of effortless wizardry, but of course it is not. I am grateful to the entire staff, but especially to Kristin Brandt, Refugio Acker-Ramirez, Stephanie Grace, David Holt, Heather Craig, and Melanie Uyeda.

This project has benefited from financial support from the UC Davis Academic Senate Committee on Research and from the dean's office at UC Davis School of Law. I am particularly grateful to Deans Kevin Johnson and Jessica Berg and to Associate Deans Afra Afsharipour and Donna Shestowsky.

Steven Sarson very kindly allowed me to read an advance copy of his fascinating new book, *The Course of Human Events: The Declaration of Independence and the Historical Origins of the United States*. I am similarly grateful to Mark A. Graber, who shared an advance copy of his coedited volume, *The Cambridge Companion to the Declaration of Independence*.

At Cambridge University Press, three anonymous reviewers provided helpful feedback, and Matt Gallaway has been an enthusiastic and supportive editor.

My deepest debt is to my family. My parents, Carl and Esther Larson, read the entire manuscript and have offered unflagging support. My wife, Elaine Lau, also read the entire manuscript and saved me from numerous infelicities of expression. Acknowledgments in other books have helped me appreciate that such spousal interest should by no means be taken for granted. Finally, my children, Carina and Elliot, are a continual source of inspiration and joy. As they move from my dependents into an independence of their own, I hope this country will provide them with the same freedoms and opportunities it has provided me.

This book is dedicated to the memory of my grandparents, Elmer and Elvera Larson and Clarence and Anne Hagen. As the children of immigrants, they understood the promise of America. As lifelong farmers and survivors of the Great Depression, they understood that we are all in this together. I hope they would have enjoyed this book, as I hope they would have enjoyed all my offspring, both of the literal and the more literary sort.

NOTE ON THE TEXT

When quoting from eighteenth-century sources, I have retained the original spelling, italicization, and capitalization. As some of the book's argument turns on these details, it is important that the original text be presented as accurately as possible. In the few instances where I have added italicization for emphasis, I have noted this in the endnotes.

ABBREVIATIONS

JCC   *Journals of the Continental Congress*, 34 vols. (Washington, DC: Library of Congress, 1904–1937)

LDC   *Letters of Delegates to Congress, 1774–1789*, 25 vols. (Washington, DC: Library of Congress, 1976–2000)

INTRODUCTION

On July 4, 2026, the United States will celebrate the 250th anniversary of the Declaration of Independence. It will be read aloud at the National Archives and in similar ceremonies across the country, echoing annual celebrations that began in 1777. In a bitterly fractured nation, enthusiasm for the Declaration of Independence is one of the few things that transcend party lines. In a 2020 Rose Garden appearance, President Donald Trump avowed his belief in the "timeless principles of the Declaration of Independence," which were part of the "big, beautiful heritage of all Americans."[1] Similarly, in a 2024 campaign event, Vice President Kamala Harris emphasized the "foundational principles that underlie ... the Declaration of Independence and all those words that are supposed to reflect the principles that we hold dear."[2] A July 2025 poll found that 66 percent of respondents felt that "believing in the principles of the Declaration of Independence" was important to being an American, behind only obeying the laws and supporting the Constitution.[3]

Given this bipartisan enthusiasm, surely the Declaration of Independence should be clearly and accurately understood. But it is not. In 1945, the eminent historian Charles Warren lamented, "It is a singular fact that the greatest event in American history – the Declaration of Independence – has been the subject of more incorrect popular belief, more bad memory on the part of participants, and more false history than any other occurrence in our national life."[4]

Over eighty years later, Warren's lament continues to ring true. Consider the following paragraph, which is a distillation of common views in the literature on the Declaration of Independence:

The Declaration of Independence was written by Thomas Jefferson and was signed on July 4, 1776, by members of the Second Continental Congress. It announced that the thirteen colonies were now thirteen sovereign and independent nations, with no formal legal connection to each other. The Declaration of Independence, which was written by hand on a large piece of parchment, is now on display at the National Archives in Washington, DC, next to the United States Constitution. Unlike the Constitution, however, the Declaration has little to say about the structure of government and consists primarily of airy generalities. Deeply rooted in natural law and a commitment to God, its central purpose was to celebrate individual liberty and the equality of all people. The Declaration views government as a necessary evil, to be endured only to the extent that it helps protect individual natural rights.

Every single sentence in this paragraph is not just wrong, but egregiously wrong. And it matters, because by getting the Declaration of Independence wrong, we are also getting America wrong. To understand America, we must understand the Declaration of Independence. And that means getting the Declaration of Independence right.

~~~

Let's start with a very simple question: When is America's birthday? Although most Americans would answer July 4, 1776, the date that the Declaration of Independence was adopted, historians and legal scholars are deeply divided. According to Garry Wills, who wrote one of the bestselling books on the Declaration, "July 4, 1776, produced twelve new nations (with a thirteenth coming in on July 15)."[5] Under this "thirteen-independent-nations" view, the United States of America did not legally exist as a nation in 1776. It did not become one until much later, perhaps with the adoption of the Articles of Confederation in 1781, perhaps with the ratification of the Constitution in 1788, or perhaps at the conclusion of the Civil War in 1865.[6] The proponents of this view believe that July 4, 1776, marks the anniversary of American independence, but not the birthday of a nation.

If these scholars are right, Fourth of July of celebrations have been going awry for a very long time. But these scholars are not right. The United States of America became an independent nation on July 4, 1776, and from that date forward presented itself as one nation to the rest of the world. To be sure, the vast majority of governmental power was exercised by the individual states. The internal organization of the nation was not definitively clarified, but all the powers of external sovereignty – the powers that marked the "United States of America" as a new nation on the global map – now vested in the Continental Congress.

This point is easy to miss if we focus solely on written constitutions rather than on the reality of how government actually functioned. The United States lacked a *written* constitution until 1781, when the Articles of Confederation were adopted, but that did not mean it lacked a *constitution.* There was an American constitution on July 4, 1776, but it was an unwritten one, like the English constitution with which colonial Americans were familiar. It was a set of practices and institutions rooted in tacit popular consent. And under that constitution, the American states were linked together as a confederated nation governed by the Continental Congress. That is, the states were confederated together from the moment of independence, and at no point functioned as completely independent nations. The Articles of Confederation later fleshed out the details of that confederation, but they did not create it. As James Wilson, a signer of the Declaration of Independence, pointed out at the Constitutional Convention, he could "not admit the doctrine that when the Colonies became independent of Great Britain, they became independent also of each other." Rather, Wilson argued, the Declaration declared the colonies "independent, not individually but unitedly."[7]

Unfortunately, state-centric views of the Declaration are prominent in wide swaths of our political and legal culture. In his First Inaugural Address, Ronald Reagan claimed, "All of us need to be reminded that the Federal Government did not create the States; the States created the Federal Government."[8] Similarly, in a 2019 decision, authored by Justice Clarence Thomas, the United States Supreme Court stated, "After independence, the States considered themselves fully sovereign nations."[9] In recent years, the Supreme Court has significantly narrowed the power of the federal government in favor of the states, in cases ranging from allowing states to evade federal law to restricting the scope of the Voting Rights Act.[10] In all of these cases, the federal government is treated with suspicion, and states are celebrated as the defining original feature of the American constitutional system.

These state-centric views could not be more wrong. The Continental Congress, the federal government of the time, made the states independent and governed the nation following independence. At no point did the states ever act like fully sovereign nations, nor were they ever considered as such. This book contends that we were *One Nation* from July 4, 1776. Although the argument will be laid out in detail in the chapters that follow, consider this question: When was the first appeal filed from a state court to a federal tribunal? The answer will likely surprise even well-informed historians. The first appeal from a state court was filed on July 4, 1776.[11] That is, the same day on which the Continental Congress declared American independence, it accepted jurisdiction over a state court proceeding, and it ultimately reversed the decision of the state court. Whatever was happening on July 4, 1776, it most emphatically was *not* the creation of thirteen independent nations, entirely separate from each other.

~~~

The most familiar part of the Declaration of Independence is, of course, its famous second sentence, which begins, "We hold the Truths to be self-evident, that all Men are created equal, that they are endowed by their Creator with certain unalienable Rights, that among these are Life, Liberty, and the Pursuit of Happiness." For good reason, this is the passage that has reverberated through the centuries, inspiring movements for the abolition of slavery, women's suffrage, and civil rights. (It has also inspired supporters of prayer in public schools and opponents of minimum wage laws.)

But few readers in 1776 would have viewed this passage as the central point of the document; it stated fairly conventional views about the origins of rights. More important was what followed: "to secure these Rights, Governments are instituted among Men, deriving their just Powers from the Consent of the Governed, [and] whenever any Form of Government becomes destructive of these Ends, it is the Right of the People to alter or abolish it." That is, people have the right to overthrow their government when it is no longer functioning as it is supposed to. This, too, was hardly a novel concept in the Anglo-American world. It had been clearly articulated by the philosopher John Locke in the late 1600s, and was part of the justification for the overthrow of James II in England's Glorious Revolution of 1688.

The primary question the Declaration had to answer was one of proof: Did the facts justify overthrowing the king of Great Britain and replacing his government with something new? To make this argument, the Declaration offered "Facts" to "be submitted to a candid World." These "Facts" – the lengthiest part of the document – are the heart of the Declaration. If accepted as sufficient, they prove the case for independence. If not, then none of the document's other assertions are relevant. Although these "Facts" have faded in historical memory, they were the most critical component of the Declaration in 1776, and they deserve our close attention.

When we read this part of the document carefully, we see a very different Declaration than the one of popular imagination. It has little concrete to say about modern disputes over the meaning of liberty and equality. But it has much to say about how we structure our government, how we shape the institutions that will decide those difficult disputes, and how we most effectively protect liberty and equality through a commitment to the rule of law.

Although sometimes portrayed as a libertarian manifesto, the Declaration evinces no hostility to government as such. Indeed, many of the complaints in the Declaration are about the *lack* of effective government. The Declaration views government as a positive good, not a necessary evil. It is only through a properly constructed government, subject to the rule of law, that liberty and equality can flourish. In short, the Declaration tells us not just that liberty and equality are important, but it tells us *how* they are most likely to be protected. This aspect of the Declaration is almost entirely unknown, but it is central to its overall argument. It commits us to be a nation *Under Law*.

~~~

Finally, we can't really discuss the Declaration of Independence until we are all on the same page – literally. That means we need to identify the actual text of the Declaration, determine who created it and for what purpose, and consider what legal status, if any, it has. Accordingly, this book begins with some preliminaries: making sure we have the correct text in front of us, identifying the Declaration's author, and situating the document within a broader legal context. Here, too, there are numerous myths about the Declaration that hinder our understanding.

The Declaration's legal status has been subject to strident assertions from widely divergent perspectives. Some view it as directly governing law, equivalent to the Constitution itself. Others dismiss the Declaration as an airy propaganda paper unworthy of a lawyer's notice. The reality is more complex: The Declaration is a legal document of continuing legal significance, one that has been cited in thousands of judicial decisions, even if its more abstract provisions are not directly enforceable by courts.

Authorship, too, has been shrouded in myth. Although Thomas Jefferson composed the first draft of the Declaration, he was not its author. That honor belongs to the Continental Congress as a whole, which issued the document in the name and voice of the American people. Interpretations of the Declaration that focus heavily on Jefferson's personal quirks veer off in the wrong direction from the very beginning.

Finally, the Declaration of Independence is *not* the parchment document enshrined in the National Archives, an artifact that has distracted many historians. Our journey through the Declaration of Independence will begin by identifying the correct text of the document, one that differs in significant ways from the document in the Archives. With the correct text in hand, we can gain a much better sense of what was actually declared on that fateful day of July 4, 1776, when a new nation under law was announced to the world.

PART I

The Document

Before considering the Declaration of Independence as a whole, we have to confront a fundamental problem, where is the Declaration and what does it actually say? Despite a proliferation of texts from 1776 to the present, all claiming to represent the Declaration, these are not simple questions to answer.

But isn't the Declaration of Independence in the National Archives in Washington, DC? Almost every American knows at least that basic fact, right? Consider the 2004 movie *National Treasure*, in which a group of treasure hunters follow a series of clues that eventually lead them to enormous riches hidden under Trinity Church in downtown Manhattan. An early clue points to the Declaration of Independence, and, after much difficulty, the treasure hunters steal it from the National Archives. With the aid of tinted glasses, they uncover a new clue written in invisible ink on the back of the document.

The plot of *National Treasure* is notoriously inane; even my eight-year-old found it ludicrously stupid. Roger Ebert found the movie "so silly that the Monty Python version could use the same screenplay, line for line."[1] As far as I am aware, though, no critic of *National Treasure* identified one of its most critical failures. When the treasure hunters were told that the next clue was in the Declaration of Independence, they rushed to the National Archives. But if the treasure hunters had been a little more careful and a little more knowledgeable about history, they might have hesitated before leaping to this assumption. Because the parchment document in the National Archives is only one possible claimant for the title of the real

Declaration of Independence, and it is not even the most compelling claimant. We can begin by tracing the Archives copy back to its living, breathing source in 1776, as the world that everyone had known was turning upside down forever.

1   WHERE IS THE DECLARATION OF INDEPENDENCE?

Even in the midst of a war, there can be pockets of tranquility. Such was the state of the pastures of Pennsylvania in the early months of 1776. The drums and cannons of the conflict that had erupted in April 1775 were but distant echoes, reverberating from battlefields hundreds of miles away. Philadelphia itself was filled with political contention of the highest order, as statesmen debated endlessly in the Pennsylvania State House, but none of that drifted down to the world of the sheep grazing away on the banks of the Delaware and Schuylkill Rivers. For these decidedly unagitated animals, the day's agenda would have been the same as it had been for thousands of years: eating grass, resting, and dozing. (The typical sheep sleeps for only around four hours a day.)[1] And, like millions of sheep before them, they would leave little imprint on history.

But one sheep in this flock was about to achieve historical immortality, destined to be permanently commemorated in a shrine of the most powerful nation the world has ever known. Regrettably, we know very little about this particular sheep. We do not know the name of its owner or where it was born. We do not know whether it was male or female. And, to be strictly accurate, there is a slight possibility that it might have been a goat. One likes to imagine that it had distinctive personality traits, perhaps leading its owner to christen it with a name, but more likely it was just another face in the herd.

At some point that year, the sheep found its way to the Philadelphia shop of parchment maker Robert Wood, located on Fifth Street, half a block away from the Pennsylvania State House, where the Second Continental Congress and the Pennsylvania Assembly were meeting.[2]

If the sheep was brought alive to Wood's shop, it may have even glimpsed the State House. But whether it was alive or dead upon entry, it was clearly dead when it left. By then, Wood had carefully removed the sheep's skin, submerged it in a lime solution, and stripped it of flesh, fat, and hair, before washing it and drying it under tension on a wooden frame. The whole process would have taken a couple of weeks to complete.[3]

Philadelphians prided themselves on their home-grown industries, and since 1771, Wood had been promoting his parchment as just as well-made and inexpensive as its imported English competitors.[4] When war broke out in 1775, most sources of imports were cut off, leaving Wood as the city's primary provider of high-quality parchment.[5] Wood seems to have made his parchment primarily from sheepskin, since he also advertised quantities of wool for sale.[6] Although his parchment could be obtained through other retailers such as stationers and printers, Wood also sold it directly to consumers in his shop.[7]

One such consumer was a Philadelphia brewer and renowned cockfighter named Timothy Matlack, a close neighbor of Wood's.[8] Despite his rather boisterous reputation, Matlack was known for his elegant handwriting, and in mid-July 1776, he had been asked to help prepare a parchment copy of a previously printed document.[9] Likely written on a parchment from Wood's shop, Matlack's transcription of the older document was later signed by dozens of other men before being filed away in government records, where it languished in obscurity until early 1777.[10]

In later years, that sheepskin covered with Matlack's handwriting came to be revered as one of America's greatest historical treasures. It is currently on display at the National Archives in Washington, DC, under the heading "The Declaration of Independence," where it is visited by over a million people a year.[11] Curiously, the notion from *National Treasure* that this document contains secret information is not as half-baked as it might seem. If the parchment were to be subjected to DNA analysis, using the emerging field of "biocodicology," one could learn conclusively whether it was made from sheepskin or goatskin, whether the animal was male or female, and we might even be able to identify some living relatives who are genetically linked.[12] Perhaps the Daughters of the American Revolution could consider a new chapter for animal members. It's one thing to be descended from a signer of the Declaration of Independence; it's a distinction of an entirely different order to be descended from a version of the Declaration itself.

The answer to the question, "Where is the Declaration of Independence?" would thus seem to have an obvious answer – it is in the National Archives in Washington, DC. Indeed, this would seem to be one of the clear, undisputed facts of American history; it could as easily be the subject of a *Jeopardy* question, for example, as the state in which Mount Vernon is located.

But it is actually not a very good answer. When the Continental Congress adopted the Declaration on July 4, 1776, the sheepskin currently residing in the Archives was probably lying in Robert Wood's Philadelphia shop in some stage of preparation. It is even possible, although just barely, that the storied "Declaration of Independence" was very much part of a live sheep, its appointment with destiny just days away.

So if the parchment in the National Archives is not the real Declaration of Independence, what is and where is it? To answer that question, we need to turn to how the document was actually produced and distributed to the American people.

PRINTING THE DECLARATION

On July 4, 1776, the Continental Congress approved the Declaration of Independence. It also ordered that the "declaration be authenticated and printed" under the supervision of the committee that had drafted it. The printed copies of the Declaration were to be sent "to the several assemblies, conventions and committees, or councils of safety, and to the several commanding officers of the continental troops." It was also to "be proclaimed in each of the United States, and at the head of the army."[13]

That night, a Philadelphia printer named John Dunlap, an immigrant from Ireland, prepared the first printed copies of the Declaration of Independence. We do not know which members of the committee supervised the printing, although it is certainly possible that Thomas

Jefferson and Benjamin Franklin (a former printer himself) were involved.[14] Dunlap prepared an initial printing, in a copy that is now at the Historical Society of Pennsylvania in Philadelphia. Numerous errors were then corrected before a final printing was issued.[15] Historians refer to this printing as the "Dunlap Broadside." Over the course of printing, some letters in the type became damaged, so not every surviving broadside is exactly identical, although the text itself is the same.[16] The paper itself appears to have been produced in the Netherlands; of the surviving copies with watermarks, all are of Dutch origin.[17] (A transcript of the Dunlap Broadside is provided in the Appendix.)

Although the precise number of copies printed on the night of July 4 is not known, a substantial number of them appear to have been provided to the Continental Congress, and John Hancock, the Congress's president, soon began forwarding them to the states. The Declaration began appearing in newspapers on July 6, 1776, following the text of the Dunlap Broadside. A copy surviving at Independence National Historical Park was used by Colonel John Nixon, who publicly read the Declaration at the State House yard on July 8, 1776. A copy in the Washington Papers at the Library of Congress appears to be the one that Washington read to his troops in New York City on July 9, 1776.[18] In Massachusetts, the state's Executive Council directed that copies of the Declaration be printed and distributed to each church in the state. After reading it to their congregations, ministers were to provide it to the town clerk for entry into their town's record books.[19]

On July 19, 1776, the Continental Congress ordered the Declaration to be handwritten on parchment and that "the same, when engrossed, be signed by every member of Congress."[20] Timothy Matlack was assigned the task of securing the parchment and preparing the document.[21] On August 2, 1776, Congress's journal stated, "The declaration of Independence being engrossed and compared at the table was signed by the Members."[22] But the signing was not a faithful reproduction of the events of July 4. Some of the members who signed on August 2 had not even been elected to Congress on July 4, and some members who were elected after August 2 continued to sign the document upon their arrival in Philadelphia. Signer Matthew Thornton of New Hampshire, for example, didn't take his seat in Congress until November 4, 1776.[23] This wasn't necessarily improper – Congress had ordered the document to be signed "by every member" and it had not specified only those present on July 4. John Adams later recalled that he had found it "absurd" that "all future members should sign the original parchment," but such a "resolution was passed and was obeyed."[24] It nonetheless created a confusing historical record by implicitly suggesting that each signer had been present for the document's adoption.[25]

The document created by Timothy Matlack in late July 1776, and signed by members of Congress beginning in early August 1776, is the document currently enshrined at the National Archives. I call this document the "ceremonial parchment." By the time the delegates attached their names, the true Declaration of Independence had already been adopted, printed, and distributed to the states. Creating the parchment copy served no obvious legal, political, or functional purpose, other than creating an elegant formal record, and perhaps binding the delegates to independence in the form of a quasi-oath.

In its first months, the ceremonial parchment was effectively a state secret. No American, outside of Congress, could have told you the names of the signatories in 1776. The Continental Congress did not send copies with the signatories' names to the states until January 1777, after military victories at Trenton and Princeton had made independence more likely to be secured.[26]

A PRINTED DECLARATION

The continued celebration of the ceremonial parchment, both through its enshrinement at the National Archives and its reproduction in various forms (the *New York Times* has reproduced it every July 4 since 1922[27]), tends to obscure a critical fact: In 1776, every person, American or European, who encountered the Declaration of Independence outside of the Continental Congress did so through a printed copy, initially through the Dunlap Broadside, and then through re-printings throughout the colonies and throughout the world.[28] One newspaper even printed the Declaration on a separate page, so that customers could post it in their homes.[29] When revolutionary Americans thought about the Declaration, they thought of a printed document, lacking any signatures, other than the names of Congress's president, John Hancock, and its secretary, Charles Thomson, which appeared at the very end. This was the Declaration that Americans knew and celebrated. As historian Julian Boyd astutely noted, the Dunlap Broadside, not the ceremonial parchment, was the "first official and perhaps the most authoritative text."[30]

Our modern tendency to view the Declaration solely through the ceremonial parchment, however, has led to a number of significant distortions. First, it tends to make the Declaration seem more distant and remote in time; it becomes a quaint home-made item, a product of quill and ink, reproducible only with hours of painstaking effort. But the Declaration was actually mass-produced with intricate machinery, wood and metal seamlessly working together to rapidly produce hundreds of identical pages. Focusing on the "anachronistic" ceremonial parchment, as one scholar has argued, "subverts the revolution of movable type."[31]

For the distribution of knowledge, the eighteenth century was primarily a culture of print, not of handwriting. As scholars Caroline Archer-Parré and Malcolm Dick have noted, "Printing helped advance general knowledge through new modes of publication and wide-ranging products – pamphlets, posters, leaflets, newspapers, journals – which had implications for the way lives were organized, structured, and documented." The eighteenth century witnessed a "build-up of printed documents" and "accumulated reliance on printed texts over the oral and written."[32] Printed pamphlets, for example, as historian Bernard Bailyn found, formed "much of the most important and characteristic writing of the American Revolution."[33] Or as historian Robert Parkinson has noted, "Printer's ink was ... the Revolution's lifeblood."[34] For Americans at the time, the Declaration was a text to be found in broadsides and newspapers, and always in print.[35]

Second, overemphasis on the ceremonial parchment tends to overstate the significance of the signers, leading to an almost cult-like reverence for these particular figures. (Admittedly, not everyone gets the details right: On July 5, 2024, Representative Marjorie Taylor Greene incorrectly stated that James Madison, Alexander Hamilton, James

Monroe, Aaron Burr, Paul Revere, and George Washington signed the Declaration.)[36] Multiple books have been published on the lives of the signers of the Declaration of Independence, but even these are an odd assortment, since some people who were present on July 4 never signed, and others who weren't later did. And no Americans, outside of the Continental Congress, would have had any idea in 1776 just who these people were, as their names appeared nowhere on the texts of the Declaration that they knew and celebrated.

Third, an overemphasis on the ceremonial parchment allows phrases such as "our lives, our fortunes, and our sacred honor" to be read as personal commitments of the delegates to Congress. As Chapter 2 will explain, it is a mistake to think of the Declaration as written in the voice of the delegates, a mistake that is easier to avoid if we focus on the Dunlap Broadside rather than the parchment.

Finally, and most importantly, the text of the documents is different, in significant ways. When we seek to understand the Declaration, we should try to understand the Declaration that was actually presented to the American people – the Dunlap Broadside – and not a text that was created for ceremonial purposes and then quietly squirreled away.[37] Historians have often made confident pronouncements about the meaning of the Declaration based on the parchment text, apparently unaware that the text of the Dunlap Broadside is strikingly different. Eli Merritt, for example, in a thoughtful book about the revolutionary period, wrote, "The Declaration twice makes reference to the 'united States of America,' and the lowercase 'united' is hardly accidental."[38] This is true if one only looks at the ceremonial parchment, but the Dunlap Broadside refers twice to the "UNITED STATES OF AMERICA," and does not indicate any distinction between the capitalization of "United" or "States." Merritt's point would have been incomprehensible to almost every American living in 1776.[39] Other scholars have simply reproduced the ceremonial parchment as "the Declaration of Independence" without any acknowledgment that varying texts exist.[40] But to even start getting the Declaration right, we need to be on the same page – literally – and that page is not the ceremonial parchment in the National Archives.

~~~

So, where is the Declaration of Independence? The best answer is wherever copies of the Dunlap Broadside are located. There are 26 known copies, 23 in the United States and three in the United Kingdom. If we had to identify a specific location, we should probably select the city which holds the most copies. For this distinction, there is a four-way tie; New York City, Philadelphia, Washington, DC, and London all have three copies of the broadside.[41] And one of the copies in Washington, DC is in the National Archives, on display in the Rotunda. But it's on the left-hand side, in an exhibit about the history of the Declaration of Independence, and not under the primary exhibit labeled "The Declaration of Independence."[42] So when the treasure hunters in *National Treasure* raced to the Archives to examine the Declaration, they weren't necessarily wrong. Their mistake was immediately pursuing the newer copy of the Declaration, not realizing that an older version, one that rolled off the printing presses on the night of July 4, 1776, was readily at hand.

2 WHO WROTE THE DECLARATION OF INDEPENDENCE?

For all of their achievements, the ancient Romans always had an awareness of the great civilizations that had preceded them. Although ancient Greece may have loomed the largest, the far older Egyptian civilization still held a powerful grip on the Roman imagination. Nowhere was this more apparent than in their capital cities. At enormous expense, they plundered ancient Egypt, shipping obelisks from the Nile Valley to Rome and later to their new capital of Constantinople on the Bosporus. Many of these obelisks still stand, most prominently in St. Peter's Square in what is now Vatican City, and in the Hippodrome in what is now Istanbul.[1]

It was no surprise that Washington, DC, a city modeled after ancient Rome in many respects, would soon desire an obelisk as well. With genuine Egyptian models sadly out of reach, a modern one was created with stone from Maryland quarries. The Washington Monument, as it was called, would lack the hieroglyphs of a genuine obelisk, but it would surpass even the Pyramids in height. At 555 feet, it was the tallest building in the world at the time of its completion in 1884. Despite its extraordinary size, it was seen as a plain, straightforward commemoration of George Washington, who was widely viewed as a plain, straightforward man.[2]

When it came time to commemorate the more worldly and complicated Thomas Jefferson, a very different approach was employed. The Jefferson Memorial, completed in 1943, was based on the Pantheon, Jefferson's favorite building in ancient Rome. Its graceful curved dome, which also evoked Jefferson's plantation home of Monticello, could not have been more different than the massive spike of the

Washington Monument. For many observers, the Jefferson Memorial perfectly captured Jefferson's erudition and love of European architecture. It seemed like the memorial Jefferson himself would have selected.

When Jefferson designed his own memorial, however, he did not invoke the Pantheon. Instead, for his grave, he chose a simple, white obelisk, a miniature version of what would later become the Washington Monument. He specified the obelisk's dimensions in exacting detail and requested that the following inscription be carved on its sides:

Here was buried

Thomas Jefferson

Author of the Declaration of American Independence

of the Statute of Virginia for religious freedom

& Father of the University of Virginia

These achievements, Jefferson claimed, were the ones for which he wished "most to be remembered."[3] The inscribed obelisk, the first "Jefferson Memorial," was erected in 1833, where it stood for fifty years until it was replaced with an even larger obelisk, twice the size that Jefferson had specified (the original obelisk was moved to the grounds of the University of Missouri at Columbia).[4]

Jefferson's obelisk is one of the more curious attempts at shaping historical memory. Nowhere does Jefferson mention his service as Governor of Virginia and as Secretary of State, Vice President, and President of the United States of America. Perhaps he thought those would be remembered anyway, and he wished to emphasize roles that were more at risk of being forgotten. In this, he was only partially successful. Scholars are familiar with Jefferson's work on the Virginia Statute for Religious Freedom, and visitors and students at the University of Virginia cannot avoid Jefferson's looming historical presence on campus. But few Americans, if asked to identify Jefferson's greatest achievements, would mention the founding of a state college or the drafting of a state law.

By contrast, Jefferson's claimed "authorship" of the Declaration of Independence has reverberated through the ages. It's one of those basic facts of American history that even young elementary students are expected to know. And not just students – a psychologist found possible evidence of mental impairment in a Texas man because "he did not know the author of the Declaration of Independence."[5] The Naturalization Test provided by the US Citizenship and Immigration Services poses this question, "Who wrote the Declaration of Independence?" The only permissible answer listed is "(Thomas) Jefferson."[6]

But this claim is false. Although Jefferson composed the first draft of the Declaration, it is not strictly accurate to describe him as its author, no matter how much he wished it were so. Treating the Declaration of Independence as the personal testament of Thomas Jefferson, as the unique expression of his distinctive mind, significantly distorts our understanding of what the Declaration of Independence actually was: a public document issued by a public body, written in the voice of the American people.[7]

CREATION OF THE DECLARATION

On June 7, 1776, Richard Henry Lee of Virginia introduced a resolution in the Second Continental Congress declaring that "these United Colonies are, and of right ought to be, free and independent States, that they are absolved from all allegiance to the British Crown, and that all political connection between them and the State of Great Britain is, and ought to be, totally dissolved."[8] After several days of debate, Congress resolved on June 10 to defer consideration of the resolution until early July in order to allow more state delegations to receive authorization to support independence. To prevent any time from being lost, however, it appointed a committee to prepare a declaration to be issued if Congress adopted the resolution.[9] The following day, Congress appointed five members to the committee: Thomas Jefferson of Virginia, John Adams of Massachusetts, Benjamin Franklin of Pennsylvania, Roger Sherman of Connecticut, and Robert Livingston of New York.[10] We do not know precisely why these five were chosen, but they did represent a wide geographical range, a factor that was likely important to Congress.[11]

The committee presumably met shortly after its appointment.[12] Nearly thirty years later, in his autobiography, John Adams stated that the committee had initially requested that he and Jefferson jointly prepare a draft and that Jefferson had proposed Adams as the initial drafter. Adams, however, insisted that Jefferson take the lead, citing a number of reasons:

> 1. That he was a Virginian and I a Massachusettensian. 2. that he was a southern Man and I a northern one. 3. That I had been so obnoxious for my early and constant Zeal in promoting the Measure, that any draught of mine, would undergo a more severe Scrutiny and Criticism in Congress than one of his composition. 4thly and lastly that would be reason enough if there were no other, I had a great Opinion of the Elegance of his pen and none at all of my own.[13]

Although there is undoubtedly some truth behind it, Adams's recollection suggests a self-effacing modesty that is not generally remembered as one of his defining personality traits. It seems more plausible that Adams was simply consumed by other work that he viewed as more important, most notably preparing draft treaties with foreign nations.[14] For his part, Benjamin Franklin was in his seventies and suffering from a severe case of gout.[15] Jefferson's later recollections of his selection were somewhat different. As he recalled, the committee had never sought Adams's involvement, but had unanimously requested that Jefferson prepare the initial draft.[16]

However he was selected, Jefferson proved to be an inspired choice. Working in a rented room on Seventh Street in Philadelphia, in a house that has now been reconstructed as part of Independence National Historical Park (his writing desk is on display at the Smithsonian), Jefferson produced an eloquent and thoughtful first draft, a draft that contains many of the phrases that we now consider among the finest in the document. Although Congress and his fellow committee members would significantly improve it, Jefferson deserves considerable credit for much of the Declaration's rhetorical genius. A lesser writer could have easily mangled the job, producing a plodding, unmemorable report. Jefferson did not. One can compare the Declaration of Independence, for example, to the Declaration and Resolves of the

First Continental Congress of 1774, which opens with this convoluted sentence:

> Whereas, since the close of the last war, the British parliament, claiming a power, of right, to bind the people of America by statute in all cases whatsoever, hath in some acts, expressly imposed taxes on them, and in others, under various pretences, but in fact for the purpose of raising a revenue, hath imposed rates and duties payable in these colonies, established a board of commissioners, with unconstitutional powers, and extended the jurisdiction of the courts of Admiralty, not only for collecting the said duties, but for the trial of causes merely arising within the body of a county.[17]

Jefferson would never have penned anything so clumsy and inelegant. Fred Kaplan, author of a substantial study of Jefferson as a writer, concludes that the Declaration is a "brilliant and powerful example of a state document as literature" and that it was "Jefferson's talent as a synthesizing mind and a brilliant writer that [gave] the document its power."[18] (Not everyone has been so impressed; John Wilkes, who strongly supported American rights in Parliament, conceded that the Declaration was "very ill written," but noted that the Americans had little use for "polished periods … harmonious happy expressions … and … beautiful diction," but instead relished "manly, nervous sense … even in the most awkward and uncouth dress of language.")[19]

When Jefferson began the initial draft, his task was quite clear – he was not writing a personal testament; he was drafting a public document to be adopted by a public body. To be effective, the document would have to be persuasive to wide swaths of the American people and to influential figures abroad. This would require stating the argument in the clearest possible terms, using the vocabulary and frames of reference that would be most widely understood. As Fred Kaplan has pointed out, the document was to be "a synthesis and a culmination, a consensus document." Jefferson had not been "assigned to be its author in the modern sense," and the Declaration would be "Congress's authoritative statement on the matter, not the voice of an individual."[20]

Late in life, in response to a claim that the ideas of the Declaration were unoriginal, Jefferson rather sarcastically pointed out that he "did not consider it as any part of my charge to invent new ideas altogether & to offer no sentiment which had ever been expressed before."[21] Jefferson noted, but did not specifically refute, Richard Henry Lee's claim that some of the Declaration was copied from Locke's *Second Treatise on Government*. Rather, Jefferson claimed that he had no books or pamphlets immediately at hand when drafting the document and that its ideas may have come from "reading or reflection."[22]

In an 1825 letter, Jefferson expanded on this notion, explaining that the object of the Declaration was "not to find out new principles, or new arguments, never before thought of" or to "say things which had never been said before," but "to place before mankind the common sense of the subject." It was to be an "expression of the american mind." Its authority rested "on the harmonising sentiments of the day, whether expressed in [conversations] in letters, printed essays, or in the elementary books of public right, as Aristotle, Cicero, Locke, Sidney etc."[23]

On this point, Jefferson was surely right. The Declaration's assertion of natural rights, of social compact theory, and of the right of the people to rebel against a tyrannical government was entirely commonplace.[24] As Julian Boyd pointed out, these ideas would have been familiar to "every pamphleteer, every lawyer, every minister of the gospel, almost every American subject of George III in the epochal year 1776."[25] They were so commonplace that they could even be found in textbooks for young students in Britain.[26] But that was precisely the point – the more commonplace the ideas, the more likely the Declaration was to persuade. In Professor Boyd's inimitable phrasing, Jefferson had "failed to be original in an enterprise where originality would have been fatal."[27] Or, as Pauline Maier argued, the Declaration "restated what virtually all Americans – patriot and Loyalist alike – thought and said in other words in other places."[28]

When Jefferson had completed his draft, he submitted it to his fellow committee members. The extent to which the committee modified Jefferson's draft is unclear. In his autobiography, John Adams claimed that he could not recall whether the committee suggested any edits.[29] Late in life, Jefferson stated that he showed the draft initially to Adams and Franklin, who made some minor changes, and that the committee then passed the draft unaltered to the full Continental Congress.[30]

But a contemporaneous letter from Jefferson to Franklin suggests that the committee was more involved and may have made substantive changes to Jefferson's draft.[31]

Whatever edits the committee made, however, were far less extensive than those made by the Congress as a whole. Line by line, members of Congress dissected the committee's draft declaration, excising whole sections and rephrasing and tightening sentences and phrases. Historian Pauline Maier aptly described Congress's work as "an act of group editing that has to be one of the great marvels of history."[32] "By exercising their intelligence, political good sense, and a discerning sense of language," she argued, "the delegates managed to make the Declaration at once more accurate and more consonant with the convictions of their constituents, and to enhance both its power and its eloquence."[33] Nearly every historian has agreed, finding that Congress's edits significantly improved the committee's draft.

The primary dissenter from this consensus was Jefferson himself, who watched in horror as "these gentlemen continued their depredations on other parts of the instrument."[34] Until the end of his life, Jefferson appears to have considered his initial draft superior, and he often sent copies of it to friends.[35] Benjamin Franklin sought to console Jefferson by telling him the tale of a hatter whose initial proposed sign, "John Thompson, Hatter, makes and sells hats for ready money," was whittled down by edits to "John Thompson" and an image of a hat. Franklin advised that he had "made it a rule … to avoid becoming the draughtsman of papers to be reviewed by a public body."[36]

Jefferson's sensitivity to edits suggests his personal investment in the document. But Congress's readiness to use a red pen should hardly have been surprising. Jefferson knew he was drafting a document for Congress, and that body had substantially edited nearly every previous state paper submitted for its consideration.[37] Of course, Congress would take care to edit a document for which every member was potentially responsible, particularly if that document was to announce the most significant political decision ever made in the American colonies. As Pauline Maier argued, "In the end, considering its complex ancestry and the number of people who actively intervened in defining its text, the Declaration of Independence was the work not of one man, but of many."[38] What "generations of Americans came to revere was not Jefferson's but Congress's Declaration."[39]

The answer to the question of who wrote the Declaration of Independence is the Continental Congress, although it is entirely fair to give Jefferson credit for a promising first draft. As Danielle Allen has put it, "I would never gainsay that [Jefferson] was a superb writer, yet he was not *the* author of the Declaration of Independence. The text was written by a group."[40] A modern analogy might be a presidential speechwriter. The speechwriter works hard to capture the president's voice and to articulate themes that the president is seeking to advance. The president then takes the speechwriter's draft and edits it, before ultimately assuming ownership of it by delivering it publicly. In such circumstances, it is entirely appropriate to attribute authorship of the speech to the president, even if someone else – often a very talented someone else – composed the initial draft. Another analogy might be a Supreme Court opinion announced by a particular justice. It is quite possible that a law clerk composed the first draft of the opinion, but it was ultimately edited by the justice and by the other justices who signed on to it. Here, too, we attribute authorship to the justice who signed the opinion, even if he or she had a very talented scribe working behind the scenes.

It is thus a significant mistake to equate Jefferson's drafting of the Declaration with his authorship of works such as *A Summary View of the Rights of British America* or *Notes on the State of Virginia*. Those publications are indisputably in Jefferson's own voice and can be profitably considered as part of his overall intellectual journey. By contrast, viewing the Declaration as primarily the product of a solitary mind leads to distinct misunderstandings of the document.

Consider, for example, Garry Wills's 1978 book *Inventing America,* with the notable subtitle *Jefferson's Declaration of Independence*. Wills argues that there are three Declarations of Independence: (1) Jefferson's draft, (2) the document ultimately approved by the Continental Congress, and (3) the document as later remembered in national myth.[41] This framework is not entirely implausible. After all, Jefferson's draft does differ from the final version, and later interpretations of the Declaration are not always firmly grounded in the world of 1776.

Wills devotes the bulk of his volume to Jefferson's draft, arguing that it was deeply rooted in Jefferson's own idiosyncratic personal intellectual history. As Wills sees it, Jefferson was profoundly shaped by William Small, a Scottish immigrant who taught Jefferson at William and Mary. In one of his more extravagant passages, Wills claims, "the real lost world of Thomas Jefferson was the world of William Small, the invigorating realm of the Scottish Enlightenment at its zenith."[42] Wills then seeks to demonstrate that some of the Declaration's most famous passages are not paraphrased from the work of John Locke, as has been widely supposed, but from the work of Francis Hutcheson, a major Scottish Enlightenment figure.[43] Indeed, Wills goes so far as to say that there is no "conclusive proof" that Jefferson even read Locke's *Second Treatise on Government*.[44] This is quibbling of the very highest order. Jefferson praised the *Second Treatise* as "perfect as far as it goes."[45] True, Jefferson didn't directly state that he had read it, but why would he? Isn't that a reasonable implication when a noted bibliophile praises a book?

Shortly after *Inventing America's* publication, historian Ronald Hamowy pointed out that Hutcheson was likely paraphrasing Locke in his own writing, and Jefferson never once named Hutcheson as an influence on the Declaration.[46] Indeed, Hamowy notes that Hutcheson "is not once quoted, cited, referred to, or recommended, in any connection, in any of Jefferson's writings."[47] When asked, later in life, for the intellectual influences on the Declaration, Jefferson stated that he had drawn on "elementary books of public rights, as Aristotle, Cicero, Locke, Sidney, &c."[48] Not Francis Hutcheson, and not any other Scottish thinker, either.

Wills never responded to Hamowy's criticisms and his "Scottish thesis" about the Declaration carries little weight with historians.[49] But one must not lose sight of the larger point: The Scottish thinkers are a distraction – a fascinating distraction, but a distraction nonetheless. Even if Wills is correct and Jefferson was personally influenced by various Scottish writers, that fact tells us nothing about the original public meaning of the Declaration of Independence. Did any other members of the Continental Congress perceive the Declaration as an expression of Scottish Enlightenment philosophy? Would any informed observer of the text have discerned a Scottish influence? If the answers, as seems probable, are no, then Jefferson's own, possibly idiosyncratic, intellectual history provides no illumination of the

Declaration itself, considered as a *public document* adopted by a *public body*. To his credit, Wills seems to recognize this point by treating Jefferson's draft as distinct from the document adopted by Congress. But we must use Wills's volume very carefully, as an exploration of Jefferson's personal views and not as an interpretation of the Declaration of Independence that was actually adopted by the Continental Congress.

Another distraction is Jefferson's religious beliefs. Allen Jayne, in a study of Jefferson's theological views, contends that the Declaration promulgated not only "Jefferson's worldview," but also his "heterodox concepts of God and man."[50] Jayne delves deeply into every nook and cranny of Jefferson's unusual religious views (one section is entitled "The Influence of Kames on Jefferson's Interpretation of Jesus"), but never explains why Jefferson's religious notions should be attributed to the Continental Congress as a whole.[51] Alan Dershowitz devoted nearly a third of a short book on the Declaration to Jefferson's personal religious views.[52] Religious principles are surely the one area where we would least expect to find widespread agreement in a multi-member public body, and the exercise of attributing a highly distinctive religious worldview to a public document is misguided from the very beginning.[53] One doubts, for example, that our understanding of, say, the Civil Rights Act of 1964 would be greatly enhanced by exploring the religious views of the congressional staffer who drafted it.

In short, we must always keep in mind that the Declaration was a public document adopted by a public body. Jefferson's personal views on politics and religion will always be interesting, but they cannot constitute authoritative interpretations of the Declaration, any more than his views on horses or wine, unless there is strong evidence that those views were shared by most other members of the Continental Congress.[54]

Indeed, one suspects that if Jefferson had died in the fall of 1776, he would be, at most, a minor footnote in American history. His long subsequent public life, however, retrospectively added luster to his role as the Declaration's drafter. Jefferson's role as draftsman was not publicized until 1783, and was not widely known until the 1790s, at a time when Jefferson had become embroiled in partisan politics.[55] We might compare him to Gouverneur Morris, who composed the final draft of the US Constitution, and is widely credited for the document's overall style. Morris's role was undoubtedly important, but he does not loom over the American imagination in anywhere near the same way as Jefferson. But they played somewhat similar roles, Jefferson as a draftsman, and Morris as an editor, of significant documents adopted by public bodies. Yet a Jefferson who died in 1776 would probably be remembered even less than Morris. It's not so much that Morris is underappreciated with respect to the Constitution (although he probably is), it's that Jefferson has been significantly overappreciated with respect to the Declaration.[56]

THE TEXT

We can now turn to the Declaration's actual text. The document begins abstractly, in the third person: "When in the Course of human Events, it becomes necessary for one People to dissolve the Political Bands which have connected them with another." It then abruptly shifts to the first person in the second sentence: "We hold these Truths to be self-evident." The Declaration thus presents a mirror rhetorical image to the US Constitution, which opens with a first-person sentence ("We the People of the United States ..."), but shifts immediately to the third person for the rest of the document.

The insistent use of the first person is one of the Declaration's most conspicuous rhetorical devices (emphases added):

We hold these Truths to be self-evident....

He has kept among *us* ... Standing Armies, without the consent of *our* Legislatures....

He has ... subject[ed] *us* to a Jurisdiction foreign to *our* Constitution, and unacknowledged by *our* Laws....

He has ...sent hither Swarms of Officers to harass *our* People....

For quartering large Bodies of Armed Troops among *us*:

For cutting off *our* Trade with all Parts of the World:

For imposing Taxes on *us* without *our* Consent:

For depriving *us* ... of ... Trial by Jury:

For transporting *us* beyond Seas to be tried for pretended Offences....

For taking away *our* Charters, abolishing *our* most valuable Laws and altering fundamentally the Forms of *our* Governments....

For suspending *our* own Legislatures, and declaring themselves invested with Power to legislate for *us* in all Cases whatsoever.

He has abdicated Government here, by declaring *us* out of his Protection and waging War against *us*.

He has plundered *our* Seas, ravaged *our* Coasts, burnt *our* Towns, and destroyed the Lives of *our* People....

He has constrained *our* fellow Citizens taken Captive on the high Seas to bear arms against their Country ...

He has excited domestic Insurrections amongst *us*....

[We] have petitioned for redress....

Nor have *we* been wanting in Attentions to *our* British Brethren.

We have warned them....

We have reminded them....

We have appealed to their native Justice....

[W]e have conjured them by the ties of *our* common kindred

We must, therefore, acquiesce....

We ... Declare, That these United Colonies are, and of Right ought to be, FREE AND INDEPENDENT STATES....

[W]e mutually pledge to each other *our* Lives, *our* Fortunes, and *our* sacred Honor."

To fully understand the Declaration, we must first understand its speaker. Who is the "we" that is speaking throughout the document? This question is more complicated than it seems. Given the care that went into drafting the Declaration, we can reasonably assume that the pronoun is consistent throughout the document and doesn't lurch around from sentence to sentence. There are at least three possible answers: (1) the Declaration is speaking in the voice of the thirteen colonies ("We, the states"); (2) it is speaking in the voice of the delegates to the Continental Congress ("We, the delegates"); or (3) it is speaking in the voice of the people of the United States ("We, the people"). Although arguments can be made for all three positions, the best answer is the last – the Declaration is the Declaration of the American people.

We, the States?

The strongest argument for a "We, the states" reading turns on the heading to the ceremonial parchment, which describes it as "The unanimous Declaration of the thirteen united States of America." What could be more straightforward than this? Indeed, one might note other pieces of text that support this reading. The document accuses the king of sending "Swarms of Officers to harass our People" and of destroying "the Lives of our People." The phrase "our people" most plausibly suggests the voice of a state. Although "our people" could plausibly be equally attributed to the delegates in Congress, it is hard to see why the people themselves would refer to "our people" rather than "us."

If we take the ceremonial parchment as the last word, then the case would seem be open and shut. Garry Wills accepted this argument in *Inventing America*. As Wills put it, "The Declaration speaks for thirteen united *states*. These new *states* pledge to each other their honor, that honor accruing to sovereignties as they take their 'free and equal station' with other nations."[57] The "'we' who 'mutually pledge our lives, our fortunes, and our sacred honour' are the 'united states' of the document's title."[58] But there are very good reasons to conclude that the ceremonial parchment does not accurately describe the document, since it is fundamentally inconsistent with the text that follows.

Most notably, when the Declaration refers to the colonies, it does so with the third person, not the first. For example: "Such has been the patient Sufferance of *these Colonies*; and such is now the Necessity which constrains *them* to alter their former Systems of Government." Or, "the Establishment of an absolute Tyranny over *these States*." The king is accused of preventing the "Population of *these States*" and introducing the same absolute Rule into *these Colonies*." In all of these instances, if the Declaration was truly speaking in the voice of the states, it should have used the first person. But it does not.

Similarly, in many places a "We, the States" reading is simply implausible as a textual matter. The Declaration condemns the British government for "transporting us beyond Seas to be tried for pretended Offences." Colonial Americans regularly accused the British government of seeking omnipotence, but even they would not have suggested that Massachusetts had somehow been hustled off to London. Nor were states, as states, directly taxed or denied the benefits of trial by jury. States, as juridical entities, would not likely refer to "our British Brethren" or to the "Ties of our common Kindred." And although Wills offers a tortured argument about states' "honor," he has no plausible explanation for why states would pledge to each other their "lives," as the Declaration does in its conclusion.

So why does the ceremonial parchment nonetheless claim that the Declaration is "The Unanimous Declaration of the thirteen united States of America?" The original caption, in the Dunlap Broadside, was "A Declaration by the Representatives of the UNITED STATES OF AMERICA in General Congress Assembled." There is no direct evidence of why the caption was changed, but it was most likely a result of the peculiar circumstances surrounding the Declaration's adoption. New York initially abstained from voting for independence, and its delegates were not given permission to approve the Declaration until after it had already been approved and issued.[59] For the ceremonial parchment, Congress wanted some way to emphasize the colonies' unanimity, but it couldn't really alter the main text, leaving tinkering with the caption as the only plausible alternative. One option was simply adding the word "unanimous" to the existing caption: "The Unanimous Declaration by the Representatives of the United States of America." But that wasn't strictly accurate, as two delegates abstained from voting.[60] Nor was "the unanimous United States of America" likely to be an appealing option. So the only way to work in unanimity was to refer to the Declaration as the unanimous declaration of the states. It was rhetorically crisper, with the clear emphasis on "unanimous," as compared to the somewhat convoluted description in the original.

Rhetorical considerations also explain the Declaration's two uses of the phrase "our people," which most strongly suggest the voice of the states. In both instances, a plural first person pronoun would have proved awkward, especially in a document that was intended to be read aloud. The formulation that the king had sent "Swarms of Officers to harass *our People*" has far better poetic meter than "Swarms of Officers to harass *us*." Similarly, only someone with a tin ear for language would write, "He has plundered our Seas, ravaged our Coasts, burnt our Towns, and destroyed our Lives," which suggests that the speaker is dead. And the rhythm of the clause demands a longer con-cluding phrase. "Destroyed the lives of our People" is much better.

In short, there is little reason to take the caption of the ceremonial parchment at face value. The delegates altered the caption from the original to make a political point about unanimity, fumbling about the best they could, and settling on what seemed to be the least bad option. But that caption (itself not publicly revealed until 1777) is fundamentally inconsistent with the text that followed. And it is that text – not a later caption – that matters.

We, the Delegates, or We, the People?

A more plausible argument can be made that the "we" of the Declaration is the delegates to the Continental Congress, who, of course, drafted and approved the Declaration. The document's language suggests the voice of live human beings far more readily than that of abstract concepts like states or colonies. The delegates personally signed the ceremonial parchment under the phrase, "we mutually pledge to each other our Lives, our Fortunes, and our Sacred Honor." And perhaps most tellingly, when the Declaration actually provides a clear reference for the pronoun "we," it refers to the delegates: "We, therefore, the Representatives of the UNITED STATES OF AMERICA, in General Congress Assembled...." This closely correlates with the caption to the Dunlap Broadside: "A Declaration By the Representatives of the United States of America, In General Congress Assembled."

It is a better argument than "We, the States," but it, too, is ultimately unpersuasive. Consider the key phrase in full: "We, therefore, the Representatives of the UNITED STATES OF AMERICA, in General Congress, Assembled ... do, *in the Name of, and by Authority of the good People of these Colonies*, solemnly Publish and Declare...." The critical phrase is "in the Name of," which is not simply rhetorical reiteration of "by Authority of." Rather, the phrase directly tells us that the Declaration is the Declaration of "the good People of these Colonies." It *names* the voice that is speaking throughout the document, and it is not the states or the delegates, but the people. The Congress had used a similar structure in other significant public documents. In its 1775 response to the king's proclamation that the colonies were in a state of rebellion, for example, Congress spoke "in the name of the people of these United Colonies."[61]

A "We, the people" reading is also more consistent with the Declaration's larger structure and theory. The Declaration begins, "When in the Course of human Events, it becomes necessary for *one People* to dissolve the Political Bands which have connected them with another ... a decent Respect to the Opinions of Mankind, requires that *they should declare* the causes which impel *them* to the Separation." This sentence is immediately followed by the first use of the pronoun "We": "We hold these Truths...." The implication is clear. The voice that announces itself is the voice of the one people who are required to justify the reasons for independence. This reading is bolstered by the Declaration's larger political theory, which states that "whenever any Form of Government becomes destructive of these Ends, it is the Right of the *People* to alter or to abolish it." In other words, it is the people, and only the people, who have the right to overthrow a government. Severing ties with Great Britain could only be done by the people themselves, so it is entirely appropriate that the document be written in the voice of those same people.

There is a further problem with a "We, the Delegates" reading: although many of the Declaration's charges refer to offenses committed against all Americans, some of them seem to refer to specific events, such as the charge that he "transported us beyond Seas for be tried for pretended Offences." This certainly didn't happen to any signer of the Declaration (nor to any colonial American, as far as can be determined). Moreover, the claim that "We have petitioned for redress" through "every stage of these Oppressions" seems to be referring to petitions sent since 1765, long before the Second Continental Congress had convened.[62]

It is one thing to determine that the Declaration speaks in the voice of the "people." It is quite another to determine who exactly those people are. The Declaration certainly wasn't speaking for the thousands of Loyalists who wished to retain their allegiance to George III. Nor was it was speaking for the thousands of enslaved persons who toiled so that wealthy men could live in leisure. It did not speak for the Indian tribes that inhabited much of the land claimed by the thirteen colonies. Nor did women or children have any say in who selected the delegates to the Continental Congress. The "people" behind the Declaration turn out to be only a small portion of the American population.

By modern standards, the Declaration's claim to be speaking on behalf of the people is ludicrous, given the vast number of people it excluded. But even now, genuine popular consent and popular sovereignty can be hard to find. We still exclude children from voting, as well as noncitizens and, in many places, persons convicted of felonies. Moreover, given low participation rates in elections, there are hardly any political decisions one could point to as representing the clear will of the majority of the American people. Yet we still contend that our governments are based on popular consent (at the least the ones that are not horribly gerrymandered).[63]

One might say the same with respect to the Declaration. Of course, it didn't speak for all of the American people. But it mattered that it purported to do so. It is the right of the "people," not states or the delegates, to determine the structure of their government. The only legitimate basis for government is popular consent, and that can only be provided by the people, a group that would fortunately come to be much more broadly defined.

THE DECLARATION'S AUDIENCE

If the Declaration was speaking in the voice of the American people, to whom was it addressed? The document's opening sentence proclaims that a "decent respect to the Opinions of Mankind requires that they should declare the causes which impel them to the Separation." This strongly suggests that the Declaration is addressed to the rest of the world, and a number of scholars have emphasized its critical international audience. David Armitage, for example, in his global history of the Declaration, concluded that it was addressed to the "collective public opinion of the powers of the earth."[64] Garry Wills felt there was an even more specific foreign nation in mind, arguing that the Declaration was a "propaganda overture, addressed primarily to France."[65] By contrast, other scholars have found the domestic audience more salient. Pauline Maier, for example, argued that the Declaration was "designed first and foremost for domestic

consumption," a view consistent with the widespread public readings of the document.[66] Thomas Hutchinson, the former governor of
Massachusetts, concluded in 1776 that despite the document's reference to the "opinions of Mankind," its real purpose was "to reconcile
the people of America to ... Independence."[67]

There is considerable truth in both positions; the Declaration had
multiple intended audiences, and we need not definitively determine
which was most predominant. Hans Eicholz has best summarized it,
arguing that the Declaration "served a dual purpose, as an appeal to
world opinion (to mankind, as stated up front), and as an appeal to the
American people, as demonstrated by its initial widespread circula-
tion throughout the former colonies."[68] The document's reference to
"Mankind" likely speaks to all humanity, both foreign and domestic.
Through it, the American people were speaking not just to the rest of
the world, but, to a considerable extent, to themselves.

~~~

So who ultimately wrote the Declaration of Independence? The best
answer is this: The initial draft was composed by Thomas Jefferson, but
the Continental Congress authored the final document in the voice of
the American people.[69] Such was the view of the chief justice of South
Carolina, William Henry Drayton, who observed in October 1776 that
the "People of America..., by the Mouths of their Representatives in
Congress" had declared independence.[70] Or, as Gouverneur Morris
put in 1778, "the people of America, through their Congress, declared
themselves free and independent."[71] In 1809, Jefferson himself had
recognized the Declaration as an "act of [a] public bod[y]" to which
he could have "no personal claim."[72] If Jefferson had retained this
humility and been a little more precise on his tombstone, he could
certainly have called himself the "principal drafter" of the Declaration
of Independence.[73] That would have been more than sufficient glory
for a memorial – drafting such a significant document (at such a high
level) on behalf of the American people was an achievement for the
ages. There was no reason to claim even more.

3 IS THE DECLARATION OF INDEPENDENCE LAW?

First-year law students are routinely surprised to learn how much of the law is truly unsettled. Instead of clear-cut black and white rules, there are often endless shades of gray. A number of legal questions simply have no definite answer, as they have never been conclusively resolved by a court. And in even cases where a clear legal standard is established, the application can vary widely. Many tort cases, for example, turn on a "reasonable person" standard. Litigants – and jurors – must rely on their subjective sense of what this standard requires in any given circumstance.

Lawyers can usually agree, however, on which sources are relevant for answering legal questions. In our system, we look to the US Constitution, state constitutions, federal treaties, federal and state statutes, federal and state administrative regulations, and the decisions of federal and state courts. This vast body of material is what we refer to generally as "the law." Does it include the Declaration of Independence? Despite the seeming simplicity of this question, it has provoked widely conflicting answers from scholars and judges.

The vast majority have taken the position that the Declaration is not law. As they see it, the document is an airy statement of ideals, of no more legal authority than Abraham Lincoln's Gettysburg Address or Martin Luther King, Jr.'s "I Have a Dream" speech. It is a propaganda paper, designed for a particular historical purpose, but with no ongoing legal significance. To equate the Declaration with "law" is to fundamentally misunderstand what law is all about. The Constitution is law, but the Declaration clearly is not.

There are a number of dissenters, however, who counter that, yes, the Declaration is law, either as a directly binding legal authority or as a fundamental statement of legal principles, such as a commitment to natural law – the overarching, unwritten law to which all other laws are presumably subject. Under this view, ignoring the centrality of the Declaration of Independence fundamentally misunderstands American law.

Both the "yes" and "no" positions raise significant points, but neither is particularly persuasive on its own terms. The "no" camp fails to understand the multiple ways in which the Declaration is relevant to the world of law, while the "yes" camp inflates the Declaration to a level equivalent to (or even superior to) the Constitution. I propose a more nuanced approach: The Declaration is a legal document of continuing legal significance, even if it is not "law" in the sense of directly imposing ongoing legal obligations on public and private actors.

"NO, IT IS NOT LAW"

We can start with the "no" camp, which is supported by the bulk of historical and legal commentary. Garry Wills, for example, asserted that the "Declaration is not a legal instrument, like the Constitution," because it has "no such force of law."[1] Law professor Frederick Schauer suggested that "the Declaration is not now part of American law, or not much of a part of American law, whether constitutional or otherwise,"[2] and law professor Mark Graber notes that the "Declaration is not the source of any important legal right."[3] Law professor Darrell A. H. Miller writes that the Declaration "is not law. It does not purport to be law and it was not intended to be law. Courts do not enforce it as law."[4] Historian Willi Paul Adams views the Declaration as a "pithy statement of beliefs; legally speaking it was … irrelevant."[5] Benno Schmidt, the former dean of Columbia Law School, took perhaps the most extreme position, claiming that "the Declaration of Independence has no standing in constitutional interpretation whatsoever."[6]

American courts, too, routinely dismiss the legal significance of the Declaration. In a 2000 opinion, Justice Antonin Scalia argued that although "a right of parents to direct the upbringing of their children is an 'unalienable right' recognized by the Declaration of Independence," the document was "not a legal prescription conferring power upon the courts."[7] Arguments about the Declaration, he asserted, should be made to legislative bodies, not the judiciary.[8]

Most American courts have embraced Justice Scalia's view. In a 1988 decision, for example, the United States Court of Appeals for the Fourth Circuit stated bluntly that "the Declaration of Independence is a statement of ideals, not law."[9] In 2024, the United States Court of Appeals for the Tenth Circuit emphasized that the Declaration "does not grant enforceable rights."[10] Another federal appellate court warned against citing the Declaration of Independence, because "general statements about inalienable rights ... tell us little about the prerogatives of an individual in concrete factual situations."[11] A federal trial court told a plaintiff that he "could reference the Declaration of Independence as it pertains to his personal beliefs, but this document does not provide a legal basis ... to challenge any action of the federal government."[12] Another noted that the "Declaration of Independence is an important historical document, but it is not law."[13] The Supreme Court of Idaho concluded that the Declaration was "aspirational, but legally inoperative."[14] A federal court in California stated, "The Declaration of Independence is not a federal law, is not part of the Constitution, and does not give rise to a federal civil rights action."[15] A New York federal court, in a frequently quoted decision, stated, "While the Declaration states that all men are endowed with certain unalienable rights including 'Life, Liberty and the pursuit of Happiness' ... it does not grant rights that may be pursued through the judicial system."[16] A Connecticut court found that a claim based on the Declaration of Independence was "anachronistic and ludicrous."[17]

American attorneys generally understand that invoking the Declaration of Independence in court is one of the surest ways to send their clients on an express journey to Loserville. That insight has failed to reach many pro se litigants. Although some have been hostile to the Declaration, including one who sought an order requiring Congress to redraft the Declaration[18] and another who sued the Declaration itself,[19] pro se litigants have generally been the most enthusiastic proponents of the Declaration in court, convinced that the document's stirring language clearly resolves legal issues in their favor. In one case, in response to a defendant's motion to dismiss, a pro se plaintiff filed a copy of the Declaration of Independence, with his autograph added to the list of signatories.[20] None of these arguments, however, has been successful, and it's easy to see why. In recent years, pro se litigants have argued that the Declaration has been violated, for example, by:

- an automaker's failure to credit payments to a delinquent account;[21]
- a sheriff's acceptance of a check in a property sale;[22]
- the Reagan Administration's provision of aid to the Nicaraguan contras;[23]
- a Biden Administration registration requirement for firearms;[24]
- a bank employee's phone call to the police about an irate customer;[25]
- the New York City Fire Department's Covid-19 vaccine requirements;[26]
- the Bureau of Land Management's removal of a bridge on land that it owned;[27]
- the Washington State Nursing Commission's suspension of a nursing license;[28]
- Georgia Power Company's termination of electricity services;[29]
- a Texas county's collection of property taxes;[30]
- the procedures of the IRS;[31]
- the Consumer Financial Protection Bureau's and Senator Elizabeth Warren's criticism of Wells Fargo;[32]
- a California jail's failure "to separate the Satanic Church from the Christian Church";[33] and
- a bank's failure to issue a reverse mortgage.[34]

These types of frivolous claims help solidify American lawyers' perceptions about the Declaration of Independence – if you are relying on the Declaration of Independence, you are almost certainly losing, and losing big time.

"YES, IT IS LAW"

The profession's conventional wisdom about the irrelevance of the Declaration to American law has not gone unchallenged, however. A handful of intrepid judges have announced that the Declaration is, in fact, directly binding law. In 1971, a Michigan federal judge, addressing a request to expunge an arrest record, concluded, in a footnote, that the "Declaration of Independence ... has never been repealed, and, is valid and binding on all governments of the United States, federal and state, as a primary obligation."[35] The only authorities offered for this assertion were President Lincoln's Gettysburg Address and Second Inaugural, as carved on the Lincoln Memorial.[36] A year later, a justice of the New York Court of Appeals (the state's highest court) claimed in a dissenting opinion that "[t]he Declaration has the force of law and the constitutions of the United States and of the various States must harmonize with its tenets."[37] In his view, a New York statute liberalizing the state's abortion laws "turned its back on ... the natural law reiterated in the Declaration of Independence."[38] In a concurring opinion striking down California's ban on interracial marriage in 1948, a justice of the California Supreme Court stated, "The Declaration of Independence is a part of the law of our land."[39] The statutes at issue, he argued, "violated the supreme law of the land as found in the Declaration of Independence."[40]

Opinions for appellate courts, which require at least two judges to agree, less commonly invoke the Declaration, but there are a few noteworthy examples. In a 1980 decision, the Wyoming Supreme Court stated, "where the law must decide whether a child will be separated from his mother, we have looked to the Declaration of Independence for guidance."[41] The court found that "the rearing of our children" was part of the "pursuit of happiness" recognized by the Declaration. An Ohio state appellate court, in a 1928 opinion arising from a bank insolvency, declared, "Our opinion is that this declaration is part of the law of this state, as much so as its Constitution and statutes. Without its adoption and maintenance there would have been no federal or state Constitution."[42] In 1899, the Court of Appeals for the District of Columbia stated, "The Declaration of Independence is not, as has sometimes been flippantly asserted, a mere string of glittering generalities. It is a bill of rights which enters fundamentally into the structure of our Government; and the one great fundamental truth, which it seeks to enforce, is the doctrine of the equality of all men before the law."[43] The Supreme Court of North Carolina took a somewhat similar approach in 1892, when it referred to a "violation of a fundamental right asserted in our own national *Magna Charta*, the Declaration of Independence."[44]

A handful of judges have sought to ground certain unwritten rights directly in the Declaration of Independence. In a 1912 decision, Oklahoma's highest court for criminal cases held, "The right of a father to defend his daughter is founded upon the law of nature, and is not and cannot be superseded by any law of society. This is an inalienable right recognized in and protected by the Declaration of Independence."[45] A Texas supreme court justice recently claimed, "Like the inalienable rights of which the Declaration of Independence speaks, the bond between parent and child was not given by law. We were endowed with it by our Creator."[46] Similarly, a federal judge in Texas concluded that the Declaration of Independence "recognizes that people have rights that are not readily taken by statutes such as parenting a minor."[47] An Illinois appellate judge has suggested that there is a constitutional right to the pursuit of happiness, based on the interaction of the Declaration of Independence and the Ninth Amendment (which states that the Bill of Rights should not be interpreted as an exhaustive list of rights).[48]

Other judges have suggested that the Declaration is a guide to interpretation. In 1897, the United States Supreme Court stated, "While such declaration of principles may not have the force of organic law, or be made the basis of judicial decision as to the limits of right and duty... it is always safe to read the letter of the constitution in the spirit of the Declaration of Independence."[49] A Texas Supreme Court justice has argued that "between two equally plausible interpretations" of a statute, a court should prefer the one "that better accommodates the inalienable rights proclaimed by the Declaration of Independence."[50] In a similar vein, Justice Arthur Goldberg of the United States Supreme Court argued, "The Declaration of Independence states the American creed."[51]

A handful of academics have taken up the case for the Declaration as law. Harvard Law School professor Mark Tushnet argued in a 1999 book that certain phrases from the Declaration (rephrased to reflect modern sensibilities) combined with the Constitution's preamble create a "thin constitution," a basis for a "populist constitutional law" in which judicial review no longer exists.[52] In his view,

"The Declaration's principles define our fundamental law" and "the Constitution requires only that the principles of the Declaration of Independence be respected."[53] Law professor Scott Douglas Gerber argued in a 1995 book that "the natural-rights principles embodied in the Declaration are not 'above' or 'beyond' the Constitution; they are at the heart of the Constitution."[54] Another enthusiast was legal scholar Charles Black, who claimed that "the doctrines of the Declaration should be taken to have the force of *law*."[55]

An especially fervent proponent was Professor Harry Jaffa of Claremont McKenna College. A student of philosopher Leo Strauss, Jaffa helped draft portions of Barry Goldwater's 1964 Republican National Convention speech, including the famous line that "extremism in defense of liberty is no vice."[56] In Jaffa's view, "the Declaration remains the most fundamental dimension of the law of the Constitution."[57] "The heart of the Declaration," he contended, was a "natural theology" and the conviction "that there is a permanent order in the universe by which human beings ought, directly or indirectly, to be guided, whether as men or as citizens."[58] What precisely follows from any of this is unclear, as Jaffa rarely descended from high theory to the particulars of actual legal disputes, other than to assert that the *Dred Scott* case was wrongly decided.[59] As one critic complained, Jaffa's view "of the Declaration as the meaning of the Constitution is almost incomprehensible."[60]

Invocations of natural law and natural rights will ring hollow for most modern American lawyers, as these concepts have essentially no role in contemporary legal practice. Law professor Stuart Banner has explained, "if a lawyer tries to discuss natural law in court, the judge will look puzzled, and opposing counsel will start planning the victory party."[61] Natural law has generally been understood to be a pre-existing, unchanging, unwritten law to which all man-made law must conform. Such an idea can be found as far back as Sophocles' play *Antigone*, written in the fifth century BCE, and it was a widely accepted component of Roman law. Many eighteenth-century Americans had at least some familiarity with natural law, although the full extent is not entirely clear. Richard Helmholz notes, "It is hard to arrive at a fully satisfactory explanation for what the authors of American independence knew about the law of nature, but there is little doubt that many of them did know something, and some of them knew quite a bit."[62] American courts invoked natural law in the eighteenth and nineteenth centuries, although only rarely to invalidate legislative action; far more common was the use of natural law to interpret a statute.[63]

For a variety of reasons, natural law arguments largely disappeared from American legal discourse in the late nineteenth and early twentieth centuries, although they have re-emerged in other forms.[64] Arguments about "fundamental rights," for example, are often indistinguishable from arguments about natural rights. Professor Banner suggests that a revitalized jurisprudence of natural law would probably make little, if any, difference to any actual legal dispute: "Lawyers would use different words in their arguments, but the substance of their arguments would remain largely the same."[65]

We can safely assume that many members of the Continental Congress had some broad familiarity with the concept of natural law and were certainly not hostile to it.[66] But the case that the Declaration requires a robust commitment to natural law is often overstated. As a textual matter, the document nowhere uses the exact term "natural law," and it is implied only twice. The first is in the opening sentence, where the Declaration asserts that the American people are claiming the "separate and equal Station to which the Laws of Nature and of Nature's God entitle them." This is a seeming mixture of both natural and divine law, although phrased in a very unusual way. A search of a database of American printed materials, for example, reveals only twenty-three uses of the term "Nature's God" prior to 1776, most of which are in poetry and none of which occur in a legal or political context.[67] Similarly, the phrase "Laws of Nature" can be easily read, as Harvard historian I. Bernard Cohen argued, as a Newtonian reference to the laws of science.[68] Alternatively, the laws of nature may merely assert the equality of nations under conventional eighteenth-century understandings of international law.[69]

The second reference is the statement that "all Men created equal, that they are endowed by their Creator with certain unalienable Rights, that among these are Life, Liberty, and the Pursuit of Happiness." Although this does not explicitly refer to the doctrine of natural law, it is a fairly straightforward explanation of the commonplace late seventeenth- and eighteenth-century view that certain rights (we might call them natural rights) predate society, and that governments are created to protect those rights.

But when the Declaration gets down to business – articulating specific complaints about the British king – nothing turns on natural rights or natural law. Complaints about deprivation of jury trials and royal control over judges' salaries, for example, are technical procedural arguments rooted in the English common law experience; no one could plausibly argue that they derived from natural law. As legal historian John Phillip Reid noted, the rights asserted in the charges "belonged only to those who had customarily possessed them from time immemorial. Only the British could make that claim, for they were English constitutional principles, sanctioned by English constitutional history, and guaranteed by English common law. Far from being a statement of abstract, natural principles, the Declaration is a document of peculiarly English constitutional dogmas."[70]

Nor did natural law arguments significantly shape the debates about the scope of British authority in the 1760s and the 1770s that led up to the Declaration. Reid found that "natural-law principles" had only a minor significance "in the debates with the mother country" and "in motivating Americans to support the Whig cause."[71] Far more important were the principles of seventeenth- and eighteenth-century English constitutionalism.[72] Reid notes that "American whigs did not in any official petition or resolution claim a natural right that was not already extant in British constitutional theory or English common law."[73] When the Declaration asserts that the king and Parliament had subjected the colonists to a "Jurisdiction foreign to our Constitution," for example, it is speaking in constitutional language, not the language of natural law.

None of this is to deny that the Declaration can be read as expressing a broad commitment to natural law; rather, the point is that such a reading is neither inescapable nor required. The document at no point squarely states that natural law should govern the internal decisions of the nation going forward; that conclusion must rest on something more substantial than the cursory and elusive statements in the Declaration itself.

An entirely different argument for the Declaration as law rests on its placement in the United States Code, the current version of which includes the Declaration of Independence, the Articles of Confederation, and the Northwest Ordinance of 1787 under the heading "The Organic Laws of the United States of America." In a tribute to Professor Jaffa, Lewis Lehrman argued that "the original intent of the Founders and the United States Code incorporated the Declaration of Independence into the Constitution of the United States."[74] Jaffa himself claimed that the Declaration has always had constitutional status "in the statutes of the United States."[75] Libertarian attorney Timothy Sandefur has argued that the Declaration "appears at the front of our law books, at volume one, page one of the United States *Statutes at Large*, and at the head of the United States Code.... It is hard to understand why we would deny the Declaration standing as law."[76] In a 2015 opinion, a Texas Supreme Court justice found it highly significant that "Congress placed the Declaration of Independence at the outset – page 1, volume 1 – of the United States Code, under this heading: 'Organic Laws of the United States of America.'"[77] Under this view, there is no need to embrace natural law – the statutory law of the United States itself enacts the Declaration of Independence as law.

Upon close examination, however, this argument proves to be basically frivolous. The United States Code, an attempt to place the statutes of the United States in some type of logical order, was not authorized by Congress until 1926. The federal statute establishing the Code directed that the compilers include the Declaration of Independence.[78] But why would an editorial decision by Congress during the Coolidge Administration conclusively ascertain the fundamental law of the United States?[79] Suppose Congress had excluded the Declaration from the Code – would that mean the Declaration was no longer law? If so, something so casually discarded must have had little legal weight to begin with. If not, whatever legal significance it holds has nothing to do with its placement in the Code.

Congress was not writing on a completely blank slate in 1926.[80] Starting in 1795, Congress had authorized the printing of collections of federal statutes in chronological order.[81] The initial volumes included the Constitution, but not the Declaration.[82] In 1814, Congress authorized a new edition and directed that it include the "declaration of independence."[83] At the time, the United States was again at war with Great Britain, so it probably seemed worthwhile to reiterate the

Declaration. In 1845, Congress approved a new set of volumes entitled the *Statutes at Large*, which would become the official source of laws going forward. Congress directed that the volumes also include the Articles of Confederation and the Constitution.[84] But this time it said nothing about the Declaration, which nonetheless appeared in the first volume.[85] The editor, Richard Peters, the son of a federal judge and a former reporter of decisions of the United States Supreme Court, was likely following the tradition of the 1814 volume – an editorial decision that hardly constitutes a definitive determination of the laws of the United States.

The history of American statutory compilations thus reveals that the Declaration has been treated in an idiosyncratic manner, not at all suggestive of a clear congressional intent to adopt the Declaration as law. No one would argue, for example, that the inclusion of the Articles of Confederation in an 1845 compilation made those Articles legally binding, and there is no better reason for thinking it did so with respect to the Declaration. If the Declaration is to be understood as law, it must be for stronger reasons than its treatment by nineteenth- and twentieth-century editors.

THE DECLARATION AS A LEGAL DOCUMENT OF CONTINUING LEGAL SIGNIFICANCE

Neither the "yes" nor "no" camp gets it quite right, and both positions are marred by the tendency to take the claims to their most extreme conclusions. The "yes" camp is incorrect to the extent that it treats the Declaration as directly governing law. The Declaration is not the Constitution or a federal statute, and treating it as such is a serious mistake. But the "no" camp also errs when it claims that the Declaration is entirely irrelevant to American law.

The best way to think about the Declaration is that it is a legal document with continuing legal significance.[86] That is, the Declaration enacted a legal change – separation from Great Britain and the termination of British rule over the thirteen American colonies. Unlike the Gettysburg Address, this had immediate, tangible legal consequences; it was effectively a national divorce decree. Moreover, that legal effect was not limited to the year 1776. The Declaration of Independence continues to inform and shape American law in a wide variety of ways.[87]

Justification for State Constitutions

Although an earlier congressional resolution had called for the formation of new state governments, a number of states cited the Declaration in the preambles to the new state constitutions they wrote following independence.[88] New York even included the complete text of the Declaration in its constitution of 1777.[89]

Severance of English Common Law

With one exception, every American state has adopted the common law of England as the primary rule of decision for its courts (Louisiana applies the civil law of the European continent). The English common law is centuries old, and states had to answer the question, "At what point will we treat this law as no longer directly binding?" There are a variety of approaches, but the most typical is to treat the Declaration of Independence as the critical date. The Washington Supreme Court, for example, has held that "the common law and statutes of England prior to the time of the Declaration of Independence constitute the rule of decision in this state."[90] The North Carolina Supreme Court has held that the "'common' law to be applied in North Carolina is the common law of England to the extent it was in force and use within this State at the time of the Declaration of Independence."[91] In Nevada, "unless superseded by state or federal law, the common law of Nevada is the statutory and common law of England as it existed at the signing of the Declaration of Independence."[92] Florida law states that the "common and statute laws of England ... down to the 4th day of July, 1776, are declared to be of force in this state."[93]

In an 1889 decision, the United States Supreme Court held that "The law of Great Britain since the declaration of independence is the law of a foreign country" and must be argued as such.[94] A 1942 federal court decision stated that questions of federal law, in the absence of a federal statute, should be decided "in accordance with the principles of the common law existing prior to the Declaration of Independence."[95]

Title to Land and State Boundaries

American courts have held that, under the Declaration of Independence, title to public lands passed immediately from the British Crown to the individual states in which the land was occupied. Although Great Britain recognized such a title only following the 1783 Treaty of Paris, the American position has always been, as the Supreme Court explained in 1827, that "the soil and sovereignty within their acknowledged limits, were as much theirs at the declaration of independence as at this hour."[96] A New York court in 1905 concluded, "By the Declaration of Independence the right, title, and interest of the British Crown in the public streets and highways vested in the people of the state."[97] The principle was equally applicable to ungranted lands within a colony.[98] A panel of federal arbitrators determined in 1849 that the "Declaration of Independence, for the day it was made, is thenceforth the title of every state."[99] Not every colony was a royal colony, directly under the control of the king. Some were governed by proprietors, who typically held title to the colony under hereditary right. But their claims, too, were extinguished by the Declaration. For example, the Delaware Supreme Court held that the Declaration terminated title to lands held by the heirs of the founding proprietor William Penn and transferred them by sovereign succession to the state of Delaware.[100] The Declaration, the Court held, "prostrated equally the Kingly and Proprietary Powers."[101]

Relatedly, the Supreme Court has held that "The Declaration of Independence has made Delaware a state with boundaries fixed as of that time."[102] The Court held "when the colonies dissolved their connection with the mother country by the Declaration of Independence … it was understood by all of them, that each did so, with the limits which belong to it as a colony.[103]

Citizenship

American judicial decisions have consistently dated the creation of American citizenship to the adoption of the Declaration of Independence on July 4, 1776.[104] Persons present in the United States on that date are presumed to be American citizens, unless they actively took steps to retain their allegiance to Britain.[105] A South Carolina court held in 1825, for example, that a Frenchman who came to South Carolina in 1774 became a citizen by virtue of the Declaration of Independence.[106] By contrast, English law contends that Americans remained British subjects until the signing of the Treaty of Paris in 1783.[107] Few current disputes turn on this distinction, but it was of considerable consequence in the late eighteenth and early nineteenth centuries, since only citizens could inherit real property in America.

Treason

The law of treason provided an important corollary to the law of citizenship. The Declaration provided firm legal support for what many colonial Americans had been arguing since the war began – that adherence to the king of Great Britain was treason.[108] On June 24, 1776, the Continental Congress adopted a resolution stating that "all persons abiding within any of the United Colonies, and deriving protection from the same, owe allegiance to the said laws, and are members of such colony." And any such person who adhered to the King of Great Britain was "guilty of treason against such colony."[109]

The American colonies had regularly imprisoned British adherents prior to the Declaration, but they had hesitated to impose the death penalty, due to the obvious legal awkwardness. As a Massachusetts man explained, "No one thing made the Declaration of Independence indispensably necessary more than cutting off traitors. It is amazingly wonderful that, having no capital punishment for our intestine enemies, we have not been utterly ruined before now ... Our Tories ... knew very well the absurdity of punishing as high treason any acts or deeds in favor of the government of the King of Great Britain, so long as we all allowed him to be King of the Colonies."[110] John Adams argued that a great benefit of the Declaration was to make it easier to "establish Tests and ascertain the criminality of Toryism."[111]

The Declaration stated that "we hold [our British brethren], as we hold the rest of Mankind, Enemies in War, in Peace, Friends." "Enemies," of course, has a technical meaning within the law of treason. Under English law, adherence to the "enemy" was treason, and the American states quickly responded with a host of treason statutes punishing aid to the British as treason. Persons who maintained their allegiance to the King now faced the very real prospect of capital punishment.[112] In 1789, historian David Ramsay observed that the "change of the public mind of America respecting connection with Great Britain" was "without parallel. In the short space of two years nearly three millions of people passed over from the love and duty of subjects, to the hatred and refinement of enemies."[113]

Requirement for Admission to the Union

Since 1864, Congress has required that territories seeking statehood create constitutions that are "not repugnant to … the principles of the Declaration of Independence." Such provisions were part of the Enabling Acts (the statutes setting forth the conditions and process for statehood) for the territories that became Nevada, Colorado, North Dakota, South Dakota, Montana, Washington, Oklahoma, Arizona, Alaska, and Hawaii.[114] It is unclear why Congress introduced this requirement in 1864, although it is possible that the Declaration was being invoked as an antislavery document.[115] One member of Congress expressed concern, claiming that this was "an entirely new condition…. The interpretations which are given to that important paper are so various and wide apart that I think it would be a very unsafe rule," but Congress adopted it anyway.[116]

Courts have taken a variety of approaches to the Enabling Acts. The Oklahoma Supreme Court, for example, concluded that the Enabling Act applied only to the state's original constitutional convention and was not "in force forever as an irrevocable limitation on the sovereign powers of the state."[117] This view is supported by the 1911 decision of the United States Supreme Court in *Coyle v. Smith*, which held that an Enabling Act provision specifying the location of Oklahoma's capitol was unenforceable after admission to statehood.[118] An alternative holding, the Court concluded, would create two tiers of states – those with full powers of statehood and those with powers limited by Enabling Acts.[119]

Some state courts, however, have recognized that the Declaration of Independence has at least some legal authority as a result of the Enabling Acts. In a 2024 decision in a residential boundary dispute,

the Arizona Supreme Court cited the state's Enabling Act and concluded that "consistent with the principles of the Declaration of
Independence and the federal and Arizona Constitutions, the ownership of property is a natural right of significant interest which we
have a duty to protect."[120] One justice refused to sign on to this language, since it "arguably suggests that through the Enabling Act, the
Declaration of Independence and its proclamation of 'natural right[s]'
similarly constrain Arizona's constitution."[121]

In individual opinions, judges have occasionally stated that the
Declaration is binding law under the Enabling Acts. A Washington
supreme court justice, for example, relied on the Enabling Act to
conclude that "no taxation without representation" was a fundamental principle of the Declaration that was binding in Washington
state.[122] A justice of the Colorado Supreme Court concluded that the
state's constitution "must not be repugnant ... to the principles of the
Declaration of Independence."[123]

The view of disbarred law professor John Eastman that "the
Declaration of Independence [has] the sanction of positive law, at least
in the eleven states admitted to the Union since the Civil War that
were statutorily bound by the principles of the Declaration" is almost
certainly overstated.[124] Nonetheless, Congress at least scrutinized
the proposed state constitutions for consistency with the Declaration
of Independence, and the document's principles may be, at least in
Arizona, governing law.

Interpretation of State Constitutions

A number of American state constitutions contain language
taken directly, or in close paraphrase, from the Declaration of
Independence.[125] The Iowa Constitution, for example, states, "All
men are, by nature, free and equal, and have certain inalienable
rights – among which are those of enjoying and defending life and liberty, acquiring, possessing, and protecting property, and pursuing and
obtaining safety and happiness."[126]

Some state supreme courts have held that these provisions recognize judicially enforceable individual rights. In 2019, for example, the
Kansas Supreme Court held that a state constitutional provision stating

"All men are possessed of equal and inalienable natural rights, among which are life, liberty, and the pursuit of happiness" protected a right to abortion. In reaching this conclusion, the justices engaged in extended analysis of the Declaration of Independence.[127] The Iowa Supreme Court has held that a similar provision in the Iowa Constitution is "not a mere glittering generality without substance or meaning" but protects citizens' "pre-existing common law rights (sometimes known as 'natural rights')."[128] Similarly, the North Dakota Supreme Court, relying in part on the Declaration of Independence, found that its state constitutional provision protects a broad array of fundamental rights.[129]

Other states have taken a more restrictive approach, concluding that these provisions do not authorize courts to strike down state statutes. The Supreme Court of New Mexico, for example, has held that the "Inherent Rights Clause has never been interpreted to be the exclusive source for a fundamental or important constitutional right."[130] The Supreme Court of Ohio has held its state constitutional provision was "a statement of fundamental ideals" that required "other provisions of the Ohio Constitution or legislative definitions to give it practical effect."[131]

Creation of a "Negative Constitution"

In June 2024, the United States Supreme Court issued two decisions involving jury rights, and both cases relied in part on the Declaration of Independence. The first case considered whether, under the federal Armed Career Criminal Act, defendants were entitled to a jury trial on the question of whether their past offenses were committed on separate occasions. The Court held that they were, and began its analysis by noting, "Prominent among the reasons colonists cited in the Declaration of Independence for their break with Great Britain was the fact Parliament and the Crown had 'depriv[ed] [them] in many cases, of the benefits of Trial by Jury.'"[132] The second case addressed whether the Securities and Exchange Commission could impose civil penalties without a jury trial. The Court held that it could not, and stated, "when the English continued to try Americans without juries, the Founders cited the practice as a justification for severing our ties to England. See Declaration of Independence ¶20."[133]

In these cases, the Court used the Declaration's charges against the king as a sort of "negative constitution." Under this approach, each charge amounts to a negative command – a blueprint of what *not* to do. An action so horrific as to be cited as a justification for independence should surely not be tolerated now. Read in this way, the Declaration effectively directs governments not to deny the benefits of trial by jury. The charges against the king can thus provide a framework that courts can enforce, or, at minimum, take into account when interpreting other constitutional provisions.

American courts have been employing this technique since at least 1799, when Chief Justice Oliver Ellsworth, presiding over a trial in Connecticut, noted, "That the king of England refused to permit the naturalization of aliens in the colonies, was one of the causes of complaint enumerated in the Declaration of Independence."[134] Although few judges have explicitly commented on the rationale behind this practice, Justice Brett Kavanaugh argued in a 2024 opinion that "[t]he pre-ratification history of America's many objections to British laws and the system of oppressive British rule over the Colonies – identified most prominently in the Declaration of Independence – can likewise inform interpretation of some of the crucial provisions of the original Constitution and Bill of Rights."[135] Justice Neil Gorsuch has noted, "The Declaration of Independence did not endorse crown prerogatives but described many as evils."[136] And in the famous 1952 *Youngstown* decision, rejecting President Truman's seizure of the steel industry, Justice Robert Jackson explained, "The example of such unlimited executive power that must have most impressed the forefathers was the prerogative exercised by George III, and the description of its evils in the Declaration of Independence leads me to doubt that they were creating their new Executive in his image."[137]

There are dozens of judicial decisions that invoke the charges against the king in this manner.[138] In a 2023 decision about jury rights, for example, the Supreme Court cited the Declaration's charges that the King had protected British soldiers by a "mock Trial" and that he had transported colonists "beyond the [sic] Seas to be tried for pretended offences."[139] Here, we can interpret the Declaration as prohibiting mock trials or transporting individuals beyond Seas to be tried for pretended offences. In a 2011 case arising from a dispute over the estate of Anna Nicole Smith's deceased husband, the Court noted, "Article III protects liberty not only through its role in implementing the separation of powers, but also by specifying the defining characteristics of Article III judges. The colonists had been subjected to judicial abuses at the hand of the Crown, and the Framers knew the main reasons why: because the King of Great Britain 'made Judges dependent on his Will alone, for the tenure of their offices, and the amount and payment of the salaries.' The Declaration of Independence ¶11."[140] Here, the Declaration can be read as imposing a command that judges should not be dependent upon the will of the executive alone.

The Declaration's commitment to judicial independence has been an especially resonant theme for American courts,[141] as has been its commitment to trial by jury.[142] (Most do not go so far as an Ohio Supreme Court justice, who quoted almost the entirety of the Declaration to object to his colleagues' reversal of a jury verdict.)[143] But a host of other charges have generated their own "negative commands" including those dealing with civilian control of the military,[144] standing armies,[145] quartering of troops,[146] taxation without representation,[147] the obstruction of naturalization laws,[148] the improper use of military tribunals,[149] the right to petition,[150] and the right to representation.[151]

~~~

So, is the Declaration of Independence law? Given all the ways in which the Declaration is relevant to law, a dismissive "no" is surely incorrect. The Declaration is far more intertwined with American law than, say, the Gettysburg Address. At the same time, a hearty "yes" doesn't fully capture the situation either, since the document lacks most of the typical attributes of directly binding law. We can avoid the pitfalls of both positions, however, by viewing it as a legal document with continuing legal significance.

One last point about law. All the legal decisions discussed in this chapter treat the adoption of the Declaration of Independence on July 4, 1776, as marking the legal separation of the United States from Great Britain. But on July 2, 1776, the Continental Congress voted to approve Richard Henry Lee's resolution for independence. Writing to his wife Abigail the next day, John Adams stated, "The Second Day of July, 1776, will be the most memorable Epocha, in the History of

America. I am apt to believe that it will be celebrated, by succeeding Generations, as the great anniversary Festival. It ought to be commemorated, as the Day of Deliverance by solemn Acts of Devotion to God Almighty. It ought to be solemnized with Pomp and Parade, with Shows, Games, Sports, Guns, Bells, Bonfires, and Illuminations from one End of this Continent to the other from this Time forward forever more."[152]

Adams astutely predicted the course of future July 4 celebrations, but he famously got the date wrong. Or did he? After all, surely John Adams, of all people, would know when the United States became independent. And one can make a plausible argument that July 2 ought to be considered the technical date of independence. The *Pennsylvania Evening Post* appears to have gotten the scoop, with a one-sentence note on the last page of its July 2, 1776 issue stating, "This day the CONTINENTAL CONGRESS declared the UNITED COLONIES FREE and INDEPENDENT STATES."[153]

But there is also a strong case for July 4. The Declaration nowhere refers to the July 2 resolution, and its voicing suggests it is doing something in the present moment. It says, "We ... publish and declare," not "we have declared" or "we have resolved," which it would have done if it was simply reporting an earlier event. "Publishing" and "declaring" legally alters the status of the parties, as in a declaration of war. The Congress did not publish its July 2 vote; instead, it published the Declaration of Independence through the Dunlap Broadside, with the July 4, 1776, date prominently displayed. Any American reading the Dunlap Broadside would have had no reason to know that there was an earlier undisclosed vote.

One might also consider the issue of finality. Suppose on July 3, 1776, a member of the Continental Congress introduced a motion to reconsider the July 2 vote. The Congress probably could have considered that motion. But once independence had been publicly "declared," through a formal Declaration of Independence now racing off of the printing presses, independence became a formal, legal, and irrevocable reality.

PART II

Creating an American Nation

On July 4, 2023, *The Atlantic* published an excerpt by the Vietnamese-American writer Beth Nguyen, from her memoir, *Owner of a Lonely Heart*. A child refugee from Vietnam, Nguyen did not know the date of her birth. As she recalled, "I envied my friends who could cite details about their own birth, down to the minute. No one in my family had a birth certificate. I spent years longing for what I thought of as evidence of my beginnings." Although her mother seemed to suggest that it made no difference, Nguyen wanted to know – for her, it was an essential part of her identity.[1]

Just as personal identity is rooted in the circumstances of one's birth, so, too, is national identity. By longstanding custom, we treat the Declaration of Independence as our national birth certificate and celebrate July 4, 1776 as our national birthday. In 2026, by this reckoning, the United States of America will be 250 years old.

But, as the fireworks soar into the sky on July 4, 2026, it is worth asking whether we are celebrating the correct date. Many scholars have insisted that we are not. At most, they have claimed, July 4 is the anniversary of independence from Great Britain, but it is not the birthday of the United States of America. The Declaration of Independence created thirteen independent nations, who only later, through the Articles of Confederation, the Constitution, or maybe even the Civil War, merged together into the nation-state we now call the United States of America. Under this view, it is appropriate to celebrate July 4 as "Independence Day," but it generated thirteen birth certificates, not one. Willmoore Kendall and George Carey, for example, argued that the "Declaration of Independence did not ... establish our independence *as a nation*. Rather, what it did was to establish a baker's dozen of new sovereignties."[2] In their view, 1789 had "a far stronger claim to marking the beginnings of our nation."[3] In his influential book *Inventing America*, Garry Wills insisted, "Not one country, but thirteen separate ones, came into existence when the Declaration was at last made unanimous on July 19, 1776."[4] Law professor Joel Richard Paul claims, "The United States did not declare independence; rather, the individual states declared their independence.... The states were allies in the struggle for independence, but they were not yet one nation."[5] Paul even argues that the very term "United States" was a "convenient fiction."[6] A prominent article by two other law professors agrees, concluding that the "American States possessed full sovereignty following the Declaration of Independence" and when the Constitution was adopted, each state was understood as a "separate sovereign possessing *all* of the rights and powers traditionally recognized by the law of nations."[7] Another scholar suggests that a "*national* identity for the United States did not congeal until after the War of 1812" and that a "*United* States of America was but an idea, an aspiration throughout much of the founding period and even through the critical years of the 1790s."[8]

The view that the Declaration created thirteen independent nations has even penetrated the highest levels of the federal judiciary. In a 2019 decision, authored by Justice Clarence Thomas, the United States Supreme Court stated, "After independence, the States considered themselves fully sovereign nations."[9] A 2011 decision from the United States Court of Appeals for the Seventh Circuit proclaimed, "From the time of the Declaration of Independence until the Constitution of 1787 took effect, the states were fully sovereign in the international sense of the term: they were States, just as modern-day France, Japan, or India are States today."[10]

Although this view is widespread, it is profoundly mistaken. The Declaration announced the birth of a union of states – a confederated republic – that stood as one nation with respect to the rest of the world.[11] To be sure, the individual colonies (now states) retained significant powers, and were potentially free to leave the American Union. There was no unitary nation-state on July 4, 1776, in the sense of a national government that had complete authority over every subunit.

But if that's the test for a nation-state, we still don't live in one, given the significant powers reserved to state and tribal governments.[12] Many federal states divide power among subunits; they are no less a nation as a result. Nor is a potential right to secession necessarily inconsistent with nationhood. The United Kingdom is no less a nation because it entertained a referendum on Scottish independence in 2014. Ethiopia recognizes a constitutional right for its subunits to secede, but it is still clearly a nation.[13] A more useful way of thinking about a nation might be how it looks on a map of the world. Would it be colored in with one color or thirteen? And with respect to the larger community of nations, there was clearly only one color – the United States of America that presented itself as one nation to the rest of the world.

This point has tended to be obscured by our modern understanding of constitutions as written documents. Under this view, the United States has had two constitutions: The Articles of Confederation, which were ratified in 1781, and the US Constitution, which was drafted in 1787. But this view leaves a gaping hole – what was the constitution of the United States from 1776 to 1781?

The answer is that the United States had an unwritten constitution, an informal set of arrangements that were nonetheless approved by popular consent.[14] This type of a constitution would have been readily familiar to the American colonists, as the English constitution was itself unwritten, consisting of a mishmash of institutions, procedures, court cases, and occasional documents accumulated over time. Historian Jonathan Gienapp observes that it was as "much a description of how law and government actually functioned as a prescription for how it ought to work" – "as much a set of habits and practices as it was a concrete set of materials."[15] Nonetheless, the English constitution was viewed with reverence, and much of the colonial dispute with Britain centered on debates over the nature of the English constitution.

A similar unwritten constitution emerged after the Declaration of Independence.[16] As Thomas McKean, a signer of the Declaration and the chief justice of Pennsylvania, stated in 1781, after the Declaration, "The powers of sovereignty were then lodged with Congress." No formal document empowered the Congress, but as McKean explained, "[A] formal compact is not a necessary foundation of government" if it is nonetheless based on popular consent.[17]

This unwritten constitution – America's first – placed control over all matters of external sovereignty in the Continental Congress, which possessed the supreme powers of war and peace, of diplomacy, and of treaty-making. The Congress drafted and ratified treaties, appointed ambassadors, controlled the Continental Army and appointed its officers, reviewed and reversed state court judgments in admiralty cases, and consistently asserted its authority over all matters of foreign relations. It is thus entirely inaccurate to claim, as some scholars have, that the states "surrendered aspects of their sovereignty" for the "first" time in the Articles of Confederation.[18]

This Part explains how the Declaration of Independence created the independent nation of the United States of America. It begins by first examining closely the actual text of the Declaration, which, contrary to many hasty interpretations, is fully consistent with a one-nation thesis. It then turns to historical practice. Americans after 1776 presented themselves as one nation to the rest of the world, recognized the Continental Congress as the governing national body, and operated as a confederate republic even without the benefit of formal articles of confederation. When later Americans reflected on the founding, they largely agreed that a nation had been created on July 4, 1776. Such was the holding of early court cases that directly considered the issue, and the consistent view of the United States Supreme Court until very recently. It was the view of eminent lawyers and statesmen like John Quincy Adams, Andrew Jackson, Joseph Story, Daniel Webster, and Abraham Lincoln. And it was the view of ordinary Americans, who have continuously celebrated the Fourth of July as the "national birthday."[19]

4 TEXT

The textual debate over the legal status of the United States of America has tended to focus almost entirely on one sentence from the Declaration's final paragraph:

> We ... solemnly Publish and Declare, That these United Colonies are, and of Right ought to be, FREE AND INDEPENDENT STATES; that they are absolved from all Allegiance to the British Crown, and that all political Connection between them and the State of Great-Britain, is and ought to be totally dissolved; and that as FREE AND INDEPENDENT STATES, they have full Power to levy War, conclude Peace, contract Alliances, establish Commerce, and to do all other Acts and Things which INDEPENDENT STATES may of right do.

Proponents of the thirteen-independent-nations argument place enormous emphasis on this passage. And it's easy to see why. After all, it explicitly refers to "Free and Independent States," not to one nation, and those states are recognized as having all the powers of "Independent States."

Such a conclusion, however, is far too quick. An emphasis on "Free and Independent States" overlooks an equally important piece of textual evidence: the critical phrase "these United Colonies." The Declaration tells us that "these United Colonies" = "Free and Independent States." It does not say that Massachusetts, for example, is an independent state, or even that thirteen colonies are now free and independent states, but that the *United Colonies* are now independent states.

The term "United Colonies" had been widely used to describe the colonies that had sent delegates to the Second Continental Congress. A Massachusetts newspaper reported in May 1775, for example, that a uniform postal system was likely to be established "throughout the United Colonies."[1] On June 19, 1775, John Hancock signed George Washington's commission as the "General and Commander in Chief of the army of the United Colonies."[2] In the July 1775 Declaration of the Causes and Necessity of Taking Up Arms, the members of Congress described themselves as "Representatives of the United Colonies of North-America."[3] That same month it was reported that the military forces gathered in Massachusetts were not "to be distinguished as the troops of any particular colony but as the forces of 'THE UNITED COLONIES OF NORTH AMERICA' into whose joint service they have been taken by the Continental congress, and are to be paid and supported accordingly."[4] In August 1775, Benjamin Franklin was appointed "Postmaster General of the United Colonies of North-America," and two other men were appointed "joint Treasurers of the United Colonies."[5]

By early 1776, "United Colonies" was effectively the standard name for the collective colonies.[6] George Washington reported in March 1776, that the British had evacuated Boston and that the city was now in the possession of the "Forces of the United Colonies."[7] Washington regularly issued proclamations under the title "General and Commander in Chief of the Thirteen United Colonies."[8] In March 1776, the Congress appointed commissioners to Canada, who were authorized to "promise in the names of the United Colonies, that we will defend and protect the people of Canada against all enemies, in the same manner as we will defend and protect any of the United Colonies."[9] The Pennsylvania Provincial Conference in late June 1776 invoked the "Respect and Obedience which are due to the Authority of the United Colonies."[10] In late June, Joseph Ward wrote to John Adams, stating "I have been waiting with earnest expectation to see the grand Declaration of Independence of the United Colonies."[11] In May 1776, the Virginia Convention resolved unanimously that its delegates in Congress should pursue a resolution "to declare the United Colonies free and independent states."[12]

When the Congress did exactly that, it was not announcing the dissolution of the United Colonies. Far from it – the United Colonies were still united, operating as before, although they were now called the United States. George Washington's army did not suddenly dissolve, to be replaced by thirteen new national armies; his commission as commander in chief did not evaporate. The Continental Congress did not cease operations. The United Colonies were now free and independent of Great Britain, but nothing in the Declaration directly states that they were now completely independent of each other.[13]

Why, then, does the Declaration state that "they have full Power to levy War, conclude Peace, contract Alliances, establish Commerce, and to do all other Acts and Things which Independent States may of right do?" We need to pay particular attention to the word "they." The Declaration does not state that "each" has the power to levy war, etc. In context, "they" suggests collective action. Consider some examples. When speaking of jurors, we might say that "they" have the power to convict or acquit, but this does not mean that any individual juror holds such power. Or, when referring to members of the US House of Representatives, we might say that "they" have the power to impeach the president. Collectively they do, but no individual member does. "They" does not necessarily mean "each."

The Declaration uses "they" similarly to describe the American states as constituted in an American union. Although Chapter 5 will consider historical evidence in more detail, it is surely noteworthy that none of the states individually exercised any of these powers after the adoption of the Declaration. The states waged war collectively, through the Continental Army and Navy. They contracted alliances collectively, through the Continental Congress. They did not create treaties with each other, did not send ambassadors to fellow states, or do anything else that suggested that the other states were foreign countries in the eyes of the law. As Alexander Hamilton explained in 1784, the Declaration of Independence asserted the "Power of *Congress* to levy war[,] conclude peace[, and] contract alliances."[14]

This view of the Declaration is supported by numerous other passages in the document, largely overlooked, that are entirely inconsistent with the thirteen-independent-nations argument.

"ONE PEOPLE"

We can start by returning to the issue of the Declaration's voice. As explained in Chapter 2, the Declaration is written in the voice of the American people, specifically the "good People of these Colonies." But is it the voice of one American people, or the voice of thirteen separate peoples, who happen to be speaking in unison?

Let us first consider the term "people," which under modern usage is routinely used to refer to the undistinguished mass of humankind.[15] "People are like that," we are told, or "the Earth contains 7 billion people." But in the eighteenth century, and especially in legal documents, the term "people" had a much more precise meaning – it referred to members of a distinct political community.[16] The first definition of "people" in Samuel Johnson's 1755 dictionary, for example, was "[a] nation; those who compose a community."[17] The Declaration uses the term "people" in this sense. By contrast, when it refers to all persons throughout the earth, it uses the terms "men," "mankind," and "human." And when it refers to individuals residing within a particular location, it uses the term "inhabitant."[18] (The Constitution of 1787 uses the terms in a similar manner).[19]

This allows us to see just how much is being accomplished rhetorically in the Declaration's opening sentence: "WHEN in the course of human Events, it becomes necessary for one People to dissolve the Political Bands which have connected them with another ... a decent Respect to the Opinions of Mankind requires that they should declare the causes which impel them to the Separation." The Declaration is situated within "human Events," that is, the broad sweep of human history, and it must be justified to all of "Mankind." But that larger humanity is divided into "peoples," and now "one People" is clearly separating itself from "another." With these words, independence is already complete.

The specific duty of this "one People" is explained in the following paragraph: "WE hold these Truths to be self-evident, that all Men are created equal ... that to secure these Rights, Governments are instituted among Men ...[and] it is the Right of the People to alter or abolish [forms of government that are destructive of these ends]." By instituting governments, "Men" divide themselves into "Peoples," and it is these "People," not "Men" in general, who have the right to alter their form of government. While all "Men" can claim the "unalienable Rights" of "Life, Liberty, and the Pursuit of Happiness," only members of a particular political community can exercise the more specific right of revolution. By severing their ties with the British people, the American people have announced their own distinct political identity as "one People," and the Declaration accordingly states that the British will now be treated "as the rest of Mankind, Enemies in War, in Peace, Friends."

The term "one People" had a distinct resonance in the Anglo-American world. Most notably, it was used to describe the Union of the Kingdoms of England and Scotland in the famous Act of Union of 1707. As Queen Anne described it, her subjects in both kingdoms had now become "One People."[20] The queen was praised for "making us One People."[21] A speech in the Scottish Parliament emphasized that the Act would create "One Kingdom, that is to say, One People, One Civil Government, and one Interest."[22] A sermon to celebrate the Act stated that "by this Incorporation, we are become one People, one and the *same* Kingdom."[23] Another sermon, preached at Oxford University, offered gratitude for "this Law that makes us One People and Nation."[24] By the special command of Queen Anne, the Church of England was directed to give thanks for the fact that the "Kingdoms of this Island" had been "happily united into One People."[25] Similarly, when colonial Americans sought redress from British wrongs, they emphasized their political unity. A 1774 New York resolution, for example, stated "it is our most earnest desire, that the connection which subsists between Great-Britain and her colonies, whereby they are made one people, may continue till the end of time."[26]

With this context, we can better appreciate the significance of the Declaration's opening reference to "one People." The Americans form a distinct political community – one people exercising their political right to self-determination. If thirteen truly independent nations were being formed, the Declaration ought to have referred to the necessity of "some peoples" or even just "peoples" separating themselves from another. But it does not. With the Declaration's very first sentence, the United States is announcing itself as "one people" to the rest of the world, and claiming the "separate and equal Station" – not "Stations" – to which it is entitled.

Other phrases in the Declaration amplify this point. One passage claims that George III is "unfit to be a Ruler of a free People." (Congress tightened Jefferson's original phrasing, which was a "people who mean to be free," but deliberately retained the singular of "people").[27] Similarly, the Declaration claims to be in the name of the "good People of these Colonies," not the "good Peoples." And it claims that George III constrained "our fellow Citizens taken Captive on the high Seas to bear Arms against their Country." The "Country" referred to here cannot be Great Britain; it must be America as a whole, a point underscored by the phrase "fellow Citizens," which connects Americans in all the states through the bonds of citizenship.

And perhaps the most significant evidence is the dog that didn't bark. Nowhere in the Declaration does it ever mention a state by name. The only reference is to the "United States of America." Unfortunately, this basic point is obscured by many sloppy modern editions of the Declaration, which list the signatories to the ceremonial parchment, and then organize the signatures under the names of their home states. The ceremonial parchment is, of course, largely beside the point; no signatures or states' names appeared on the publicly circulated Declaration, the Dunlap Broadside. But, critically, even the ceremonial parchment does not include the names of states. The signatures are loosely grouped by state, but at no point is any state's name directly provided.[28] The inclusion of states' names is an entirely inaccurate intrusion by later editors, beginning with a 1777 edition by Baltimore printer Mary Katherine Goddard.[29] James Wilson, a signer of the Declaration, knew better. When creating a large display parchment of the Declaration in the 1780s, he ensured that no state names appeared next to the signatories.[30]

"UNITED STATES OF AMERICA"

One of the strongest pieces of evidence against the thirteen-independent-nations argument is one of the easiest to overlook, because our typographic conventions have changed significantly since the late eighteenth century. In formal writing, nouns generally were capitalized; adjectives and pronouns were not. (Modern German still follows this rule). Benjamin Franklin, for example, America's most eminent printer and a member of the Declaration's drafting committee, had long insisted on the regular capitalization of nouns.[31] Both the Dunlap Broadside and the US Constitution adhere to this practice. For example, the Declaration uses phrases such as "separate and equal Station," "unalienable Rights," and "absolute Despotism," and the Constitution uses phrases such as "insure domestic Tranquility" and "needful Rules and Regulations."[32] In all of these cases, the noun is capitalized, but the adjective is not.

When the Declaration capitalizes adjectives, it does so when the adjective is functioning as an integral part of a larger noun phrase, such as "General Congress" or "Legislative Bodies." A more modern example would be "city hall." If we had a rule requiring capitalization of nouns, we would surely write "City Hall" and not "city Hall."

With this in mind, one can see just how critical it is that the Declaration declares that these "United Colonies are, and of Right ought to be, FREE AND INDEPENDENT STATES." Both "United Colonies" and "FREE AND INDEPENDENT STATES" must be read as complete noun phrases, not simply nouns modified by adjectives. The "United Colonies" are a distinct legal entity, not just a group of "Colonies" who happened to be "united." Similarly, the Declaration recognizes an entity of "FREE AND INDEPENDENT STATES," not just a group of "States" that happen to be "free and independent."

The capitalization of "United Colonies" was consistent with both the Declaration's drafting history and with the earliest newspaper reprintings. Richard Henry Lee's handwritten motion for independence, upon which this language was based, did not generally capitalize nouns, but it did refer to the "United Colonies."[33] Newspapers that followed the practice of capitalizing nouns naturally rendered the phrase as "United Colonies."[34] (The one exception was the *New York Gazette*, which referred to the "united Colonies," although it had elsewhere referred to the "United States."[35]) But what is perhaps most revealing is how the phrase was rendered in the large number of newspapers that did not generally capitalize nouns. Of those seventeen newspapers, sixteen nonetheless capitalized "United Colonies," making the phrase even more visually distinctive and strongly suggesting that the "United Colonies" were perceived as a distinct legal entity.[36]

(Only the *Maryland Gazette* rigorously extended non-capitalization to the "united colonies."[37])

The newspapers' treatment of "Free and Independent States" is equally instructive. Thirteen newspapers exactly followed the Dunlap Broadside's use of small capitalization and printed it as "FREE AND INDEPENDENT STATES."[38] Another four printed it as "*Free and Independent States.*"[39] Five printed it as "FREE AND INDEPENDENT STATES."[40] (As with "United Colonies," the *Maryland Gazette* continued to be the outlier, printing "free and independent states."[41])

These points are easy to miss if we look only to Jefferson's own draft or to the ceremonial parchment. Jefferson's approach to capitalization was highly unusual. Among other eccentricities, he consistently refused to capitalize the first words of sentences, even in his draft of the Declaration.[42] Close examination of Jefferson's capitalization is unlikely to yield many insights. And the ceremonial parchment, prepared by Timothy Matlack, is even more unusual. Over a hundred years ago, Carl Becker commented on the capitalization in the ceremonial parchment, archly noting that the "capitalization and punctuation, following neither previous copies, nor reason, nor the custom of any age known to man, is one of the irremediable evils of life to be accepted with becoming resignation."[43] Consider, for example, Matlack's rendition of the Declaration's opening lines: "When in the Course of human events, it becomes necessary for one people to dissolve the political bands which have connected them another, and to assume among the powers of the earth ...." Or, from the grievances: "For abolishing the free System of English Laws in a neighbouring Province, establishing therein an Arbitrary government, and enlarging its Boundaries so as to render it at once an example and fit instrument for introducing the same absolute rule into these Colonies." The caption to the ceremonial parchment includes the phrase "united States," but this almost certainly reflects Matlack's own eccentricities as a scribe and not any considered congressional decision.[44]

Finally, we should turn to how the Declaration describes the new nation. The Dunlap Broadside twice refers to the "UNITED STATES OF AMERICA." Since it employs all capital letters, it is not immediately apparent whether it should be rendered as "United States of America," or "united States of America." We have some hints from the drafting history. John Adams's draft copy uses "United States of America" in the caption and "united States of America" in the conclusion,[45] but Jefferson's copy submitted to Congress uses "UNITED STATES OF AMERICA" in the caption and "United States of America" in the conclusion.[46]

Contemporary newspapers can provide further evidence of common understanding. Some newspapers followed the Dunlap Broadside exactly by reprinting the document's caption in block text as "UNITED STATES OF AMERICA."[47] But others printed it as "United States of America,"[48] or as "UNITED STATES OF AMERICA."[49] Similarly, some newspapers followed the Dunlap Broadside by printing the reference in the concluding section as "UNITED STATES OF AMERICA,[50] but others printed it as "United States of America,"[51] or as "UNITED STATES OF AMERICA."[52] Significantly, no newspaper printed it as "united States of America," the form used in the caption to the ceremonial parchment. In other words, every American in 1776 who had access to printed copies of the Declaration would have understood that it declared the independence of the "United States of America." (The 1777 Goddard printing had "United States" in the caption, and a 1781 printing of the Declaration ordered by Congress eliminated most capitalization of nouns, but it twice capitalized "United States of America.")[53]

Yet some of our most eminent historians have stumbled on this basic point. Gordon Wood, for example, claimed that the Declaration referred to the "united States of America."[54] Forrest McDonald was even more insistent, arguing that "in keeping with eighteenth-century convention, nouns in the document are capitalized, and what the delegates represent are united States – that being not a name, but 'united' being merely an adjective describing the stance of the states in opposition to Britain."[55] McDonald appears to have relied solely on Timothy Matlack's eccentric transcription of the Declaration on the ceremonial parchment, entirely unaware that all other versions of the Declaration – the ones actually presented to the American people – fatally contradict his argument.

~~~

The Declaration can thus be plausibly read as announcing the existence of a new nation – the United States of America, whose citizens are announcing themselves as "one people" on the world stage. It is hardly sufficient to gesture to the "Free and Independent States" language as if that somehow conclusively resolved the issue; if anything, the capitalization is more supportive of a confederated states argument. And claims based on "united States of America" in the ceremonial parchment are even more frivolous, effectively finding the denial of nationhood in a lowercase letter penned by a scribe with a penchant for erratic capitalization.

Fortunately, we don't have to rely on the text alone, as we can test this interpretation against actual historical events. Did anyone at the time understand the Declaration in this way, and did they act as if one confederated nation had emerged on July 4, 1776? As we shall see, there is overwhelming evidence that they did.

5   HISTORY

If the Declaration of Independence created thirteen independent nations, with no legal connection between them, what might we expect to see? In such a world, we would see each state sending ambassadors to other states and to foreign countries. We would see tariffs imposed on goods shipped from one state to another. All disputes over international shipping issues would be decided by each state, with no appeal to any other body. There would be no notion of United States citizenship or of treason against the United States. No one would ever refer to the United States as a nation, a state, or an "it."

Such a world was theoretically possible, of course, but it was not the world that actually existed in 1776 and afterwards. Instead, Americans consistently acted as if they were citizens of a nation called the "United States of America" and they authorized the Continental Congress to speak to the rest of the world on their behalf as one nation.

THE VIEW FROM 1776

Numerous individuals and groups closely connected with the Declaration of Independence regularly spoke of the Declaration as creating one American nation, which they referred to in the singular, as an "independent state." These statements significantly undercut the notion that revolutionary Americans understood the Declaration as creating thirteen entirely separate nations.

In the first half of 1776, many localities issued their own "declarations of independence," urging the Continental Congress to cut ties with Great Britain.[1] These local declarations lent support to Congress's claim to speak on behalf of the people of the United States. A number of these declarations deliberately linked independence to nationhood. On May 27, 1776, the town of Malden, Massachusetts, for example, called for the creation of an "American republic" and instructed its delegate that "it is now the ardent wish of our souls that America may become a free and independent state."[2] Topsfield, Massachusetts, hoped that, "for the safety of the United Colonies," the Continental Congress would "declare *America* to be independent of the Kingdom of *Great Britain.*"[3] Palmer, Massachusetts, declared it "absolutely necessary for the safety of the United Colonies to be independent from *Great Britain,* and declare themselves entirely a separate State."[4]

Similar views had been percolating for months. The Reverend Moses Mather of Connecticut published a pamphlet in 1775, arguing that "Great Britain and America" were "two countries" that were "entirely distinct and several."[5] Joseph Ward wrote to John Adams in October 1775 from the Continental Army camp, noting his expectation that Congress would publish "the Confederacy of the Colonies" and complete "the Republic of America."[6] In November 1775, an anonymous writer noted that "we expect soon to break off all kind of connection with Britain, and form into a GRAND REPUBLIC of the AMERICAN UNITED COLONIES."[7] In January 1776, a writer in the *New England Chronicle* considered it "the indispensable duty of the united colonies of America *immediately* to form themselves into an independent constitution, or a *republic state.*"[8] In his highly influential pamphlet *Common Sense*, Thomas Paine equated independence with a continental union. As he put it, "the most powerful of all arguments is, that nothing but independence, i.e. a continental form of government, can keep the peace of the Continent and preserve it inviolate from civil wars."[9] "Independence," he argued, "is the only Bond that can tye and keep us together."[10] Accordingly, he proposed a "Continental Charter" to govern the "United Colonies."[11]

The notion of America as an independent state was widespread. In March 1776, the Continental Congress's Committee of Secret Correspondence issued instructions to Silas Deane, who was sent as an American agent to France. The instructions noted the likelihood that the "Colonies should be forced to form themselves into an independent state."[12] William Whipple, a signer of the Declaration from New Hampshire, observed in May 1776 that Virginia had instructed its delegates to "declare the Colonies a free and independent state."[13] The New Hampshire legislature instructed its delegates to "join with the other Colonies in declaring the thirteen United Colonies a free and independent State."[14] A New Yorker argued in June 1776 that "America bids fair to be the most glorious state that has ever been on earth."[15] An opponent of independence understood this clearly, warning that our "new legislators would persuade us, that when these Colonies have shaken off the British yoke they will calmly set down with one heart and one voice to form themselves into a great Republic."[16]

In late June 1776, the Pennsylvania Provincial Conference of Committees, which had been formed to bypass the recalcitrant Pennsylvania Assembly, announced that the colony was willing "to concur in a Vote of the Congress, declaring the United Colonies free and independent States, provided the forming the Government, and the Regulation of the internal Police of this Colony be always reserved to the People of the said Colony."[17] The reservation of certain internal rights is striking; if Pennsylvania were to be a truly independent nation after independence, such a reservation would have been entirely unnecessary. But Pennsylvanians understood that they would continue to be in union with the other colonies after independence.

In a June 29, 1776, submission to the *Pennsylvania Evening Post,* an anonymous author (possibly Thomas Paine) stated that "until, as other nations have done before us, we agree to call ourselves by some name, I shall rejoice to hear the title of the United States of America, in order that we may be on a proper footing to negociate a peace."[18] In a July 1, 1776, letter, John Adams noted that the vote on independence was imminent, and exulted, "May Heaven prosper the new born Republic – and make it more glorious than any former Republics have been."[19] Two days later, he wrote to his wife Abigail that "the two Countries" of Great Britain and America "should be sundered forever."[20] In a second letter to Abigail he noted that the Declaration "will cement the Union."[21] In addition to adopting the Declaration on July 4, 1776, the Continental Congress also appointed Benjamin

Franklin, John Adams, and Thomas Jefferson to design "a seal for the United States of America."[22] If the United States of America had no existence as a legal entity, why would it need a seal?

Consider how an intelligent reader construed the Declaration nine days after its adoption. Ezra Stiles was a preacher, a lawyer, an amateur scientist, a member of the American Philosophical Society, a founder of what would become Brown University, and one of the most learned men in America. He would be appointed president of Yale in 1778. If anyone was capable of understanding written texts, it was Stiles. He received his copy of the Declaration on July 13, 1776, and he did not understand it as creating thirteen independent nations. Far from it. Stiles observed, "The *thirteen united Colonies* now rise into an *Independent Republic* among the Kingdoms, States & Empires on Earth. May the ... Lord ... shower down his Blessings upon it, & ever keep it under his holy Protection."[23]

Other readers and listeners agreed. On July 28, 1776, the Declaration was read to Continental Army soldiers at Fort Ticonderoga. An observer noted, "the language on every man's countenance was, Now we are a people! We have a name among the states of this world."[24] In Savannah, Georgia, the state's president and executive council celebrated the Declaration in August 1776 by publicly reading the Declaration aloud to four different audiences. In the evening, they held a mock funeral procession for George III, who they swore would never "rule again over these United States of America," and explained their understanding of the Declaration: "America is free and independent; that she is, and will be, with the blessing of the Almighty, great among the nations of the earth."[25] The chief justice of South Carolina concluded in October 1776 that there "has suddenly arisen in the World, a new Empire, stiled, The United States of America."[26]

Two signers of the Declaration expressed their views clearly in early debates over the Articles of Confederation. In late July 1776, New Jersey signer John Witherspoon compared the proposed Articles to the "existing confederacy," thus showing his understanding that a confederacy already existed in 1776.[27] A few days later, Pennsylvania signer Benjamin Rush argued, "We are now a new Nation." Rush described himself as a "Citizen of America" and noted, "We are dependent on each other – not totally independent states."[28]

It has sometimes been argued that the use of the term "Congress" implies that the Continental Congress was primarily an international convention, a gathering of ambassadors, much like the later Congress of Vienna.[29] This notion has little historical support. Revolutionary Americans routinely used the term "Congress" to describe governing and deliberating bodies within states. Massachusetts, for example, convened a "Provincial Congress" in 1774, and twice in 1775.[30] North Carolina convened five "Provincial Congresses" between 1774 and 1776.[31] New York held a "Provincial Congress" between April 1775 and June 1776.[32] New Jersey held "Provincial Congresses" in May, June, August, and October 1775.[33] The New Hampshire constitutional convention of 1776 described itself as the "Congress of New Hampshire."[34] The South Carolina constitutional convention of 1776 described itself as a "congress."[35] The New Jersey Constitution of 1776 was drafted by the "Provincial Congress, New Jersey," which described itself as meeting "in congress assembled."[36] When Americans referred to the "Continental Congress," they were not referring to a distinctive international body; it was simply the governing body of the Continent, a congress like those of the individual states, just with a far broader jurisdiction. In short, a Continental Congress.

CONFEDERATION

The confederation of the American colonies had been linked to independence since the very beginning. Richard Henry Lee's June 7, 1776, motion for independence included two related proposals: "That it is expedient forthwith to take the most effectual measures for forming foreign Alliances. That a plan of confederation be prepared and transmitted to the respective Colonies for their consideration and approbation."[37]

There were conflicting views on timing. Some delegates felt that independence should be declared first before turning to the terms of a confederation. Others, such as John Adams, felt that a formal confederation should come first.[38] The Continental Congress initially tackled all at once. On June 11, 1776, it appointed five men to the committee to draft the Declaration, and the next day it appointed five men to a committee to form foreign alliances, and twelve men to a committee to draft articles of confederation (Benjamin Franklin and John Adams were appointed to both the Declaration committee and the foreign alliances committee).[39]

The confederation committee consisted of a delegate from each state, other than New Jersey, and it was chaired by Pennsylvania delegate John Dickinson.[40] Dickinson's committee worked quickly, and on July 12, 1776, it presented a draft to the full Congress for consideration.[41] Since this draft is the closest in time to the Declaration of Independence itself, it likely provides the best sense of how the delegates understood the American Union.[42]

The draft was titled "Articles of Confederation and Perpetual Union." Although we often shorten this to just "Articles of Confederation," the full title bears emphasis. "Perpetual Union" is just as significant as "Confederation." It was understood that the American states were in perpetual union with each other.[43]

Revolutionary Americans did not need to invent the concept of a confederation, as two European examples were quite familiar, the older Swiss confederation and the more recent Dutch confederation. In a July 1776 speech in the Continental Congress, New Jersey delegate John Witherspoon invoked both as models.[44] In 1579, Dutch provinces seeking to break away from Spanish rule formed the United Provinces of the Netherlands. The provinces pledged to "ally, confederate and unite ... to hold together eternally in all ways and forms as if they were but one province," while reserving significant internal powers to themselves.[45] Most external powers, including governing overseas territories, were granted to the central government, which was also empowered to resolve disputes between provinces and to control coinage.[46]

The German theorist Samuel von Pufendorf expounded on the nature of confederacies in an influential 1672 treatise. In the English translation owned by John Adams, Pufendorf explained that confederacies "are carried on with this Design, that the several States shall for ever link their Safety one within the other, and in order to this mutual Defence, shall engage themselves not to exercise certain parts of the sovereign Power, other than by a common Agreement and

Approbation." This was quite different from a mutual defense treaty, where the parties merely agreed to act together in a particular war; it was far stronger – a commitment that "none of us ... will make use of our Right, as to the Affair of Peace and War, except by the general Consent of the whole Confederacy."[47]

The first three articles of the Dickinson committee draft addressed broad issues. Article One announced a name: "The name of this Confederacy shall be 'The United States of America.'" Article 2 provided that the "Colonies united themselves so as never to be divided by any Act whatever, and hereby severally enter into a firm League of Friendship with each other, for their common Defence, the Security of their Liberties, and their mutual and general Welfare." Article 3 stated that "Each colony shall retain and enjoy as much of its present Laws, Rights, and Customs, as it may think fit, and reserves to itself the sole and exclusive Regulation and Government of its internal police, in all matters that shall not interfere with the Articles of this Confederation."[48]

One might have expected the draft Articles to then turn to the Continental Congress and its powers. Instead, the next ten articles proceeded to lay down a series of restrictions on the actions of states. That is, the initial concern was not so much empowering the national government, but restricting the powers of the states. And the restrictions were significant. States were completely prohibited from engaging in any sort of foreign relations without the consent of Congress; prohibited from entering into treaties with each other; required to respect the privileges and immunities of citizens of the other states; barred from passing imposts or duties that conflicted with treaties made by the United States; barred from keeping standing armies; required to submit to the determinations of Congress with respect to financial losses or expenses incurred in prosecuting the war; barred from granting titles of nobility; barred from engaging in war without the consent of Congress; and obligated to respect the boundaries and territories of the other states.[49]

After articulating these restrictions on states, the draft Articles turned to the powers of Congress, granting the "United States assembled" the "sole and exclusive" powers of war and peace, of maritime captures, trying crimes committed on the high seas, sending and receiving ambassadors, entering into treaties and alliances, resolving boundary disputes between states, coining money, regulating affairs with the Indians, and regulating the Continental Army and Navy.[50]

In short, the draft Articles emphatically treated the "United States of America" as a confederated *nation* – one in which all external powers were granted to the federal government and in which states had no role to play in foreign affairs. From the perspective of any foreign observer, the United States of America was one nation on the map of the world. Gouverneur Morris, a signer of the Articles, noted in 1778 that "America is an independent power."[51] This understanding of the United States is the understanding of the drafters of the Declaration of Independence. We stood as one nation – not thirteen – with respect to the rest of the world.

Dickinson's draft, was, of course, just a draft proposal by a committee, and it would be extensively debated in Congress in July and August 1776. One of the most controversial aspects of the Dickinson draft was granting each state an equal vote in the Congress. Larger states argued that voting should be based on state population, whereas smaller states insisted on equal voting rights. John Adams argued for voting by population, claiming that the confederation would "make us one individual only; it is to form us, like separate parcels of metal, into one common mass."[52] Similarly, James Wilson argued, "It is strange that annexing the name of 'State' to ten thousand men, should give them an equal right with forty thousand. ... As to those matters referred to Congress, we are not so many states; we are one large state."[53] It was an issue that would bedevil American politics for years, eventually resulting in the compromise of the 1787 Constitution providing for population-based representation in the House of Representatives and equality of states in the Senate. There were also deep disagreements over how to handle taxation and the states' western land claims.[54]

The members of Congress agreed on some points, and they deleted several provisions from Dickinson's draft, including those dealing with congressional power over state boundaries and control over western lands, but ultimately, they were unable to resolve their deeper disagreements, and on August 20, 1776, the Articles of Confederation were tabled indefinitely.[55] For many delegates, it seemed better to say nothing on the subject of confederation than to risk potential disunion by forcing certain issues to a vote before a consensus had emerged.[56] Congress resumed debate on the Articles in April 1777 and it took until November 1777 to agree on a final text. By this point, Congress had fled to York, Pennsylvania, following the British capture of Philadelphia.

The final version of the Articles followed the Dickinson draft in granting significant powers to the national government. The "United States, in Congress assembled" were granted the "sole and exclusive right and power" of (1) "determining on peace and war"; (2) "sending and receiving ambassadors"; (3) "entering into treaties and alliances"; (4) "establishing rules for deciding, in all cases, what captures on land or water shall be legal"; (5) "granting letters of marque and reprisal in times of peace"; (6) "appointing courts for the trial of piracies and felonies committed on the high seas"; (7) "establishing courts for receiving and determining, finally, appeals in all cases of captures"; (8) "regulating the alloy and value of coin struck by their own authority"; (9) "fixing the standard of weights and measures throughout the United States"; (10) "regulating the trade and managing the affairs with the Indians not members of any of the states"; (11) "establishing and regulating post offices from one State to another throughout all the United States"; (12) "appointing all officers of the land [and naval] forces of the United States"; and (13) "making rules for the government and regulation of the said land and naval forces, and directing their operations." The "United States, in Congress assembled," was also appointed "the last resort on appeal in all disputes and differences now subsisting, or that hereafter may arise between two or more states concerning boundary, jurisdiction or any other cause whatever."[57]

The clear intent, at least with respect to external relations, was to create a unitary nation. From the perspective of any foreign power, there was only one nation – the United States of America. Congress alone was empowered to speak for that nation; the states were required to be mute. John Adams forcefully made this point to the French foreign minister in 1781, noting: "By this Constitution, all Power and Authority, of negotiating with foreign Powers is expressly delegated to the United States, in Congress assembled. It would therefore be a publick Disrespect and Contempt offered, to the Constitution of the Nation if any Power Should make any Application, whatever, to the Governors, or Legislatures of the Separate States."[58] Alexander Hamilton agreed, pointing out that war and peace were "among the first rights of sovereignty, and does not the delegation of them to the general confederacy, so far abridge the sovereignty of each particular state?"[59] Similarly, Benjamin Rush, a signer of the Declaration, explained that the states were not sovereign under the Confederation, because they lacked the power to make war and peace; Congress was the "only sovereign power in the United States." "No individual State as such," he argued, "has any claim to independence. She is independent only in a union with her sister States in Congress."[60]

But Congress's powers were not limited to external affairs. We are sometimes told that the Articles created a government that operated only on states, not on individuals. This is clearly incorrect, as James Madison noted in *The Federalist No. 40*:

> In cases of capture, of piracy, of the post-office, of coins, weights and measures, of trade with the Indians, of claims under grants of land by different States, and above all, in the case of trials by Courts-martial in the army and navy, by which death may be inflicted without the intervention of a jury, or even of a civil Magistrate; in all these cases the powers of the confederation operate immediately on the person and interests of individual citizens.[61]

A member of the Continental Army about to be hung for desertion, for example, would probably have some choice words to say if informed that future historians would deny that the Confederation government operated directly on individuals.

The Articles' restrictions on states were equally significant. States were required "to assist each other" against all attacks made upon them; to recognize the privileges and immunities of citizens of other states; and to extradite criminal suspects to other states. States were forbidden from taxing the property of the United States or any other state; interfering with freedom of speech and debate in Congress; arresting members of Congress in civil suits; sending embassies to foreign countries, making treaties with foreign countries, entering into treaties or alliances with other states without the consent of Congress; granting titles of nobility; laying any imposts or duties that conflicted with treaties made by the United States; keeping vessels of war or bodies of armed men in time of peace, engaging war, or granting letters of marque and reprisal without the consent of Congress. Finally, states were required to "abide by the determinations of the United States, in Congress assembled, on all questions which, by this confederation are submitted to them." The "union shall be perpetual" and the Articles "inviolably observed by every State."[62] The chief justice of South Carolina, William Henry Drayton, lamented that Congress had "assume[d] almost all the important powers of government" and complained about the document's "great and humiliating restrictions" on the sovereignty of states.[63]

In short, as Jack Rakove observes in his substantial study of the Continental Congress, "the framers of the Articles intended to vest certain sovereign powers in Congress and to subordinate the states to its decisions."[64] The "idea that the confederation was essentially only a league of sovereign states," he continues, "was ultimately a fiction. Congress was in fact a national government burdened with legislative and administrative responsibilities unprecedented in the colonial past."[65] In a circular letter transmitting the Articles to the states, Congress stated that they were designed to "form a permanent union," claimed that under them our "brethren and fellow-citizens" would be "forever bound and connected together by ties the most intimate and indissoluble," and argued that the Articles were "essential to our very existence as a free people."[66] Delegates to the Confederation Congress routinely referred to the United States as a "nation."[67] George Washington would later refer to the Articles as "our national Constitution."[68] James Wilson, a signer of the Declaration, referred to them in 1785 as the "constitution of the United States."[69]

The provision of the Articles that has tended to generate the most historical interest and debate is Article Two, which stated, "Each State retains its sovereignty, freedom, and independence, and every power, jurisdiction, and right, which is not expressly delegated to the United States, in Congress assembled."[70] This article has sometimes been interpreted as suggesting that each state was effectively an independent nation. But close attention to the article's history and text suggests that this conclusion is greatly overstated.

The Article was submitted by North Carolina delegate Thomas Burke, who arrived in Congress in early 1777, as an amendment to language in the Dickinson draft. Burke noted that the amendment was not initially seconded, because "it was at first so little understood."[71] But it eventually passed by a large margin, and was not seen as making a fundamental change. One scholar, for example, argues that it was "supremely unimportant and simply restated the intention of the congress with respect to the sources and limits of its authority."[72] Another suggests that "it is questionable whether this redefinition of the theoretical nature of the union actually altered most delegates' perceptions of the extent and character of congressional authority."[73] Indeed, scholars have noted that there was surprisingly little attention paid to difficult questions of sovereignty and the nature of the Union in the debates over the Articles.[74]

The Article states that each state "retains" the powers not granted to the confederacy. But it does not conclusively resolve what any of those powers were. For example, foreign affairs powers had never been exercised by the colonies as colonies, and they had not been exercised after independence, either, so there were no such powers for the colonies to retain. States could not retain what they had never possessed. Even Thomas Burke thought the "United States ought be as One Sovereign *(power)* with respect to foreign Powers, in all things that relate to War or where the States have one Common Interest"[75] and that "the American States stand in no other relation to Britain, than as an independent Empire at war with her."[76]

Although the delegates to Congress expected that ratification would happen quickly, Maryland dragged its feet and did not ratify until February 1781, after Virginia agreed to cede its western lands to the United States. The Articles were deemed effective on March 1, 1781. The ratification was celebrated in the *Pennsylvania Gazette,* which noted that the states were now "finally consolidated into a perpetual confederacy" and the "United States of America ... are growing up into consequence among the nations."[77] But, functionally, the Congress continued to function as it always had, the primary difference being that its directives were now labeled "ordinances," rather than "resolutions."[78]

Scholars describing the Articles of Confederation have often reached for analogies to modern international institutions. Gordon Wood, for example, suggested that the United States under the

Articles was "similar in many respects to the present-day European Union, held together by a kind of treaty."[79] Akhil Reed Amar contends that the United States were "not much more than the 'United Nations.'"[80] And Gregory Maggs has suggested they were little more than a "mutual defense treaty," apparently similar to NATO.[81]

These analogies are very poor fits for the actual Articles of Confederation. No country joining the EU, the United Nations, or NATO, thought that it was entering into a "perpetual union" with other countries; none thought that it was surrendering all control of foreign policy to a central government; and, certainly in the case of NATO and the UN, none thought it was allowing a central government to reverse decisions of its own courts. The Articles contemplated a far stronger union and central government than anything contemplated by the United Nations, NATO, or the EU. True, it was not as a strong or perfect a union as it would be under the Constitution, but it was a union nonetheless.

THE PRACTICE OF GOVERNMENT

Perhaps the most important evidence of American nationhood between 1776 and 1781 lies in the actual practice of government. Although the Articles of Confederation had not been ratified, the states nonetheless acted as if they were formally confederated and it was widely understood that the United States of America was a distinct nation among the nations of the world. As historian Peter Onuf has pointed out, "The American states did not behave as independent sovereignties were expected to behave: they did not act like true states."[82] Rather, they "behaved as if Congress had a superintending jurisdiction."[83]

The Second Continental Congress convened in May 1775, and it quickly assumed the attributes of a de facto national government. By early August 1775, the Congress had created the Continental Army, appointed its officers and prescribed its regulations and pay scales, authorized bills of credit, created uniform regulations for the colonial militias, authorized the Continental Post Office, and taken control over foreign relations.[84] On December 4, 1775, the Congress unanimously resolved that it would be "very dangerous to the liberties and welfare of America, if any Colony should separately petition the King or either house of Parliament."[85] As Pauline Maier has suggested, even prior to independence, Congress had "an authority and even an eminence above and beyond that of any separate colony, and, indeed, far beyond what the colonists conceded to Parliament."[86] Jack Rakove notes, "For most intents and purposes, the Americans were already acting as if they were an independent nation: waging war, creating new governments, issuing money, and enacting other expedient measures."[87]

After independence, Congress continued to carry out these functions without any formal Articles of Confederation. As historian Jerrilyn Greene Marston put it, "while agreement on the Articles of Confederation proved impossible to achieve in 1776, a functioning confederation did not."[88] When the Articles were finally ratified in 1781, they did not create new national powers, which had been exercised for years. Rather, the Articles finally clarified and defined those powers, placing them on a firm textual foundation.

One example is interactions with Indian nations. Even prior to independence, Congress had taken steps to centralize control of Indian relations,[89] and a committee of the Confederation Congress later assumed that the power to deal with the Indian tribes, which had been previously "possessed by the King," had passed "entire to the Union."[90] The Articles of Confederation would explicitly grant Congress the "sole and exclusive power of ... regulating the trade and managing all affairs with the Indians, not members of any of the States." But it was not breaking new ground – it was simply confirming what Congress had been doing for years.

Historian Edmund Cody Barnett concluded that Congress largely complied with the Articles even prior to ratification.[91] It was a de facto national government, even though its precise legal status remained formally undefined.[92] Or as historian Richard Morris argued, "The central government alone possessed those attributes of external sovereignty which entitled it to be called a state in the international sense, while the separate states, possessing a limited or internal sovereignty, may rightly be considered a creation of the Continental Congress, which preceded them and brought them into being."[93]

The earliest states to form new governments, New Hampshire and South Carolina, did so in early 1776, but only after consulting with the Continental Congress.[94] Moreover, both state constitutions fully recognized Congress's authority. New Hampshire's constitution, adopted on January 5, 1776, stated that it was forming a new government because that measure had been "recommended by the Continental Congress." It also stated that the colony confided in the "prudence and wisdom" of the Continental Congress.[95] Similarly, the South Carolina Constitution of March 26, 1776, provided for elections to the Continental Congress, and stated that "the resolutions of the Continental Congress, now of force in this colony, shall so continue until altered or revoked by them."[96]

On May 10, 1776, the Continental Congress adopted John Adams's resolution calling for the establishment of new governments in the colonies.[97] A preamble to the resolution added five days later stated that the "exercise of every kind of authority under the [crown of Great Britain] should be totally suppressed."[98] In his autobiography, Adams claimed that it was "on all hands considered by Men of Understanding as equivalent to a declaration of Independence."[99]

In short, the states, as states, were called into being by federal action. As historian Peter Onuf has put it, "statehood was conferred on a state by other states because of its membership in the union and representation in Congress. In some sense, then, statehood derived from Congress and participation in the common cause.... To become a state in revolutionary America was to forgo what we consider the essential prerogatives of sovereignty."[100] Or in Martin Flaherty's terms, "By that resolution the national government called the states into existence rather than the other way around."[101]

Significantly, none of the state constitutions looked like the constitutions of truly independent nations. None claimed the powers of national defense or foreign affairs, and ten of them provided for elections of delegates to Congress.[102] As Richard Morris argued, "If any of the former colonies pretended to be sovereign states, as the terms were understood even then in international law, they failed to make apparent those intentions."[103]

Congress approved draft treaties in September 1776 between the "United States" and foreign powers; no state was specifically named in the draft.[104] The Treaty of Alliance with France in early 1778 did name the individual states, but referred to itself as a treaty between "two contracting Parties," the United States and France, and stated that each party would "in the manner *it* may judge most proper, make all the efforts in *its* Power, against their common Enemy."[105] When a French minister appeared in Philadelphia in August 1778, the Continental Congress greeted him with elaborate ceremony. The *Pennsylvania Packet* was struck by "the Representatives of the United States of America, solemnly giving public audience to a Minister Plenipotentiary from the most powerful Prince in Europe." Such an event would have been inconceivable four years earlier, but now the Almighty had "stationed America among the powers of the earth, and cloathed her in robes of Sovereignty."[106]

In early 1777, the Continental Congress, after a lengthy debate, voted on whether states had the authority to meet with each other without the approval of Congress. Under a thirteen-independent-nations view, this should have been an easy question to answer – of course, one independent nation can speak to another independent nation. But, after extensive debate, the Congress found itself evenly divided on this point and took no conclusive action.[107] Three signers of the Declaration argued strenuously against state authority. James Wilson contended that any actions that were "wholly continental ... of course required the approbation of Congress."[108] John Adams noted that "the same principles of equity & reason should govern us as if we were united by a confederacy" and that the "four New England states bore the same relationship to the congress that four counties bore to a single State" and they had "no right to touch upon Continental Subjects."[109] Benjamin Rush agreed, contending that states meeting to discuss continental business "usurped the powers of congress as much as four counties would usurp the powers of legislation in a state should they attempt to tax themselves."[110] He speculated that at some point the states might become "independent of each other, but I can conceive of no temporal punishment to be severe eno' for that man who attempts to dissolve, or weaken the union for a century or two to come."[111]

The priority of the nation over states was particularly pronounced in admiralty cases.[112] In November 1775, at the urging of George

Washington, Congress recommended that each colony provide for a court to deal with prize cases, that is, cases of captured enemy ships. Significantly, however, Congress provided that no enemy ships could be seized without a commission from Congress and that "in all cases an appeal shall be allowed to the Congress."[113] This was the first time that appeals had been authorized from a colonial court to a federal body. Historian Henry Bourguignon noted, "This insistence also tells us something of the attitude of many delegates to Congress as early as November, 1775, toward the need for final control by a central authority of questions touching the rights of other nations."[114]

Significantly, the first appeal from a state court to the Congress was filed on July 4, 1776.[115] That is, when the Declaration of Independence was adopted, there was already federal jurisdiction over certain kinds of state cases. It's hard to imagine a starker violation of the thirteen-independent-nations argument than this. The case came from Pennsylvania, and on September 9, 1776, Congress appointed a committee of five members to hear the appeal.[116] The committee found the appeal meritorious and reversed the judgment of the state court.[117] Congress continued to appoint ad hoc committees for the next seven appeals from state courts, before resolving in January 1777 to create a permanent standing Committee on Appeals.[118] The Articles of Confederation authorized Congress to appoint a court for "determining finally appeals in all cases of capture," but barred members of Congress from serving on the court. Congress nonetheless continued to employ the Committee on Appeals, on which its members served, until 1780.

The jurisdiction of the Committee on Appeals became the subject of a lengthy dispute with the state of Pennsylvania. In a case arising from the ship *Active*, Pennsylvania had refused to follow the directions of the Committee on Appeals, claiming that a state law prohibited Congress from reconsidering any factual matters that had been decided by a jury.[119] The Continental Congress was appalled and insisted on its power to review state court decisions in admiralty cases. In March 1779, by a vote of 11 states to 2 (Pennsylvania and New Jersey dissented), Congress approved a resolution drafted by a committee appointed to look into the matter. The committee was chaired by none other than Thomas Burke, the most ardent supporter of states' rights in Congress.[120] But even Burke had nothing but condemnation for the notion of states' rights in this context:

> That Congress is by these United States invested with the supreme sovereign power of war and peace:
>
> That the power of executing the law of nations is essential to the sovereign supreme power of war and peace:
>
> That the legality of all captures on the high seas must be determined by the law of nations:
>
> That the authority ultimately and finally to decide on all matters and questions touching the law of nations, does reside and is vested in the sovereign supreme power of war and peace:
>
> That a control by appeal is necessary, in order to compel a just and uniform execution of the law of nations.

Accordingly, no state "could destroy the right of appeal and the re-examination of the facts reserved to Congress."[121]

Although the Committee on Appeals had sometimes been colloquially referred to as a "court of appeals," Congress officially created a new "Court of Appeals in Cases of Capture" in January 1780.[122] This was now a true judicial body, staffed by judges who were not members of Congress, and it can be appropriately considered the nation's first federal appellate court.[123] Significantly, it was created over a year before the formal adoption of the Articles of Confederation. The court heard over sixty appeals before its dissolution in 1787, and in numerous cases reversed decisions of state courts.[124]

Perhaps the most conclusive piece of evidence for American nationhood following the Declaration of Independence is the circular letter sent by a unanimous Continental Congress under the signature of President John Jay to the states on September 13, 1779. The letter addressed the question of "[w]hether the United States have put themselves in a political capacity to redeem" the bills of credit issued by the Congress. This was a significant issue, because "our enemies" had argued "that the confederation of the states remains yet to be perfected; that the union may be dissolved, Congress be abolished, and each state, resuming its delegated powers, proceed in future to hold and exercise all the rights of sovereignty appertaining to an independent state."[125] That is, there was a fear that individual states might soon act like independent nations.

Congress disavowed this view entirely, in a statement that should be better known among constitutional historians. Since it is the most extensive official analysis of the legal status of the United States of America prior to the adoption of the Articles, it is worth quoting at length:

> For every purpose essential to the defense of these states in the progress of the present war, and necessary to the attainment of the objects of it, these states now are as fully, legally, and absolutely confederated as it is possible for them to be. Read the credentials of the different delegates who composed the Congress in 1774, 1775, and part of 1776. You will find that they establish an union for the express purpose of opposing the oppressions of Britain, and obtaining redress of grievances. On the 4th of July, 1776, your representatives in Congress, perceiving that nothing less than unconditional surrender would satisfy our enemies, did, in the name of the people of the thirteen United Colonies, declare them to be free and independent states, and 'for the SUPPORT of that declaration, with a firm reliance on the protection of Divine Providence, did mutually pledge to each other their LIVES, their FORTUNES, and their SACRED HONOR.' Was ever confederation more formal, more solemn, or explicit? It has been expressly assented to and ratified by every state in the union.... [F]or every purpose of the present war, and all things incident to it, there does at present exist a perfect solemn confederation.

Accordingly, while "its objects remain unattained," the confederation cannot "be dissolved, consistent with the laws of God or man." Moreover, the confederation would outlast the war and would be as enduring as the "United Provinces of the Netherlands and the United Cantons of Switzerland."[126] Note in particular Congress's interpretation of the Declaration's "free and independent states" language, which is often trotted out as the centerpiece of the thirteen-independent-nations argument. Congress did not read it that way at all; instead, it was the creation of a formal, solemn, and explicit confederation. A month later, even Thomas Burke agreed that "for every purpose of common defence and common Exertions in the progress of the present War and for the conclusion thereof, the States are unquestionably, united by former acts of the Several States."[127]

A dispute from Maryland in 1780 provides further insight into the nature of the union. The state had enacted a law that, read literally, seemed to prohibit the export of provisions from Maryland to the other states. A writer in the *Pennsylvania Gazette* explained in 1780 that the statute should not be read in such a way. He argued,

> We are but one people, from one end of the continent to the other.... The union, the confederacy, necessarily imply mutual assistance and free intercourse and commerce.... An act of any State to the purpose would be void in itself, as being against the fundamental laws of the union.... Every man knows that no State can constitutionally enact a law contrary to the spirit of the Union with the other States. This is paramount and supersedes all laws.[128]

This statement is particularly noteworthy, because not only were the Articles of Confederation not in effect, the only state that had failed to ratify was Maryland. Yet this writer viewed it as an obvious truth – that "every man" knows – that Maryland was constitutionally bound by the principles of the union.

Similar views were expressed in the early 1780s. In 1782, John Jay described the United States as "independent nation" and, after reviewing the diplomatic history following the Declaration of Independence, claimed there was "not a single instance in which Congress have derogated from the Practice and conduct of an independent nation."[129] John Adams, writing in 1781, observed that with the Declaration of Independence the United States of America had "assumed an equal Station among the Nations," and he proposed an alliance between the "two Nations" of the United States and the Netherlands.[130] In 1784, Alexander Hamilton observed that "Our Sovereignty and Independence began by a Feodoral Act."[131] Under the Declaration of Independence, which was the "fundamental constitution of every state," Congress "had complete Sovereignty."[132] The Union, he argued, was "pre-existing" at the time of the Articles of Confederation," which were a "modification & abridgement of Foederal authority."[133] The Union pre-existed the Articles of Confederation, and although the Articles limited federal powers in some respects, they still left "Congress the full and exclusive powers of War Peace and Treaty."[134]

Hamilton expanded on these ideas in a 1787 speech in the New York Assembly. After reciting the passage from the Declaration declaring the colonies independent, he noted, "Hence we see that the union and independence of these states are blended and incorporated in one and the same act; which, taken together clearly imports, that the United States had in their origin full power to do all acts things which independent states may of right do; or, in other words, full power of sovereignty."[135] A written constitution, Hamilton argued, was irrelevant to the existence of governmental powers. "A government may exist without any formal organization or precise definition of its powers. However improper it might have been that the federal government should have continued to exist with such absolute and undefined authority this does not militate against the position that it did possess such authority."[136]

LOYALTY, CITIZENSHIP, AND TREASON

Strong indications of nationhood can also be found in how revolutionary Americans thought about allegiance and loyalty. In 1774, the First Continental Congress adopted the Articles of Association, in which colonial Americans pledged not to import British goods. To enforce these articles, committees were established throughout the colonies. Individuals who continued to import British goods were routinely denounced as "enemies to their country" and subjected to social ostracism.[137]

When the war broke out in April 1775, it became common to speak of treason against America. The Pennsylvania Committee of Safety convicted four men in October 1775, for example, of "holding a traitorous correspondence with some of the British ministry, and of having communicated intelligence that has a tendency to exasperate them against the Americans."[138] In early 1776, the committee charged two men with "treasonable practices against America."[139] On June 21, 1776, the New York Provincial Congress issued an arrest warrant for David Matthews, charged with "treasonable Conspiracies against the Rights and Liberties of the united Colonies of America."[140]

The nationalist rhetoric continued after independence. In late 1776, the Pennsylvania Council of Safety jailed a man named John Biles for the offense of "Treason against the United States of America" and seven men for the offense of being "Enemies to the United States."[141] In 1778, the nascent state of Vermont brought a charge of treason against David Redding, a suspected Loyalist. The indictment claimed that the case was between the "United States of America" and "David Redding," who was charged with "enemical Conduct against this and said United States."[142]

On June 24, 1776, the Continental Congress resolved that "all persons, members of, or owing allegiance to any of the United Colonies … who shall levy war against any of the said colonies within the same, or be adherent to the king of Great Britain, … giving to him … aid and comfort, are guilty of treason against such colony."[143] In many ways, this was a functional declaration of independence, declaring allegiance to the king to be treason. The Congress called on the colonies to pass legislation punishing treason. Although treason would be prosecuted at the state level throughout the war (a practical decision, given the lack of a federal criminal court system), state treason statutes would have a strong nationalist overlay. Pennsylvania's 1777 treason statute, for example, punished taking a commission from the enemies of the "United States of America," assisting enemies at open war with the "United States of America," or conspiring to betray "the United States of America into the hands or power of any foreign enemy."[144]

Oaths of loyalty and allegiance were similarly cast in nationalistic terms. Prior to independence, members of the Continental Army took oaths, not to individual colonies, but to the "United Colonies of America."[145] Following independence, county committees of safety required individuals to swear oaths of loyalty to the "United States of America."[146] On July 13, 1776, for example, James Rankin pledged to a county committee in Pennsylvania that he would "behave, in all respects, as becomes a good citizen of the United States of America."[147] The Continental Congress required federal officials to take an oath of loyalty "to the United States."[148] In early 1777, General Washington issued a proclamation requiring persons who had taken an oath to Great Britain to "take the oath of allegiance to the United States of America."[149]

Provisions in the United States Constitution confirm that national citizenship had long existed. Article One requires representatives to have been citizens of the United States for seven years and senators to have been citizens for nine years. Since the Constitution was drafted in 1787, the obvious implication is that United States citizenship existed by at least 1778; that is, it could not possibly be a product of the Articles (ratified in 1781) or of the Constitution itself.

Here, too, analogies to the United Nations or NATO fall particularly flat. No one has ever spoken of being a citizen of the United Nations or NATO or pledged an oath of allegiance to them. Indeed, the very notion is absurd. But that's what Americans did after the Declaration: proudly described themselves as United States citizens, condemned treason against the United States, and pledged their allegiance to the United States of America.

THE ADOPTION OF THE CONSTITUTION

The debates over the drafting and ratification of the United States Constitution provided an opportunity for Americans to reflect on what the Declaration of Independence had wrought. Perhaps the most thoughtful analysis came from James Wilson, the most brilliant legal mind at the Philadelphia convention. As a signer of the Declaration of Independence, Wilson spoke with considerable authority. When Luther Martin of Maryland, who would become a virulent anti-Federalist, claimed on June 19, 1787, that the Declaration had "placed the 13 States in a state of Nature towards each other" and "that they would have remained in that state till this time, but for the confederation," Wilson was apoplectic.[150]

According to James Madison's notes of the proceedings, Wilson stated that "he could not admit the doctrine that when the Colonies became independent of G. Britain, they became independent also of each other." To prove this point, he read directly from the Declaration of Independence, concluding that "the *United Colonies* were declared to be free & independent States" and that they were "independent, not *Individually* but *Unitedly*." Under the Declaration, the states were as "confederated as they were independent."[151]

These views were central to Wilson's political philosophy. In an earlier speech at the convention, he recalled that in 1776 America was viewed as "one nation of brethren."[152] In a 1785 pamphlet, Wilson argued, "To many purposes, the United States are to be considered as one *undivided, independent* nation; as possessed of *all the rights,* and *powers,* and *properties,* by the law of nations *incident* to such." "The act of independence," Wilson continued, "was made before the articles of confederation. This act *declares,* that 'these UNITED *Colonies,*' (not enumerating them separately) '*are* free and independent States; and that, as free and independent States, THEY have full power to do *all* acts and things which independent States may, of right, do.'" Significantly, Wilson emphasized that the powers of the Continental Congress had been vested by "the union of the whole." National powers that predated the Articles of Confederation had never been exercised by the states, and were therefore untouched by the provision reserving powers to the states. States, Wilson explained, could not reserve what was never theirs to begin with.[153]

Wilson's June 19, 1787 remarks in the Constitutional Convention were echoed by Alexander Hamilton, who "assented to the doctrine of Mr. Wilson" and "denied the doctrine that the States were thrown into a State of nature."[154] Rufus King of Connecticut agreed, arguing that "The States were not 'sovereigns' in the sense contended for by some. They did not possess the peculiar features of sovereignty. They could not make war, nor peace, nor alliances, nor treaties." "If the Union of States comprises the idea of a confederation," he continued, "it comprises that also of consolidation. A Union of the States is a union of the men composing them, from whence a *national* character results to the whole.... If they formed a confederacy in some respects – they formed a Nation in others."[155] Later that month, Elbridge Gerry argued that "we never were independent States, were not such now, & never could be even on the principles of the Confederation."[156]

Similar views were expressed in the debates over ratification in the states. At the Pennsylvania convention, James Wilson argued that he considered "the people of the United States as forming one great community" and he read from the Declaration of Independence, which he described as "made by the representatives of the United States and recognized by the whole Union."[157] In South Carolina, Charles Cotesworth Pinckney described the Declaration as an "admirable manifesto, which for importance of matter and elegance of composition stands unrivalled" and argued that it "sufficiently confutes the ... doctrine of the individual sovereignty and independence of the several states." He noted, "The separate independence and individual sovereignty of the several states were never thought of by the enlightened band of patriots who framed this declaration; the several states are not even mentioned by name in any part of it, as if it was intended to impress this maxim on America, that our freedom and independence arose from our union." He urged his colleagues to "consider all attempts to weaken this union, by maintaining that each state is separately and individually independent, as a species of political heresy."[158]

In *The Federalist*, written to persuade New York to ratify the Constitution, John Jay stated, "To all general purposes we have uniformly been one people – each individual citizen everywhere enjoying the same national rights, privileges, and protection. As a nation we have made peace and war – as a nation we have vanquished our common enemies – as a nation we have formed alliances and made treaties, and entered into various compacts and conventions with foreign States."[159] His coauthor James Madison similarly mocked the pretensions of state independence, asking, "Was then the American Revolution effected, was the American Confederacy formed, was the precious blood of thousands spilt ... not that the people of America should enjoy peace, liberty, and safety; but that the Governments of the individual States ... might enjoy a certain extent of power, and be arrayed with certain dignities and attributes of sovereignty?"[160] (Later in life, Madison described the Declaration of Independence as "the fundamental Act of Union of these States."[161])

Similar points were made in newspaper discussions. Tench Coxe, writing in late September 1787, stated that the "Declaration of Independence completed the separation between the two countries," with the obvious implication that the United States was now a country.[162] A New Jersey resident argued in November 1787 that the Declaration had "opened the door by which our entrance into national importance was first made" by declaring "ourselves an *independent nation*."[163] Considering that he wished to feel himself "more a citizen of the United States than of New Jersey alone," he concluded that our "advancement and prosperity, nay, our very existence as a nation depends on our Union."[164]

In 1789, South Carolinian David Ramsay, the first significant historian of the American Revolution, explained that the "rejection of British sovereignty not only involved a necessity of erecting independent constitutions, but of cementing the whole United States by some common bond of union. The act of independence did not hold out to the world thirteen sovereign states, but a common sovereignty of the whole in their united capacity."[165] This point was echoed in congressional debates in 1791 by Representative John Vining of Delaware, a former delegate to the Continental Congress, who argued that the Declaration of Independence had made "the United States ... a free and independent nation" and that under the Declaration the United States "derive[d] all the powers appertaining to a nation thus circumstanced."[166]

THE CURIOUS CASE OF NORTH CAROLINA AND RHODE ISLAND

Only two American states – Texas and Hawaii – can claim undisputed status as formerly foreign nations. The Republic of Texas was admitted to the Union as a state in 1845, and the former Kingdom of Hawaii became a United States territory in 1898 and a state in 1959.

Were there others? Some scholars have suggested that two of the original states may have been outside of the Union for a brief period. Under Article Seven, the "Ratification of the Conventions of nine States" was deemed "sufficient for the Establishment of this Constitution between the States so ratifying the Same." Unlike the Articles of Confederation, which required unanimity for adoption and amendment, the Constitution recognized that some states might not ratify, and, if they did not, they were arguably no longer part of the American Union.

As it turned out, North Carolina and Rhode Island dragged their feet on ratification, and at the time of George Washington's inauguration, they had not ratified, and they did not send representatives to Congress or vote in the electoral college. North Carolina finally ratified on November 21, 1789, and Rhode Island on May 29, 1790.

There is certainly a nontrivial argument that these two states were, for a period, no longer part of the United States of America and were legally independent nations with a formal status no different than the Kingdom of Spain. A Providence town meeting in March 1789, for example, claimed that Rhode Island now stood "perfectly alone, unconnected with any State or Sovereignty on Earth."[167] James Iredell of North Carolina lamented, after the failure of the first ratifying convention, that his state was now "out of the Union," an argument echoed by other disappointed Federalists.[168] But the argument should be carefully examined, because it is not quite as straightforward as one might think.

A large problem with this argument is that its logic extends not just to North Carolina, but also to Virginia and New York, which were the tenth and eleventh states to ratify. If the Constitution became effective on June 21, 1788, when the ninth state, New Hampshire, ratified, then all of the remaining four states were seemingly out of the Union. Virginia was only out for four days, ratifying on June 25, 1788, but New York was potentially out for a month, not ratifying until July 26, 1788.

The potential effects of being out of the Union would be dramatic. To take just one example, Article Two of the Constitution required that the president be a "natural-born citizen, or a Citizen of the United States, at the time of the adoption of this Constitution." A strict interpretation of Article Seven would suggest that a Virginian born on June 24, 1788, would be ineligible to the presidency. (Could it have made a difference? President John Tyler was born in Virginia on March 29, 1790, less than two years later). Similarly, New Yorkers born during a one-month period would have been barred from the nation's highest office.

But this seems a very strained and hyper-legalistic way of approaching the issue. Did a Constitution designed to create a "more perfect Union" really contemplate the immediate *dissolution* of that Union upon the ratification of the ninth state? Even if all the states had quickly ratified, some states would have inevitably been the last four. Were they all out of the Union the moment state nine beat them to the punch? When Virginia ratified, it thought that it was providing the ninth vote; the news of New Hampshire's ratification had yet to reach Richmond.[169] Could a state be out of the Union without even knowing it? A more plausible reading of Article Seven is that it allowed states to affirmatively leave the Union if they consciously chose to do so, but failure to ratify immediately would not be viewed as a clear indication of such intent. At some point, though, a persistent failure to ratify would justify the ratifying states in treating the recalcitrant states as foreign territory.

This view seems consistent with the patient approach that Congress took to North Carolina and Rhode Island at the time. In late July 1789, Congress enacted a comprehensive system of federal tariffs on imports. It included a provision noting that the "States of Rhode Island and Providence Plantations, and North Carolina, have not as yet ratified the present Constitution of the United States" and therefore the act did not extend to collecting customs duties in those states. Accordingly, foreign goods brought from those states into the ratifying states would still be subject to federal duties. Significantly, however, goods of "their own growth or manufacture" were not subject to any federal tariffs, suggesting that Congress did not truly view these states as foreign territory.[170] Historian William S. Powell has pointed out that prior to ratification North Carolina nonetheless "complied with the regulations of the national government" and citizens of other states had free movement into North Carolina.[171]

On September 16, 1789, Congress enacted a provision stating that all the "privileges and advantages to which ships and vessels owned by citizens of the United States" would extend to ships owned by North Carolina and Rhode Island citizens until January 15, 1790.[172] This suggested that both states would lose certain privileges if they had failed to ratify by then. North Carolina ratified two months later, leaving only Rhode Island in an anomalous legal position.

In early February 1790, Congress extended the expiration date for Rhode Island's shipping privileges to April 1, 1790.[173] After months of foot-dragging, the Rhode Island legislature finally called for a ratifying convention. When the convention assembled in early March 1790, it adjourned almost immediately without taking any vote.[174] This inaction appears to pushed members of Congress to the breaking point. In mid May 1790, the US Senate passed a bill that would have blocked all commercial intercourse between the United States and Rhode Island.[175] A few weeks later, Rhode Island finally ratified.

In short, the claim that Rhode Island and North Carolina were out of the Union requires some definite starting point – on what date did they leave the Union? For reasons already discussed, it seems overly formalistic to insist that this occurred upon ratification by the ninth state. Might one point to definitive rejections of the Constitution? Rhode Island initially refused to call a ratifying convention, although it put the question to a popular vote in March 1788, where it failed by a decisive margin (in an election largely boycotted by many Federalists).[176] But since Article Seven did not provide for ratification by a popular vote, this is not necessarily clear evidence of rejection.

North Carolina initially held a convention at Hillsborough in the summer of 1788. The delegates hoped for additional amendments to the Constitution; accordingly, they "thought it proper neither to ratify nor to reject the Constitution."[177] One convention leader claimed that this decision was a delaying tactic, designed to focus attention on the amendments that other states had proposed.[178] Thomas Jefferson had argued for such a strategy earlier that year, stating, "I wish with all my soul that the nine first Conventions may accept the new Constitution, because this will secure to us the good that it contains, which I think great and important. But I equally wish that the four latest conventions, whichever they may be, may refuse to accede to it till a declaration of rights be annexed."[179] As Pauline Maier has noted, "The delegates had no intention of staying out of the union forever."[180] A delegate who favored delay argued that "[h]e could not conceive that the adopting states would take any measures to keep this state out of the union."[181] The same convention that declined to ratify also recommended to the legislature "that whenever Congress shall pass a law for collecting an impost in the states aforesaid, this state shall enact a law for collecting a similar impost on goods imported into this state, and appropriate the money arising therefrom, to the use of Congress."[182] Sending import duties to the United States Congress does not seem like an action that a foreign nation would typically take. The North Carolina governor informed President Washington in May 1789 that "[t]hough this state be not yet a member of the union under the new form of government, we look forward with the pleasing hope of its shortly becoming such."[183]

In other words, the precise boundaries of if, when, and how North Carolina and Rhode Island left the Union, are far from clear. Although clearly not governed by the Constitution, they might have been viewed as part of the United States in some broader sense, perhaps analogous to a federal territory that held a legal right to leave the Union. Had Congress carried through with its threat to exclude Rhode Island from the benefits of union, the state's status as a foreign nation would have been hard to deny. But Congress never reached that point, and it is not clear that North Carolina and Rhode Island were ever formally and legally entirely outside the American Union.

~~~

The history recounted in this chapter supports the interpretation of the Declaration's text offered in the prior chapter. Although contrary views were not unknown, the weight of the evidence suggests that the states entered into the world functionally confederated on July 4, 1776, and that they existed as a legal entity, the United States of America, governed by the Continental Congress.[184] It is very difficult to reconcile the numerous expressions of nationhood with the notion that there were thirteen separate nations, entirely unconnected with each other. As Justice Oliver Wendell Holmes remarked in 1921, "a page of history is worth a volume of logic."[185] Theoretical arguments about the nature of the American union are useful only insofar as they are supported by actual historical facts. And those facts cut very strongly against the thirteen-independent-nations thesis.

6 MEMORY

The view that the Declaration of Independence created an American nation isn't just supported by the document's text and history; it is also supported by how the Declaration has endured in legal, political, and cultural memory. If the Declaration created thirteen independent nations, then courts, legal analysts, political figures, and the American public have been getting it wrong for a very long time. The one-nation view is amply supported by judicial decisions that have carefully considered the issue, by the public statements of some of the leading lawyers of the nineteenth century – Joseph Story, Daniel Webster, and Abraham Lincoln, and by the long public tradition of celebrating the Fourth of July as the birthday of the American nation.

ONE NATION IN THE COURTS

Judges have sometimes made flippant and erroneous statements about the Declaration. In an opinion in a gun control case, for example, a Maryland federal judge recently claimed, "Undoubtedly, there are historical facts that are unassailable. For example, everyone would agree that the Declaration of Independence was signed on July 4, 1776."[1] And a California appellate court asserted that the Declaration was "written by the 33-year old Thomas Jefferson" and "was signed by 56 of our founding fathers" on "July 4, 1776."[2] But the Declaration was not, in fact, signed on July 4, 1776, by anyone other than John Hancock and Charles Thomson. It was adopted on that date, but it was not initially signed by the other delegates until August 1776. Even more foolish was the New York County Court judge who stated "those Thirteen separate and independent Colonies created a Continental Congress by signing the Articles of Confederation," apparently unaware that it was the Continental Congress that had drafted the Articles of Confederation.[3]

But these cases are outliers; none of them turned on those points and their errors are not consequential. Far more instructive are the cases where judges grappled directly with the legal status of the United States of America in the period between the adoption of the Declaration of Independence and the adoption of the Articles of Confederation. In these cases, we find a consistent rejection of the thirteen-nations view.[4]

The earliest judicial decision I have located is a 1788 case from Pennsylvania, presided over by Edward Shippen (the father of Margaret "Peggy" Shippen, the wife of Benedict Arnold). The case involved the treatment of out-of-state seizures of Loyalist property. Shippen explained that the "first body that exercised any thing like a sovereign authority, was the Congress of the then United Colonies, who superintended the whole, and, by the like common consent, were invested with such general powers as were necessary for the prosecution of the war. We afterwards divided ourselves into several distinct governments, by the name of States; still leaving the general power in Congress," which was "in a great measure undefined."[5] Although the colonies had become "free and independent States," Shippen continued, "they appear not to be such distinct sovereignties as have no relation to each other but by general treaties and alliances, but are bound together by common interests, and are jointly represented and directed as to national purposes, by one body as the head of the whole."[6]

Five years later, the issue reached the United States Supreme Court for the first time in *Chisholm v. Georgia*, which raised the question of whether federal courts could hear civil lawsuits brought by a citizen of one state against another state. The Court held, 4–1, that they could (a holding later altered by the Eleventh Amendment). In the 1790s, the justices had not yet developed the practice of issuing a single opinion of the Court, so each justice offered a separate opinion.[7]

In addressing the question, Chief Justice John Jay (unlike the other justices) felt it worthwhile to review the history of the revolution. On this point, he spoke with some authority, having previously served as president of the Continental Congress, where he had issued the September 13, 1779, circular letter stating that the colonies were legally confederated. "The Revolution, or rather the Declaration of Independence," Jay now wrote, "found the people already united for general purposes, and at the same time providing for their more domestic concerns by State conventions, and other temporary arrangements." The people "continued to consider themselves, in a national point of view, as one people; and they continued without interruption to manage their national affairs accordingly."[8] Prior to the Constitution, Jay observed, "the United States had by taking a place among the nations of the earth, become amenable to the laws of nations; ... the United States were responsible to foreign nations for the conduct of each State, relative to the laws of nations, and the performance of treaties."[9]

The legal status of the Declaration of Independence returned to the Supreme Court in a much more direct manner in the 1795 case of *Penhallow v. Doane's Administrators.* The state of New Hampshire had refused to obey a 1777 decision of the Continental Congress's Committee on Appeals and a 1783 decision of the Court of Appeals in Cases of Capture. New Hampshire insisted that the Continental Congress had no authority to reverse state court judgments in prize cases, a power it had asserted since 1775.[10]

The Supreme Court was thus squarely confronted with the question of the legal status of the Continental Congress following the Declaration of Independence. The Court did not have the option of simply concluding that the issue was contested or that there were various views on the subject; it had to decide which view was legally correct. The litigants in front of them required a definite answer; a significant amount of money was riding on the Court's determination. The Court took the question seriously; the parties were represented by some of the nation's leading lawyers, and oral arguments extended over eight days.[11]

The lawyers arguing on behalf of New Hampshire's position argued that the "Colonies totally independent of each other before the war, became distinct, independent, States, when they threw off their allegiance to the British crown, and Congress was no longer a Convention of Agents for the Colonies, but of Ambassadors from sovereign states."[12] Any resolutions of Congress with respect to prize cases were merely recommendations to the sovereign states.[13] Congress, they claimed, "had no power to erect Courts before the Confederation."[14]

The opposing lawyers countered, "On the declaration of independence, a new body politic was created; Congress was the organ of the declaration; but it was the act of the people, not of the state legislatures." The Continental Congress possessed a "national sovereignty, extending to all the powers of war and peace," which obviously extended to cases of ships captured at sea. True, there was no written constitution, but a "formal compact is not essential to the institution of government." Congress derived its authority "from the whole people of America, as one united body."[15] If thirteen completely independent nations had been created, they sarcastically asked, "How did we get along? Were there 13 different wars?"[16]

As in *Chisholm*, the justices delivered their opinions separately, but they were unanimous in upholding the authority of the Continental Congress. Two of the six justices did not participate: Chief Justice John Jay was in England negotiating a treaty, and Justice James Wilson was recused.[17] Justice William Cushing of Massachusetts thought the issue was resolved by the Court of Appeals' 1783 decision and he did not directly address the legal status of the Continental Congress.[18] But the other three directly rejected New Hampshire's extreme claims.

Justice William Paterson delivered the first opinion. As a delegate to the Constitutional Convention, Paterson had proposed the New Jersey plan, which favored the smaller states, and he was certainly not hostile to states' rights. But Paterson had no patience with the argument New Hampshire was advancing here. As Paterson saw it, when the war broke out the American people "grew into union, and formed one great political body, of which Congress was the directing principle and soul. As to war and peace, and their necessary incidents, Congress, by the unanimous voice of the people, exercised exclusive jurisdiction, and stood, like Jove, amidst the deities of old, paramount and supreme." "The truth is," Paterson continued, "the States, individually, were not known nor recognized as sovereign, by foreign nations, nor are they now." Paterson pointed out that New Hampshire's delegate to the Continental Congress had supported Congress's authority over prize cases in 1779, and if New Hampshire was unwilling to comply, "she should have withdrawn herself from the confederacy."[19]

Justice James Iredell of North Carolina thought that the powers of Congress were "gradually enlarged, either by express grant, or by implication arising from a kind of indefinite authority, suited to the unknown exigencies that might arise." Prior to the adoption of the Articles, Iredell noted, it was "unquestionable" that Congress exercised "high powers of … external sovereignty." Because he concluded that Congress's authority was clearly established by 1783 (when the Court of Appeals had issued a decision in the case), he did not need to directly answer whether the court was lawfully established prior to the adoption of the Articles, but he did note the argument that "Congress possessed this authority before, and the Articles of Confederation amounted only to a solemn confirmation of it." Like Justice Paterson, he observed that New Hampshire had supported congressional authority in 1779, and "once given, no state could, by any act of its own, disavow and recall the authority previously given, without withdrawing from the confederation."[20]

Justice John Blair of Virginia had heard the case while sitting as a circuit judge in the lower court, and his Supreme Court opinion relied largely on his circuit court opinion. The Congress, Blair concluded, "acted in all respects like a body completely armed with all the powers of war; and at all this I find not the least symptom of discontent among all the confederated states, or the whole people of America; on the contrary, Congress were universally revered, and looked up to as our political fathers, and the saviours of their country." The powers of war easily included reviewing state court judgments in prize cases, and if New Hampshire wished to exempt itself from this review, her only remedy was "withdrawing herself from the confederacy." "[W]hile she continued a member, and had representatives in Congress, she was certainly bound by the acts of Congress."[21]

Although the *Penhallow* decision has faded into almost complete obscurity, its significance should not be overlooked. As one observer at the time put it, the case raised the question of "whether the United States were one sovereign power before the confederation, or whether they were thirteen distinct sovereignties."[22] Although only two justices directly answered that question, no justice agreed with New Hampshire's position that Congress lacked the power to create a court of appeals with the power to reverse judgments of state courts prior to the adoption of the Articles of Confederation. The two justices who did answer the question offered resounding defenses of Congress's authority and of the nationhood of the United States at the time of the Declaration of Independence (as had the two recused justices in earlier statements). Contemporary observers understood just how significant the decision was. One man who attended the handing down of the justices' opinions noted, "it is all over with the Sovereignty of New Hampshire."[23] The *New-Hampshire Gazette* complained, "the sovereignty of New-Hampshire is completely annihilated."[24] In an 1809 United States Supreme Court decision, Chief Justice John Marshall stated, "By the highest judicial authority of the nation it has been long since decided, that the court of appeals erected by congress had full authority to revise and correct the sentences of the courts of admiralty of the several states, in prize causes."[25]

One possible dissenting voice came from Justice Samuel Chase of Maryland, who joined the Supreme Court in 1796. In his first opinion as a justice, Chase argued that the Declaration of Independence did not declare that the "United Colonies jointly, in a collective capacity, were independent states etc. but that each of them was a sovereign and independent state."[26] But Chase quickly qualified this conclusion by noting that although "the several States retained all internal sovereignty, ... Congress properly possessed the great rights of external sovereignty."[27] Chase saw "but one safe rule," that is, "all the powers actually exercised by Congress, before [the adoption of the Articles of Confederation] were rightfully exercised, on the presumption not to be controverted, that they were so authorized by the people they represented, by an express, or implied grant."[28] So, despite his somewhat broad statements, even Justice Chase seems to have concurred with the recognition of Congress's authority over the states in admiralty cases.

Although the Supreme Court would not return to the issue directly until the twentieth century, early nineteenth-century lawyers and judges treated the issue as resolved. St. George Tucker's influential 1803 edition of Blackstone's *Commentaries* stated, "By the declaration of independence, the colonies became a separate nation from Great Britain."[29] A South Carolina judge noted in 1812 that "[b]y the declaration of Independence, the United States became an independent nation."[30] The eminent Philadelphia lawyer William Rawle argued in 1805 that "The independence of America was a national act. The avowed object was to throw off the power of a distant country; to destroy the political subjection; to elevate ourselves from a provincial, to an equal state in the great community of nations."[31] In 1806, Nathan Dane, a former member of the Continental Congress and a founder of Harvard Law School, described July 4, 1776, as the date of the "birth of the American nation."[32] In an 1829 treatise, Dane argued that with the Declaration, "The people of all the colonies linked together in mutual assistance, and made themselves one united people, completely independent as a *sovereign nation*," under which the states were "all subordinate to the powers vested in the General Government."[33]

The legal status of the United States in 1776 was addressed again by the United States Supreme Court in the 1936 case of *United States v. Curtiss-Wright Export Corporation*. The United States Congress had authorized President Franklin Roosevelt to declare an arms embargo on Bolivia, if he deemed it necessary. After he declared an embargo, a grand jury indicted the Curtiss-Wright Export Corporation and four of its corporate officers for selling fifteen machine guns to Bolivia.[34]

Under Supreme Court precedents at the time, there was some doubt as to the legality of Congress granting such open-ended authority to the president, at least in domestic affairs. And the Supreme Court in 1936 was consistently invalidating Roosevelt's New Deal measures. But the Court viewed this case differently, because it involved foreign affairs. The Court's 7-1 opinion, delivered by Justice George Sutherland, went into considerable detail discussing the origins of the federal government's authority over international relations: "As a result of the separation from Great Britain by the colonies, acting as a unit, the powers of external sovereignty passed from the Crown not to the colonies severally, but to the colonies in their collective and corporate capacity as the United States of America." "Even before the Declaration," the Court observed, the colonies were a unit in foreign affairs, acting through a common agency – namely the Continental Congress." Citing *Penhallow*, the Court held that when "the external sovereignty of Great Britain in respect of the colonies ceased, it immediately passed to the Union." The Court noted that the Declaration of Independence declared the "United (not the several)

Colonies to be free and independent states." Accordingly, although the powers of the federal government with respect to internal affairs had to be specifically enumerated in the Constitution, its external powers did not, because the "states never severally possessed international powers."[35]

The *Curtiss-Wright* decision has generated a fair amount of criticism, and there are aspects of it that one might legitimately question. Why is the criminal prosecution of American citizens and an American company viewed as a matter entirely related to foreign affairs? And even if the foreign affairs powers were originally unconstrained by any constitutional document, isn't it possible that the Constitution nonetheless imposed some limits?[36]

But, setting aside those concerns, the Court in *Curtiss-Wright* got its basic history right.[37] It correctly understood that the thirteen states had never acted as individual, completely sovereign and separate nations, and that the United States of America was clearly one nation, at least with respect to the rest of the world, on July 4, 1776.[38]

The issue returned to the Supreme Court in a series of cases involving the new technology of offshore oil drilling. Although the states clearly held title to their coasts to the low tide line, did they own the seabed beyond it? Rejecting claims brought by California, Texas, Louisiana, and Maine, the Court held that the three-mile strip from the low tide line was owned by the United States.[39] As the Court explained in *United States v. California*, "we cannot say that the thirteen original colonies separately acquired ownership to the three-mile belt or the soil under it." The acquisition of this belt was "accomplished by the national Government" and "protection and control of it has been and is a function of national external sovereignty."[40]

STORY, WEBSTER, AND LINCOLN

In the early 1830s, the Nullification Crisis brought the issues of nationhood to the forefront. The state of South Carolina had enacted a law purporting to nullify – that is, to declare void within the state – a federal tariff that South Carolinians perceived as favoring northern interests. Under South Carolina's view, it was free to determine what federal laws could be constitutionally applied within the state. This theory of nullification was strongly supported by the vice president of the United States, John C. Calhoun, a South Carolinian himself.

Nullification was quickly and widely condemned by politicians of all partisan stripes. The sitting president, Andrew Jackson, who had been elected as a champion of states' rights, nonetheless readily concluded that South Carolina had gone too far. In a proclamation, Jackson lectured South Carolina on the origins of the nation. "[B]efore the Declaration of Independence, we were known in our aggregate character as *the United Colonies of America.* That decisive and important step was taken jointly. We declared ourselves a nation by a joint, not several acts, and when the terms of our confederation were reduced to form, it was in that of a solemn league of several States, by which they agreed that they would collectively form one nation for purpose of conducting some certain domestic concerns, and all foreign relations."[41] Jackson continued, "Under the royal government we had no separate character; our opposition to its oppressions began as *United Colonies.* We were the *United States* under the confederation…. In none of these stages did we consider ourselves in any other light than as forming one nation."[42]

Jackson's arguments would be elaborated by two of the most significant legal figures of the era, Supreme Court Justice Joseph Story and Senator Daniel Webster. Although Webster hailed from New Hampshire, he represented Massachusetts, Story's home state, in the United States Senate. The men developed a close working alliance, described by Story's biographer as "one of the most extraordinary in American law and politics."[43]

Joseph Story was one of those people who would make even the most talented feel like underachievers. He was appointed to the United States Supreme Court in 1812 at the ripe old age of 32. Beginning in 1829, he served simultaneously as the Dane Professor of Law at Harvard Law School. He wrote nearly a dozen treatises on all aspects of American law. One of his most influential works was his widely acclaimed *Commentaries on the Constitution of the United States,* first published in 1833. The United States Supreme Court continues to cite it regularly.[44]

Story had no use for nullification and for state-centric views of the founding more generally, and he sought to educate his fellow

Americans about the proper understanding of the Declaration. The First Continental Congress, he argued, was "the first general or national government" and it was "organized ... with the consent of the people, acting directly in their primary, sovereign capacity." The Congress exercised "*de facto* and *de jure* a sovereign authority; not as the delegated agents of the governments *de facto* of the colonies, but in virtue of original powers derived from the people." This government, Story asserted, persisted until the ratification of the Articles in 1781.[45]

As Story saw it, the "declaration of independence of all the colonies was the united act of all." It was "not an act done by state governments then organized; nor by persons chosen by them. It was emphatically the act of the whole *people* of the united colonies, by the instrumentality of their representatives...." It was "an act of original, inherent sovereignty by the people themselves." "The people of the united colonies made the united colonies free and independent states, and absolved them from all allegiance to the British crown. The declaration of independence has always been treated, as an act of paramount and sovereign authority, complete and perfect *per se*, and *ipso facto* working an entire dissolution of all political connection with and allegiance to Great Britain. And this not merely as a practical fact, but in a legal and constitutional view of the matter by courts of justice."[46]

Story explained that the actions of Congress in 1776 "could in no other manner be justified or accounted for, than upon the supposition, that a national union for national purposes already existed, and that the congress was invested with sovereign power over all the colonies for the purpose of preserving the common rights and liberties of all."[47] Indeed, "before the declaration of independence these colonies were not, in any absolute sense, sovereign states; that that event did not find them or make them such; but that at the moment of their separation they were under the dominion of a superior controlling national government, whose powers were vested in and exercised by the general congress with the consent of the people of all the states."[48]

Story concluded, "From the moment of the declaration of independence, if not for most purposes at an antecedent period, the united colonies must be considered as being a nation *de facto*, having a general government over it created, and acting by the general consent of the people of all the colonies. The powers of the government were not, and indeed could not be well defined. But still its exclusive sovereignty, in many cases, was firmly established; and its controlling power over the states was in most, if not in all national measures, universally admitted."[49]

Story's ally Daniel Webster delivered a similar critique of nullification theories. Webster had a national reputation as a constitutional lawyer, having argued many of the major cases of the Marshall Court.[50] Story viewed Webster as second only to John Marshall as a "constitutional lawyer and statesman."[51] In 1833, Webster delivered an important speech rebutting John Calhoun, who was now serving as senator from South Carolina. Calhoun had justified nullification by arguing that the Constitution was a mere compact among the states. Webster found the compact theory historically unjustified. As he explained, "In 1789, and before this Constitution was adopted, the United States had already been in a union, more or less close, for fifteen years … Before the Confederation of 1781, they had declared independence jointly, and had carried on the war jointly, both by sea and land; and this not as separate States, but as one people." They did not "come together for the first time" with the Articles of Confederation, but "there was a bond of union already subsisting between them." They were "associated, united States; and the object of the Confederation was to make a stronger and better bond of union."[52] In a letter to Webster, James Madison praised him for his "very powerful speech" that "crushes 'nullification.'"[53]

A young lawyer in Illinois paid careful attention to the views of Story and Webster, and took them deeply to heart. When Abraham Lincoln was confronted with the unprecedented secession of the southern states, he turned, as he often had throughout his career, to the Declaration of Independence. In a February 1861 speech at Independence Hall, Lincoln stated, "I have never had a feeling politically that did not spring from the sentiments embodied in the Declaration of Independence."[54] In his First Inaugural Address, he argued, "The Union is much older than the Constitution. It was formed in fact, by the Articles of Association in 1774. It was matured and continued by the Declaration of Independence in 1776. It was further matured, and the faith of all the then thirteen States expressly plighted and engaged that it should be perpetual, by the Articles of

Confederation in 1778. And finally, in 1787, one of the declared objects for ordaining and establishing the Constitution, was 'to form a more perfect union.'"[55]

In his July 4, 1861 address to Congress, Lincoln laid out the historical case against secession in more detail. It was a "sophism" to assume "that there is some omnipotent, and sacred supremacy, pertaining to a *State*.... Our States have neither more, nor less power, than that reserved to them, in the Union, by the Constitution – no one of them ever having been a State *out* of the Union." The Declaration of Independence had declared the "United Colonies" to be "Free and Independent States," but "even then," Lincoln argued, "the object plainly was not to declare their independence of *one another*, or of the *Union*; but directly the contrary, as their mutual pledge, and their mutual action, before, at the time, and afterwards, abundantly show." Since the states had never existed outside of the Union, Lincoln asked, "whence this magical omnipotence of 'State rights,' asserting a claim of power to lawfully destroy the Union itself?" "The Union," he argued, "and not themselves separately, procured their independence, and their liberty. By conquest, or purchase, the Union gave each of them, whatever independence, and liberty, it has. The Union is older than any of the States; and, in fact, it created them as States."[56]

THE NATIONAL BIRTHDAY IN POPULAR CULTURE

We celebrate the Fourth of July as our national birthday, and have been doing so for a very long time. We have not celebrated other possible contenders, such as the dates on which colonial legislatures authorized their congressional delegates to vote for independence; July 2, 1776, the date Congress voted for independence; the date of the ratification of the Articles of Confederation; the dates of the signing or the ratification of the Constitution; or the date on which the new federal government under the Constitution began operating. Americans have stubbornly insisted that July 4, 1776 – and only July 4, 1776 – is the national birthday. If the Declaration of Independence created thirteen independent nations, however, our Fourth of July celebrations are wildly off track – we should be celebrating independence from

Great Britain, but not the birth of a nation. But they are not off track. Celebrating the Fourth of July as the birth of our nation is entirely appropriate, and the Americans who celebrated it as such in the late eighteenth century (most of whom were alive on July 4, 1776) and their descendants have been getting it exactly right.

The first anniversary of the Declaration in 1777 was celebrated with cannon salutes, decorated navy ships, military parades, ringing church bells, and extravagant fireworks across the eastern seaboard.[57] The Continental Congress celebrated with an "elegant dinner," concluding with toasts to those "who fell gloriously in defence of freedom and the righteous cause of their country."[58] A Philadelphia newspaper described the "Anniversary of the Independence of the United States of America" and declared, "Thus may the fourth of July, that glorious and ever memorable day, be celebrated through America, by the sons of freedom, from age to age till time shall be no more."[59] (One dour member of the Continental Congress was less than enthused, finding the day "poorly spent in celebrating the Anniversary of the Declaration of Independence" and complaining about the "great Expenditure of Liquor.")[60]

The second anniversary, in 1778, was more restrained, at least in Philadelphia, which had been freed from British occupation only two weeks earlier. Nonetheless, Congress held a celebratory dinner, an orchestra played, and cannons were fired.[61] The *Pennsylvania Gazette* republished the Declaration at the request of a reader who (foreshadowing similar natal imagery in Abraham Lincoln's Gettysburg Address) sought to "excite the good People of the United States to a Remembrance of their Birth into a world of Freedom."[62] The third anniversary, in 1779, featured an extensive fireworks display, organized by a French army officer.[63]

The Fourth of July quickly came be to seen as the national birthday. In 1786, a South Carolina newspaper described the "Fourth of July" as an "auspicious natal day."[64] In 1787, the *Providence Gazette* referred to the Fourth of July as "the anniversary of our national birthday,"[65] and the *Pennsylvania Evening Herald* claimed that it "crowned the toils of America with freedom and sovereignty."[66] In 1788, New York City honored "our national birthday" and commemorated the "magnanimous Worthies who signed that sacred Instrument the

Declaration of Independence," a document that was published in the "name of the People of America."[67] The next year, a New York newspaper, under the headline "The Day!," offered a verse: "Now ye patriotic band, Hail your Country's natal day! Saviours of a happy land! Sov'reign, free America."[68] In his 1789 history of the American Revolution, South Carolinian David Ramsay observed that the Fourth of July has "ever since been consecrated by the Americans to religious gratitude, and social pleasures. It is considered by them as the birth day of their freedom." With the Declaration, Ramsay continued, the "Americans no longer appeared in the character of subjects in arms against their sovereign, but as an independent people."[69] In 1790, John Hancock, now serving as the governor of Massachusetts, delivered an address to the state legislature, stating, "The Fourth of July, 1776, was the birthday of a Nation; ... not only the nation of which we were a part, but all the nations of the world will probably derive great and lasting blessings from it."[70] In 1791, a writer in a New York newspaper described the Fourth of July as "the birthday of a nation." "Ought not Americans, then," he asked, "to celebrate the nativity of their nation!" He called for "every trueborn son of America" to "join heart and hand in celebrating their great and annual festival."[71] That same year a Massachusetts newspaper referred to July 4 as the "birthday of our Nation" and America's "natal day,"[72] and a Philadelphia newspaper published an "Ode for the Fourth July, 1791," which concluded, "We celebrate thy natal day."[73] In South Carolina, the day was celebrated as "America's natal day."[74] A New York newspaper celebrated the Fourth in 1792 as the "separation of one country from the jurisdiction of another."[75] A 1794 Independence Day orator in Augusta, Georgia, described the "glorious 4th of July 1776" as "the birthday of a nation."[76] An eighteen-year-old Daniel Webster celebrated the Fourth as the "birth of a nation" in an Independence Day speech in Hanover, New Hampshire in 1800.[77]

Many of these celebrations involved reading the Declaration of Independence aloud, as occurred in New Haven in 1788, New York in 1791, Philadelphia in 1793, and Boston in 1802, traditions that have continued to this day.[78] One such celebration occurred in Washington, DC in 1821, when Secretary of State John Quincy Adams delivered a Fourth of July oration. After reading the entire Declaration of

Independence aloud (apparently from the original ceremonial parchment in possession of the State Department), Adams noted, "From the day of this Declaration, the people of North America were no longer the fragment of a distant empire... They were a *nation*, asserting as of right, and maintaining by war, its own existence. A nation was born in a day."[79] If asked what America had "done for the benefit of mankind," one should answer that "America, with the same voice which spoke herself into existence as a nation, proclaimed to mankind the inextinguishable rights of human nature, and the only lawful foundations of government."[80]

The most extraordinary anniversary was undoubtedly the fiftieth in 1826. Thomas Jefferson and John Adams, who had served together on the Declaration's drafting committee and later became presidents of the United States, died on that day.[81] Historian Michael Hattem notes that the "symbolism and significance of their near-simultaneous deaths on the fiftieth anniversary of independence are hard to exaggerate."[82] Many Americans saw the hand of God at work.[83] (It is not entirely implausible that both men somehow willed themselves to stay alive until the fiftieth anniversary.) The date was, of course, of special significance to Thomas Jefferson, who had described the Fourth of July as the "nation's birthday" and the "anniversary assemblage of the nation on its birthday."[84] The Declaration of Independence, he stated, "made us a nation."[85]

In 1831, John Quincy Adams, now a former president of United States, delivered another Independence Day address. It is worth quoting at length, with the original punctuation and emphases:

> The Declaration of Independence was a manifesto issued to the world, by the delegates of thirteen distinct, but UNITED colonies of Great Britain, in the name and behalf of their people. It was a united declaration. Their union preceded their independence; nor was their independence, nor has it ever since, been separable from their union. Their language is, "We, the Representatives of the *United* States of America, in General Congress assembled, do, in the name and by the authority of the good PEOPLE of these Colonies, solemnly publish and declare that these *United Colonies*, are, and of right ought to be, free and independent States." It was the act of one people. The Colonies are not named; their number

is not designated; nor in the original Declaration, does it appear from which of the Colonies any one of the fifty-six Delegates by whom it was signed, had been deputed. They announced their constituents to the world as one people, and unitedly declared the Colonies to which they respectively belonged, united, free and independent states.[86]

Adams repeatedly returned to this theme throughout his address, arguing,

> The Declaration was joint, that the United Colonies were free and independent states, but not that any one of them was a free and independent state, separate from the rest. ... The Declaration of Independence was a social compact, by which the whole people covenanted with each citizen of the United Colonies, and each citizen with the whole people, that the United Colonies were, and of right ought to be, free and independent states.[87]

The document, he asserted, "announced the severance of the thirteen United Colonies from the rest of the British Empire, and the existence of their people from that day forth as an independent nation."[88] Strident assertions of state sovereignty, Adams argued, were "hideous" and "in direct contradiction to the Declaration of Independence, and incompatible with the nature of our institutions."[89]

~~~

Although later memories of the Declaration of Independence are no substitute for direct evidence from 1776, they do provide powerful confirmation of the nationalist interpretation. Far too many modern accounts seem to consider the argument for thirteen independent nations to be conclusively resolved by the language of the Declaration and the language of the Articles, with perhaps a dash of international law theory thrown in for flavor.[90] Yet, later Americans read this same language in the Declaration and the Articles of Confederation and came to a quite different conclusion – the Declaration of Independence made the United States a nation.

To conclude that the Declaration created thirteen completely independent nations, one has to conclude that the first justices of the United States Supreme Court interpreted the Declaration incompetently; that later judicial decisions interpreted the Declaration incompetently; that Thomas Jefferson, John Quincy Adams, Joseph Story, Daniel Webster, Andrew Jackson, and Abraham Lincoln all interpreted the Declaration incompetently; and that ordinary Americans have been stupidly celebrating the nation's birthday on the wrong date for nearly 250 years. And one would also have to conclude that the better, more thoughtful, and more historically informed interpretation of the Declaration was that offered by the Southern nullifiers in the 1830s and the Southern secessionists in the 1860s. There is little reason to accept such an implausible conclusion; it is far more probable that courts, statesmen, and the American people have, in fact, been getting it right.

PART III

Making Government Work

One of the most persistent myths about the Declaration of Independence is that it is an abstract statement about individual liberty and equality, and that it has nothing significant to say about the actual mechanics of government. Justice Antonin Scalia, for example, claimed, "If you want aspirations, you can read the Declaration of Independence." By contrast, "There is no such philosophizing in our Constitution, which, unlike the Declaration of Independence … is a practical and pragmatic charter of government."[1] Law professor Sai Prakash states, "Though [the Declaration] gets the patriotic juices flowing, it hardly qualifies as a blueprint for government…. [its] principles tell us nothing concrete."[2] The political scientist Martin Diamond concluded that "the Declaration was not prescribing any particular form of government at all" and it can provide "no guidance whatsoever" on what those forms should be.[3] A duo of political philosophers were even more emphatic, arguing, "the Declaration itself gives no guidance on how or in what ways such governments ought to be built. Put otherwise, in no sense can the Declaration be considered a manual for the construction of new governments, and those who prefer to read it as such had better go back to the text."[4]

Going back to the text is an excellent idea. But we need to do a better job than the analysts quoted above. Their review of the Declaration generally begins and ends with the second paragraph. A careful reading of the entire document, however, allows a very different picture to emerge. The heart of the Declaration consists of detailed charges against the King, and they were by far the most critical part in 1776. As Pauline Maier argued, "Independence was justified only if the charges against the King were convincing and of sufficient gravity to warrant the dissolution of his authority over the American people."[5]

British critics of the Declaration understood that the entire dispute turned on the accuracy of the charges. John Lind, in *An Answer to the Declaration of the American Congress*, conceded that if the charges of "unwarrantable jurisdiction," "tyranny," and "usurpation" were true, it would be "the duty of every man to unite in procuring redress to injured subjects." But the charges, he insisted, "were unsupported, even by the shadow of a proof."[6] Accordingly, he devoted nearly all of his 128-page response to carefully dissecting each charge. Only later did he reference other parts of the document, claiming, "Of the preamble I have taken little or no notice. The truth is, little or none does it deserve."[7] Similarly, Thomas Hutchinson, the former governor of Massachusetts, focused primarily on "the false representation made of the facts which are alledged to be the evidence of injuries and usurpations, and the special motives to Rebellion."[8]

Admittedly, the British critics scored some points in their reviews of the Declaration. Some of the charges against the King are almost entirely opaque; others do not have an obvious factual basis. Pauline Maier observed, "Today most Americans, including professional historians, would be hard put to identify exactly what prompted many of the accusations Jefferson hurled against the King, which is not surprising since even some well-informed persons of the eighteenth century were perplexed."[9] Carl Becker felt that "when one has found the particular act to which in each case the particular charge was intended to refer, one is likely to think the poor king less malevolently guilty than he is made out to be."[10]

But, for understanding the Declaration's larger vision of government, we do not need to get into an historical back and forth on the accuracy of each specific charge.[11] What mattered is that the drafters of the Declaration thought they were true and that they justified revolution. What they saw was horrifying. They perceived a "Design to reduce [the Americans] under absolute Despotism." "The History of the present King of Great-Britain," they announced, "is a History of repeated Injuries and Usurpations, all having in direct Object the Establishment of an absolute Tyranny over these States. To prove this, let Facts be submitted to a candid World."

These "Facts" are the heart of the Declaration of Independence. Each Fact describes behavior that renders the King and Parliament unfit to rule. When we read these Facts carefully, and in conjunction with each other, we can begin to understand the Declaration's vision of how government is supposed to work. The Declaration demonstrates a profound commitment to constitutional self-government and to the rule of law. It seeks a government that is both empowered to act energetically to advance the public interest, but at the same time constrained by legal rules and procedures. And although the outlines are less distinct than in a formal constitution, it also offers significant structural guidance, highlighting those elements that are most essential for self-government to flourish.

7 THE IMPORTANCE OF GOVERNMENT AND LAW

The Declaration of Independence, we are often told, is deeply skeptical of government in general. In a massive reference work entitled *A Companion to the American Revolution*, for example, one finds this confident assertion: "the Declaration gives voice to a political philosophy of extremely limited government."[1] Libertarian attorney Timothy Sandefur agrees, stating, "The Framers saw majority rule as a useful but dangerous device, to be employed sparingly in order to protect freedom."[2] These interpretations rely almost entirely on the Declaration's second paragraph, which, to be fair, is susceptible to aggressively anti-government readings. But the second paragraph must be read in context, with careful attention to the charges against the King. When we do this, a very different vision of government emerges, one in which government is not a necessary evil, but a positive good.

GOVERNMENT AND LAW AS POSITIVE GOODS

One of the Declaration's most prominent themes is the importance of law in a well-governed society. Indeed, a significant number of the charges against the King are not about bad laws, but about the King's obstruction of good laws. The failure to provide good laws was as fully pernicious as the creation of bad laws. Consider the following charges (emphases added):

He has refused his Assent to *Laws* ....
He has forbidden his Governors to pass *Laws* ....

He has refused to pass other *Laws* ....

He has... obstruct[ed] the *Laws* for Naturalization of Foreigners; refusing to pass others to encourage their Migrations hither ....

He has ... refus[ed] his Assent to *Laws* for establishing Judiciary Powers ....

He has subjected us to a Jurisdiction ... unacknowledged by our *Laws* ....

For abolishing the free System of English *Laws* in a neighbouring Province ....

For ... abolishing our most valuable *Laws*.

This lack of law – a failure of government – is one of the primary objections that the Declaration makes to British rule.

Consider the very first charge that the Declaration makes against the King: "He has refused his Assent to Laws, the most wholesome and necessary for the public Good." Laws, in other words, are both wholesome and necessary. A "wholesome" law is one that improves society in some way. The word derives from early Scandinavian terms for "health" and it came to imply a promotion of well-being.[3] In *Hamlet*, Marcellus famously says of Christmas Eve: "And then, they say, no spirit can walk abroad; / The nights are wholesome; then no planets strike, / No fairy takes, nor witch hath power to charm."[4] George Washington directed military officers to keep their quarters "clean & wholesome."[5] In the 1760s, Benjamin Franklin sought to replace Pennsylvania's proprietary governor with a royal governor, who would be more "at Liberty to join with the Assembly in enacting wholesome Laws."[6] An associate of George Washington noted in 1773 that "the Increase or Population of a Country is in a great Degree owing to its wholesome Laws and good Government."[7] Good laws are a desirable feature of a well-functioning society, providing a healing and improving effect on the body politic.

As the first charge asserts, certain laws are also "necessary." The concept of necessity pervades the Declaration. The document begins, "When in the Course of human Events, it becomes necessary for one People to dissolve the Political Bands which have connected them with another." Later it refers to the "Necessity which constrains [the Colonies] to alter their former Systems of Government." At the end, it resigns itself to the inevitable: "We must, therefore, acquiesce in the Necessity, which denounces our Separation." The Americans really had no other choice – separation was necessary and required. So, too, with laws. Some laws are simply necessary for the proper functioning of society. A society without laws is no society at all.

Subsequent charges drive this theme home. The King has "forbidden his Governors to pass Laws of immediate and pressing Importance." Not only are such laws necessary, but they are "immediate and pressing." The King has "refused to pass other Laws for the Accommodation of large Districts of People" and has "obstruct[ed] the Laws for the Naturalization of Foreigners." He has "obstructed the Administration of Justice, by refusing his Assent to Laws for establishing Judiciary Powers." In all of these ways, the King has failed to provide his American subjects with the good laws that they require.

Later charges condemn Parliament, along with the King, for "abolishing the free System of English Laws in a neighbouring Province" and for "taking away our Charters, abolishing our most valuable Laws, and altering fundamentally the forms of our Governments," and for "suspending our own Legislatures." In other words, a complete deprivation of laws and government. And to emphasize the horrors of such deprivation, the Declaration condemns the King for allowing colonial legislatures to lapse, with the result that that the colonies remained "in the mean time exposed to all the Dangers of Invasion from without, and Convulsions within."

The Declaration ultimately concludes that George III is a "Tyrant, unfit to be the Ruler of a free People." It is noteworthy, then, how many of the charges are not about bad laws, but about the absence of good laws and the failure to provide competent government. Such failures can be just as tyrannical and despotic as the imposition of bad laws. A year earlier, in the Declaration of the Causes and Necessity of Taking Up Arms, the Continental Congress had claimed "government was instituted to promote the welfare of mankind, and ought to be administered for the attainment of that end." This vision – of government as an active force for positive good – could not be more distant from the minimalist, night-watchman state that we are sometimes told the Declaration demands.

In his important book *The Heart of the Declaration: The Founders' Case for an Activist Government,* historian Steve Pincus argues that the drafters of the Declaration were deeply influenced by what he calls the "Patriot Whig" movement in eighteenth-century British politics. The Patriot Whigs favored an energetic imperial state, promoting "state investment in the most dynamic elements of the economy" and supporting "commercial society, the Bank of England, the manufacturing sector, and well-designed trading companies."[8] Their political opponents, by contrast, mostly favored lowing the tax burden on wealthy English landowners.[9]

Although American colonists enthusiastically supported the Patriot Whig government of the 1750s, they were profoundly alienated by the brief administration of George Grenville in the 1760s, which viewed the primary purpose of the colonies as revenue sources to pay down Britain's national debt.[10] Unpopular policies like the Stamp Act soon followed. Grenville's administration quickly fell, but its general approach was renewed in the early 1770s under Lord North. In Pincus's view, "the Declaration of Independence needs to be understood as the ultimate statement of the eighteenth-century Patriot program in favor of a government that would aim to promote prosperity for the largest number of people."[11] The goal was to "fashion an American version of the Patriot state that had existed in Britain before the accession of George III."[12]

Even if one does not fully embrace Pincus's connection between English Patriot Whigs and the American founders, he is on to something significant: there is no reason to paint the founders as reflexively opposed to governmental power. One prominent drafter of the Declaration, John Adams, understood this clearly. As he saw it, with the Declaration, "The Legislatures of the Colonies will exert themselves, to manufacture, Salt Petre, Sulphur, Powder, Arms, Cannon, Mortars, Cloathing, and every Thing, necessary for the Support of Life. Our civil Governments will feel a Vigour, hitherto unknown."[13] The legislatures rose to the challenge. As historian William J. Novak recently pointed out, "The early American state legislative record was replete with powerful statutes regulating almost every aspect of state economic and social life in time of war and transition. The public powers exercised in the name of wartime necessity, public safety, and public welfare were as extensive as imaginable."[14] The goal was governmental vigor, not governmental torpor, and governments that would enact the good laws the British had conspicuously failed to provide.[15]

PRESERVING THE CONSTITUTION AND THE RULE OF LAW

The United States Constitution of 1787 and the recognition of judicial review in *Marbury v. Madison* loom so large over our understanding of American constitutional government that it is easy to overlook the importance of constitutional arguments in earlier periods. One of the most important passages in the Declaration of Independence, for example, is not one that typically receives much attention. The Declaration claims that the King "has combined with others to subject us to a Jurisdiction foreign to our Constitution, and unacknowledged by our Laws; giving his Assent to their Acts of pretended Legislation." The "others" in this charge are the members of Parliament. Because colonial Americans consistently rejected parliamentary legislative authority over the colonies, they refused to even mention the body by name, and its acts were denounced as merely "pretended Legislation." (Later, the Declaration dismissively refers to Parliament as "their Legislature.") The argument, quite simply, was that all of these British statutes were unconstitutional, at least as applied to the colonies.

The charge of unconstitutionality was not an innovation of the Declaration – it had been a rallying cry since the 1760s. The American critique of British policies turned almost entirely on the meaning of the larger British (and, to some extent, the earlier English) constitution.[16] As the eminent historian Jack Greene put it, "Fundamentally, the American Revolution was the unforeseen consequence of the inability of the disputants to agree upon the nature of the constitution of the British Empire."[17] From the very beginning of the colonial dispute with Britain, Americans argued not only that Britain had enacted bad policies, but that those policies were unconstitutional. When the Stamp Act was enacted in 1765, Americans insisted that Parliament could not constitutionally tax the colonies without American representation in

Parliament. Richard Henry Lee noted in June 1775 that the "original cause of our present unhappy difference is the lately assumed right and practice of Parliament, to raise revenue on the subject in America, contrary to the clearest principles of justice and the English constitution."[18] Many members of Parliament agreed. Lord Camden insisted in 1766 that taxation of the colonies "was illegal, absolutely illegal, contrary to the fundamental laws of this constitution.... Taxation and representation are coeval with and essential to this constitution."[19] William Pitt thought that the Americans had a "constitutional right, of giving and granting their own money."[20] Thomas Walpole argued in 1775 that "no privilege of our Constitution was ever better ascertained, more generally understood, or more confidently believed, than the privilege which *Englishmen*, for a long succession of ages, have enjoyed, of being taxed only with their own consent, or that of their representatives."[21]

Although English constitutional arguments dated back at least to Magna Carta in 1215, they had come to the fore in the seventeenth century. The Petition of Right of 1628, the execution of Charles I in 1649, the overthrow of James II in 1688, and the adoption of the Bill of Rights in 1689 were all celebrated as landmarks of the English constitution, even though there was no formal written document specifying the powers of government. After the 1707 Act of Union with Scotland, one could refer to a "British Constitution" that included an "English Constitution" as one of its component parts. As historian Jonathan Gienapp has explained, "By the eighteenth century, the most basic fact about the British constitution was that it was fundamental and supreme. From the seventeenth century through American independence, Britons and American colonists alike spoke confidently about the paramount status of their common constitution. Anything that violated its requirements was, by definition, null and void."[22]

Constitutional arguments reverberated throughout the conflict, beginning with objections to the Stamp Act, and accelerating starkly as British measures grew more oppressive in 1774.[23] The Stamp Act Congress of 1765 asserted that "no taxes ever have been, or can be constitutionally imposed on them, but by their respective legislatures."[24] An attack on the Tea Act, published in a New York newspaper under the title "Constitutional Catechism," included this exchange: "QUERY. How do you prove the tea *duty* to be *unconstitutional?* ANSW: Because it is a tax in direct opposition to a fundamental maxim of the British constitution, whereby we can *only* be taxed by our own consent, or that of our own representatives."[25] In 1775, the Virginia Committee of Safety adopted a new flag, which stated, "Virginia. For Constitutional Liberty."[26] The Maryland Convention complained in May 1776 of the "unconstitutional and oppressive acts of the *British* Parliament for laying taxes in *America.*"[27] A town meeting in Palmer, New Hampshire denounced the "repeated inroads on the Constitution, and gigantick strides of despotick power over the Colonies."[28] George Washington, writing to John Hancock on July 10, 1776, observed that the Declaration "will secure us that freedom and those privileges which have been refused us, contrary to the voice of nature and the British constitution."[29] In August 1776, the President and Council of Georgia complained that George III had "trampled upon the Constitution of our Country."[30]

In all of these complaints, colonial Americans voiced a constitutional perspective that pervades the Declaration: the king and Parliament are *bound* by the Constitution, and any acts that transcend the Constitution have no legal force. Such acts were "Usurpations," as the Declaration twice describes them – acts unsanctioned by law. A widespread belief that the British had persistently failed to follow the law goes a long way to explaining why so many lawyers, a class not typically in the vanguard of revolutionary movements, played such a prominent role in justifying and leading the American cause. As early as 1765, British General Thomas Gage noted that the "Lawyers are the Source from whence the Clamors have flowed in every Province."[31]

The Declaration views the British monarchy as a constitutional monarchy, an understanding that was widely shared both in England and in the colonies. The notion that the king was bound by law goes back to least to the early thirteenth-century treatise known as *Bracton*, which famously stated that the "king must not be under man but under God and under the law."[32] Subsequent English developments fleshed out what this might mean, and by the late seventeenth century, it was understood that there were significant constitutional and legal restraints on royal power. A primary justification for the overthrow of James II, for example, was his refusal to comply with statutory law

The very first right asserted in the English Bill of Rights of 1689 was that "the pretended power of suspending the laws or the execution of laws by regal authority without consent of Parliament is illegal." Few, if any, legal authorities in Britain would have disputed this basic claim.

With respect to Parliament, however, the Declaration was breaking more ground. By the late eighteenth century, a notion of parliamentary supremacy had emerged in Britain, under which Parliament was effectively the judge of its own actions, unconstrained by any other body, since English courts lacked the power of judicial review.[33] But the Declaration nonetheless insists that Parliament is as fully bound by the constitution as the king. Colonial Americans could thus claim that unconstitutional acts of Parliament were no law at all and therefore carried no obligation to be obeyed.

This is not to say that the Declaration explicitly embraced a commitment to judicial review. Colonial Americans may well have thought that the ultimate constitutional determination was to be made by the people at large, rather than by courts.[34] But it's not all that big a step from concluding that unconstitutional laws do not have to be obeyed to concluding that judges are equally bound to ignore unconstitutional laws, as the American constitutional system would quickly come to recognize. At minimum, the Declaration recognizes that the people are entitled (and even required) to overthrow their government when there have been repeated violations of the Constitution. As the Declaration puts it, "when a long Train of Abuses and Usurpations … evinces a Design to reduce them under absolute Despotism, is their Right, it is their Duty, to throw off such Government."

The Declaration's commitment to constitutionalism is rooted in a broader commitment to the rule of law more generally – the recognition that government is bound by the same laws as everyone else and that it must follow established rules and procedures. On May 17, 1775, the members of the Continental Congress processed from the State House to attend the commencement ceremonies at the College of Philadelphia.[35] The College's provost, William Smith, delivered an oration in which he set forth the widespread understanding of the rule of law. "The government of your country," Smith proclaimed, "is a government of *laws* … where your liberties, your lives, your property, depend not on the will of *one* man, nor of a number of men;

but on the known and established rules of *justice*."[36] As Chief Justice John Marshall would later put it in *Marbury*, "The government of the United States has been emphatically termed a government of laws, and not of men."[37]

The exact opposite of the rule of law was "arbitrary" power – rule by the whim of government officials.[38] Referring to the Quebec Act of 1774, which extended the province of Quebec and reintroduced its French-based civil law, the Declaration denounces the King and Parliament for "abolishing the free System of English Laws in a neighbouring Province, establishing therein an arbitrary Government, and enlarging its Boundaries, so as to render it at once an Example and fit Instrument for introducing the same absolute Rule into these Colonies." Arbitrary government and absolute rule – the antitheses of the rule of law. This complaint is echoed in other charges, which accuse the King of seeking to impose "absolute Despotism" and "absolute Tyranny." Parliament, too, was denounced for "declaring themselves invested with Power to legislate for us in all Cases whatsoever." This assertion of parliamentary sovereignty was, as John Phillip Reid observed, "a British abrogation of the English constitutional principle that Americans cherished above all others, the rule of law."[39]

The Declaration is thus far from indifferent as to how government should function. It is imbued with references to constitutional government and the rule of law. Unconstrained, arbitrary power is unacceptable. Dictatorship, tyranny, absolute rule, and the divine right of kings are impermissible forms of government. The only acceptable forms are those governed by constitutional principles and the rule of law.

UNDER GOD?

This book's title, *One Nation Under Law*, evokes a far more familiar phrase, "One Nation, Under God." That phrase comes from the Pledge of Allegiance, or at least the Pledge as altered by Congress in 1954. The original Pledge of Allegiance, written in 1892 by the socialist Francis Bellamy, used the phrase "one Nation indivisible," making an obvious connection between the unity of the nation and its indivisibility following the Civil War.[40] When Congress inserted the phrase "under God," as a way to distinguish the United States from the supposed godless Communism of the Soviet Union, it interrupted this basic connection.

If we were seeking a pithy summary of the principles of the Declaration of Independence, "under God" is quite far afield. A far more accurate description is that the document commits us to be a nation "under law." The Declaration's purported religious content has often been grossly overstated, as we can see from examining the document's four generic references to a deity (none of which are overtly Christian).[41]

The first is the reference to "Nature's God" in the preamble. But "Nature's God" is a peculiar phrase. In 1770, Dr. Thomas Young published an article in a Boston newspaper explicitly linking the "Religion of Nature's God" to the "Religion of Nature," that is, deism, which he preferred to orthodox Christianity.[42] In a thorough study of the phrase, Matthew Stewart concluded that "'Nature's God,' the God of Thomas Young and the presiding deity of the American Revolution, is another term for 'Nature.'"[43] At most, a reference to "Nature's God" is a concession that God created nature. More likely, it means only that the world is subject to the natural laws of science.

The second reference is that "all Men … are endowed by their Creator with certain unalienable Rights." This, too, is far from a deeply religious statement. In the eighteenth century few people would have rejected the existence of a Creator. In the absence of a theory of evolution, there was no other explanation for the existence of complex structures like human organs. After all, how could there be a creation without a Creator? No rational person, for example, would believe in watches but not in watchmakers. Even now, science has no answer to the question of why there is something rather than nothing. So hardly anyone in the eighteenth century would have rejected the notion of a divine creation. But that is about as far as many of them went. A number of leading political figures were not conventional Christians and embraced various theories, such as deism, which held that God had created the world, but then left it entirely to its own devices.[44] The Declaration is simply making the unremarkable acknowledgment that there is a Creator; it doesn't even explicitly state that the Creator is a god. As Steven Green, a noted historian of religion, has pointed out, the reference "reflects the influence of the prevailing rationalist thought of the period."[45]

The third and fourth references come near the end and were added by the Continental Congress to Jefferson's draft.[46] The delegates appealed "to the Supreme Judge of the World for the Rectitude of our Intentions" and invoked a "firm Reliance on the Protection of divine Providence." These, too, are fairly generic assertions. "God" is not directly mentioned, and there is nothing referencing any specifically Christian belief.

Finally, one might note that the Declaration's concluding sentence, in which Americans pledge to each other their "sacred honor," sits quite uneasily with basic tenets of Christianity, which emphasized humility. The Christ of the New Testament was not known for bristling at any perceived slights to his honor. Stridently asserting one's "honor" and declaring it to be "sacred," as the Declaration does, is far more consistent with the pagan virtues of ancient Greece and Rome, in which many of the document's drafters were steeped.[47] A seventeenth-century English translation of the Roman poet Juvenal, for example, contains the phrase "sacred honor," but it is not regularly found in Christian writings of the seventeenth and eighteenth centuries.[48]

In short, the Declaration is not an especially religious document; there is simply a generic assumption that a Creator exists. Nowhere does the Declaration say anything about the nature of God or invoke a particular religious faith or text. By contrast, the Declaration is imbued with references to the centrality of law to the new nation that was being created. If the Pledge of Allegiance was going to be tampered with (and it really shouldn't have been), a far more accurate description of the Declaration would have been "One Nation Under Law" rather than "One Nation Under God."

8   THE STRUCTURE OF GOVERNMENT

The drafters of the Declaration of Independence were profoundly concerned with the "form" of government, and attention to "form" is one of the document's primary themes. The term makes an early appearance, in the famous second paragraph. Revolution, the Declaration tells us, is justified when "any Form of Government becomes destructive of these Ends." Since the phrase could have easily read, "any Government becomes destructive of these Ends," the inclusion of the word "form" is significant – we are immediately on notice that governmental "form" will matter. In quick succession, the term appears twice more. The people are to lay the "Foundation" of a new government "in such Form, as to them shall seem most likely to effect their Safety and Happiness." And, "Mankind are more disposed to suffer, while Evils are sufferable, than to right themselves by abolishing the Forms to which they are accustomed." Finally, the king is charged with "altering fundamentally the Forms of our Governments."

In the eighteenth century, the term "form" had a slightly more definite meaning than it has today; it implied something clearly constructed, with a fixed shape. George Washington made the connection to architecture explicit in a 1776 letter to his brother: "To form a new Government, requires infinite care & unbounded attention; for if the foundation is badly laid the superstructure must be bad."[1] And it was taken extremely seriously. As John Adams wrote in early 1776, "It is the Form of Government, which gives the decisive Colour to the Manners of the People, more than any other Thing."[2] A writer in a Connecticut newspaper exulted in April 1776 that "the happy time is approaching, that a glorious state of independence shall take place, and produce such a wise and steady form of government, as will promote happiness, justice, union, and mutual confidence among all the various denominations of men, throughout this extensive empire."[3] In June 1776, a writer in the *New York Journal* proclaimed, "The important day is come, or near at hand, that America is to assume a form of government for herself.... The affair now in view is the most important that ever was before America ... If our civil Government is well constructed, and well managed, America bids fair to be the most glorious state that has ever been on earth. We should now at the beginning lay the foundation right."[4]

Not surprisingly, then, the Declaration of Independence has much to say about the appropriate form of government. Certain forms are entirely unacceptable: rule by a "Tyrant," "Despotism," "arbitrary Government," and "absolute Rule" are all categorically denounced. But it's not just those extreme examples. Even within non-despotic governments, there are better and worse forms, and the Declaration accordingly advances a broad vision of how legislative, executive, and judicial powers should be structured.

LEGISLATIVE POWER

The heart of a properly constituted government – the one indispensable element – is a representative assembly. The Declaration states that the King has "refused to pass other Laws for the Accommodation of large Districts of People, unless those People would relinquish the Right of Representation in the Legislature, a Right inestimable to them, and formidable to Tyrants only." The use of the term "Right" is particularly striking; this is the only right specifically mentioned in the Declaration other than the opening reference to the rights of life, liberty, and the pursuit of happiness. Popular representation in a legislative assembly is not just a desirable feature of government, but the bare constitutional minimum, the foundation on which everything else rests. The First Continental Congress had explained this point in 1774, asserting that "the foundation of English liberty, and of all free government, is a right in the people to participate in their legislative council."[5] (A similar argument had been made by the noted

British abolitionist Granville Sharpe; in 1774 John Dunlap reprinted in Philadelphia Sharpe's pamphlet entitled *A Declaration of the People's Natural Right to a Share in the Legislature, Which Is the Fundamental Principle of the British Constitution of State.*)[6]

In asserting this right, the Declaration was rejecting one of the worst aspects of the eighteenth-century British political system. Parliamentary districts were horribly apportioned. Certain miniscule areas, the so-called rotten boroughs, were entitled to a member, whereas some large cities had no representation in Parliament at all. British apologists justified this malapportionment under the theory of "virtual representation," which asserted that members of Parliament were supposed to look out for the interests of the entire nation, thus making all Britons "virtually represented" in Parliament even if they didn't directly elect a member themselves. The theory was regularly deployed to counter American complaints about taxation without representation – true, Americans were not represented in Parliament, but neither was Manchester.[7] Not surprisingly, colonial Americans were unpersuaded, and over the course of the 1760s and 1770s they increasingly insisted on actual – not virtual – representation. Thomas Jefferson famously asked in 1774, "Can any one reason be assigned why 160,000 electors in the island of Great Britain should give law to four millions in the states of America?"[8] As Bernard Bailyn noted, the Americans wanted government to be an "accurate mirror of the people, sensitively reflecting their desires and feelings." Through their representatives, the people would be directly "acting in the conduct of public affairs."[9]

American representation in Parliament was a possible solution, but it was not enthusiastically embraced. The Declaration and Resolves of the First Continental Congress concluded that the colonies "cannot properly be represented in the British parliament" due to their "local and other circumstances."[10] The colonists nonetheless persistently argued the corollary proposition – since colonial Americans were represented only in their colonial assemblies, only those assemblies, and not Parliament, could constitutionally tax American subjects.

The importance of representative assemblies reverberates throughout a number of further charges. The Declaration states that the King had "dissolved Representative Houses repeatedly, for opposing with manly Firmness his Invasions on the Rights of the People." The term "Representative Houses," rather than "Legislative Houses," helps underscore the critical role of representation. These houses will protect the "Rights of the People"; they are not antagonistic to the people's rights, but the primary guarantor of those rights. Historian Jonathan Gienapp has noted that eighteenth-century Americans were convinced that liberty "could be realized only under a truly representative government, a government that embodied one's consent and thus could be said to be acting in accordance with that will."[11] A similar view is expressed earlier in the document, when the Declaration states that the people can overthrow oppressive governments and "provide new Guards for their future Security." Representative assemblies are the ideal guards, precisely because they are *representative* of the people. As Gienapp has explained, for colonial Americans, "one protected liberty not by disabling government but rather by empowering government in the right kind of way. This meant, above all, constructing representative institutions that, by embodying the people's will, protected the people's liberty."[12]

In an especially interesting charge, the Declaration explains what happens after the King had dissolved representative assemblies. The "Legislative Powers, incapable of Annihilation, have returned to the People at large for their exercise." The result is a state "exposed to all the Dangers of Invasion from without, and Convulsions within." That is, in the absence of a representative assembly, the people themselves will directly exercise the legislative powers. But this is clearly an undesirable outcome, not quite complete anarchy, but something very close. Only a properly structured representative assembly can adequately defend the state from external invasion and internal convulsions. This concern is echoed in the later charge that the King and Parliament had "suspend[ed] our own Legislatures."

At the heart of the dispute between Britain and America was the Declaration's condemnation of the King and Parliament for "imposing Taxes on us without our Consent." The principle that taxation required consent had deep roots in English history. Under Magna Carta of 1215, the king could impose certain taxes only by the "common counsel" of the kingdom. The Petition of Right of 1628 explicitly stated that taxes could only be imposed by "common consent, in parliament." Charles I's subsequent unilateral extension of the so-called "ship money" (a tax imposed on certain maritime counties) to inland counties was one of the grievances contributing to his overthrow. As Parliament put it in 1641, the imposition of this tax was "contrary to and against the laws and statutes of this realm, the right of property, the liberty of the subjects, former resolutions in Parliament, and the Petition of Right."[13]

For colonial Americans, these precedents were not just curious historical artefacts; they embodied the foundational principle of English constitutional law.[14] A writer in April 1775 pointed out that "throughout America" there was "unanimity" on "the principle that taxation and representation are inseparable."[15] The New York Assembly argued that it was "essential to Freedom, and the undoubted right of Englishmen, that no Taxes should be imposed on them without their Consent given personally, or by their Representatives."[16] This deep connection between taxation and representation is further evidence that the Declaration is not indifferent to the structure of government. Outside of direct consent, as in New England town meetings, representative assemblies must exist as a mechanism to provide consent to taxation.

The importance of such assemblies is emphasized in one of the Declaration's more maligned charges, the complaint that the King had "called together Legislative Bodies at Places unusual, uncomfortable, and distant from the Depository of their public Records, for the sole Purpose of fatiguing them into Compliance with his Measures." British critics thought this referred to a 1768 incident in which the royal governor of Massachusetts required the assembly to meet in Cambridge rather than in Boston, and they could scarcely contain their derision.[17] Thomas Hutchinson pointed out that the legislature itself had often removed to Cambridge in times of smallpox, so it was not "unusual." The meeting rooms at Harvard College were not "uncomfortable." And a move of four miles was not distant from public records. Hutchinson could not fathom how this "unimportant dispute between an American Governor and his Assembly" could possibly be a "ground to justify Rebellion."[18] John Lind thought the charge was "so truly ridiculous … that it is hardly possible to answer it with any becoming gravity" and speculated that it might have been "inserted by an enemy ... to throw an air of ridicule on the declaration in general."[19]

But the Declaration may be referring to another incident. In 1774, Thomas Gage, the governor of Massachusetts, following Parliament's direction in the Boston Port Act, moved the assembly from Boston to Salem, which was much less convenient than Cambridge.[20] The underlying facts, however, are less important than the underlying concern. If a king could "fatigue" legislative bodies into compliance with his own will, then the entire purpose of a representative body would be destroyed. It would become an organ of monarchical power, rather than a body of the people. Similarly, if forced to meet at places distant from public records, the legislature would find it much more difficult to legislate intelligently, and the people's right to adequate representation would be diminished.

All of the charges relating to legislative power are ultimately rooted in the Declaration's vision of self-government. The heart of this vision – one might even say the heart of the Declaration itself – is its insistence on elected representative assemblies. Professor Kermit Roosevelt III has argued that there is no requirement in the Declaration "that government be democratic" or that "people should have an equal voice in government," but this overlooks significant portions of the document.[21] While the Declaration does not denounce constitutional monarchy as such, it nonetheless insists that any proper form of government must contain a representative assembly in which the people have a voice, ensuring that government is, as Abraham Lincoln would later put it, "of the people, for the people, and by the people."[22]

EXECUTIVE POWER

In some ways, the entire Declaration of Independence is an essay on the misuse of executive power, as it lays out multiple instances in which George III had abused his authority. And it is tempting, especially in light of the ferocious attack on monarchy unleashed in Thomas Paine's *Common Sense*, to similarly read the Declaration as a condemnation of monarchy. But the document is much more equivocal and seems to tolerate a constitutional monarchy constrained by law.

The Declaration asserts, "A Prince, whose Character is thus marked by every act which may define a Tyrant, is unfit to be the Ruler of a free People." That is, the problem is not that George III is a prince, but that he is a tyrant. He has abused his monarchical powers in ways that render him completely unfit for office. As the Declaration further claims, "The History of the present King of Great-Britain is a History of repeated Injuries and Usurpations, all having in direct Object the Establishment of an absolute Tyranny over these States." The language is anti-tyranny, not anti-monarchy.

There were two strong reasons counseling against overt attacks on monarchy in the Declaration. The first was practical politics; the Americans were desperate for foreign support, and as Stephen Lucas has pointed out, independence "was not likely to be won without support from European monarchies, neither of which would be favorably impressed with a Declaration that inveighed against kingship."[23] The second reason was more deeply rooted in principle. For most of the dispute, the colonists had imagined a British empire in which the king played a coordinating role. Parliament would govern Great Britain; colonial assemblies would govern the colonies, and all would be united around a common king (a view not dissimilar to the British Commonwealth that emerged in the twentieth century). Indeed, the Declaration denounces the King for failing to veto acts of Parliament, a complaint that sits quite uneasily with a condemnation of monarchical power in general. The King had been a beloved figure in the American colonies for much of the eighteenth century, and even in the first weeks of the war, American troops claimed to be fighting for the King, while denouncing the British forces as fighting for Parliament.[24]

By July 4, 1776, however, George III was clearly a "Tyrant." And it was not just that he was a "Tyrant," but that his "Character" was marked "by every act which may define a Tyrant." The revolutionaries placed enormous stock in personal character and virtue, and by these measures, the character of George III fell woefully short.[25] Ideally, however, one would not have to depend entirely on the personal virtues of those who govern. As James Madison would later put it, "If men were angels, no government would be necessary. If angels were to govern men, neither external nor internal controls on government would be necessary. In framing a government which is to be administered by men over men, the great difficulty lies in this: you must first enable the government to control the governed; and in the next place, oblige it to control itself."[26] Accordingly, the Declaration has much to say about how to appropriately structure the executive power, to ensure that it protects the rights of self-government without degenerating into tyranny.

The Veto

Nowhere is the Declaration more conflicted than in its varying assertions about the King's veto. The charges against the King begin with a lengthy denunciation of instances in which the King had disallowed colonial legislation, a power exercised through the Privy Council. The very first charge is that the King had "refused his Assent to Laws, the most wholesome and necessary for the public Good." The second charge says that the King had "forbidden his Governors to pass Laws of immediate and pressing Importance, unless suspended in their Operation till his Assent should be obtained; and when so suspended, he has utterly neglected to attend to them." The third charge condemns the King for refusing "to pass other Laws for the Accommodation of large Districts of People." Later, the King is condemned for "refusing his Assent to Laws for establishing Judiciary Powers."

From these charges, it is tempting to conclude that the Declaration is generally hostile to a broad power of executive veto. George III was clearly abusing his powers, and restriction, or even elimination, of veto powers might be seen as an appropriate response. But the rest of the charges suddenly turn in a completely different direction. The Declaration states, "He has combined with others to subject us to a Jurisdiction foreign to our Constitution, and unacknowledged by our Laws; giving his Assent to their Acts of pretended Legislation." That is, George III had approved acts of Parliament that colonial Americans thought were unconstitutional. The argument now is not that the King had vetoed too much, but that he had vetoed too little. Under this understanding of royal power, the King was required to veto any attempt by Parliament to unconstitutionally extend its jurisdiction over the colonies.

And here colonial Americans ran into a very serious conundrum. As Samuel Beer put it, "To suppose that the monarch had a sphere of authority beyond that of parliament – that he could rule where parliament could not – was to overlook the fact that there had been a seventeenth century."[27] Although the last Stuart monarch, Queen Anne, had vetoed an act of Parliament in 1707, no monarch had exercised the power since. Legal historian John Phillip Reid observed, "We may be certain that every lawyer knew that no Hanoverian king had ever exercised the veto, and we may suspect that every competent lawyer knew that no Hanoverian king – or any British monarch in the future – would ever again veto an act of Parliament."[28] George III took his constitutional responsibilities seriously, and understood, as one historian has noted, "that the great mistake of the Stuarts had been to attempt to enlarge their prerogative powers by curtailing those of Parliament. His duty, he knew, lay in *upholding* the rights of Parliament."[29] The monarch could advise and consult, but could not deny (this remains the status of royal veto in the United Kingdom today).

Thomas Jefferson struggled with this issue in his *A Summary View of the Rights of British America*. He complained that George III had wantonly exercised his veto power over colonial legislatures, for "the most trifling reasons, and sometimes for no reason at all." So why would one want to entrust him with a veto over acts of Parliament? Despite the long disuse of such a veto, Jefferson argued that it was now "the great office of his majesty, to resume the exercise of his negative power, and to prevent the passage of laws by any one legislature of the empire, which might bear injuriously on the rights and interests of another."[30]

In short, colonial Americans were demanding that the King assert a royal power that had laid dormant since the time of the Stuarts. To British critics, this demand sounded like a revival of the constitutional theories of Charles I, who had insisted on complete royal autonomy over the colonies, with no role for Parliament at all. As one archly noted, "Who would have expected to have found such very zealous advocates for royal prerogative among the puritannical inhabitants of New England[?]" It was "absurd," he argued, "to found the independence of any British colony upon the principles and actions of kings."[31]

In his fascinating book, *The Royalist Revolution: Monarchy and the American Founding*, Harvard professor Eric Nelson argues that we need to take this aspect of the revolutionary dispute seriously – for much of the 1760s and 1770s, colonial Americans were in fact arguing for increased royal power. In his view, they were "effectively proposing to turn back the clock on the English constitution by over a hundred years – to separate the king from his Parliament and his British ministers and to restore ancient prerogatives of the Crown that had been extinguished by the whig ascendancy."[32]

This American demand was never going to be acceptable in Britain, and it placed American and British constitutional views into an irreconcilable conflict. As John Phillip Reid put it, "The dynamics of the eighteenth-century British constitution had produced a constitutional dilemma. American liberty – the right to be free of arbitrary power – could not be secured under parliamentary supremacy. British liberty – the representative legislature over the crown – could not be secured without parliamentary supremacy."[33]

It is therefore not surprising that the Declaration ends up in an equivocal position on the veto, denouncing the King for both vetoing too much and vetoing too little. Many early state constitutions limited or eliminated their governor's veto powers, in line with the Declaration's condemnation of the King for disallowing colonial legislation. As Gordon Wood has explained, "it seemed abominable that a single person should have a negative over the voice of the whole society."[34] Eventually, however, the veto came back, in later state constitutions, and, most notably, in the president's veto over acts of Congress in the Constitution of 1787. The presidential veto, however, requires a written explanation and is subject to override by supermajorities of Congress (as are most gubernatorial vetoes by their state legislatures).[35] The American constitutional tradition thus seems to recognize that a veto power is important, but that it should not be absolute. In this way, the Declaration's conflicting views on the veto power can perhaps be reconciled.

The Duty to Follow the Law

Although the entire Declaration can be read as a condemnation of George III's failure to follow the law, there are specific charges that relate to the legal obligations of the executive authority.

For example, "He has endeavoured to prevent the Population of these States; for that Purpose obstructing the Laws for Naturalization of Foreigners."[36] That is, the King has obstructed the law, by refusing to comply with it. Complying with the law is not optional; it is a mandatory duty imposed upon the executive. In a similar vein, the Declaration charges the king with suspending various laws and then "utterly neglect[ing] to attend to them."

In one of its more forceful charges, the Declaration asserts that the King has "abdicated Government here, by declaring us out of his Protection and waging War against us." That is, the king has failed to enforce the laws and has withdrawn the legal protections to which the Americans were entitled. This amounts to an "abdication" of government, leaving the Americans free "to institute new Government, laying its Foundation on such Principles, and organizing its Powers in such Form, as to them shall seem most likely to effect their Safety and Happiness."

It had long been understood that kings were supposed to rule on behalf of their people. In 1774, Thomas Jefferson had argued that the king was "the chief officer of the people, appointed by the laws, and circumscribed with definite powers, to assist in working the great machine of government, erected for their use, and consequently subject to their superintendance."[37] It is a notion similarly expressed in the Constitution's requirement that the president "take care that the laws be faithfully executed." The president – and any executive – is not above the laws, but is bound by and subordinate to them.

Civilian Control of the Military

The Declaration pointedly denounces the King for seeking to "render the Military independent of and superior to the Civil Power." This poses two distinct problems. First, by making the military *independent* of civilian control, it frees the military to do whatever it wants. Second, by making the military *superior* to civilian power, it makes the military supreme, and subordinates civilian government to military authorities, rendering the right of representation meaningless. It is, in short, a military despotism.

Since the seventeenth century, Anglo-American constitutional thought had placed considerable emphasis on civilian control of the military, ensuring that Parliament, and not the king, was firmly in control.[38] The Petition of Right of 1628 had complained about the use of military jurisdiction over civilians and the 1689 Bill of Rights had asserted that it was illegal for the king to keep a standing army in peacetime without the consent of Parliament.

These principles are echoed in the Declaration's charge that the King had "kept among us, in Times of Peace, Standing Armies, without the Consent of our Legislatures." Here, the Declaration's skepticism of military authority is linked with its earlier insistence on the importance of representative assemblies. The people, and only the people, are entitled to decide whether standing armies are to be permitted. If so, they will be subject to popular control and less likely to commit atrocities, such as the Declaration's claim that the King and Parliament had "quarter[ed] large Bodies of Armed Troops among us."

The principle of civilian control of the military was not just an abstract ideal; it was the heartfelt conviction of George Washington, who consistently insisted on his subordination to the Continental Congress during the course of the war and memorably resigned his commission at the end of it. It also supports the Constitution's designation of the president – a civilian – as the commander-in-chief of the United States armed forces.

"Swarms of Officers"

One of the Declaration's more colorful charges is that the King had "erected a Multitude of new Offices, and sent hither Swarms of Officers to harass our People, and eat out their Substance." This appears to be a reference to the American Board of Customs Commissioners, located in Boston.[39] British critics were quick to pounce on the hyperbolic nature of this charge. Thomas Hutchinson sneeringly noted, "Thirty or forty additional officers in the whole Continent, are the *Swarms* which eat out the subsistence of the boasted number of three millions of people."[40] Smuggling was a pervasive problem in colonial America, and the Declaration did not dwell on the reason for the appointment of these officers. John Lind wondered, "Will the Americans confess, that the class of *smugglers* so numerous in that country, as to entitle them to be called – by way of eminence – *the people*?"[41] As Stephen Lucas observed, "Congress could hardly assail George III as a tyrant for appointing a few dozen men to enforce the laws against smuggling, so it clothed the charge in vague, evocative imagery that gave significance and emotional resonance to what otherwise might have seemed a rather paltry grievance."[42]

The charge evokes a biblical plague of locusts, and many commentators have fallen to the temptation of viewing this passage as a condemnation of bureaucracy and government more generally. But careful attention to the passage in context suggests that the problem is not government officials as such, but unaccountable government officials. The charge is directed at the King directly, rather than the King acting with Parliament. In other words, the King has created these offices using only his royal authority. Moreover, these officers would be effectively unaccountable strangers in the land, British residents "sent hither" and paid by the King rather than by the colonial assemblies.

The fundamental problem was the creation of executive offices that were entirely disconnected from popular control and unauthorized by any legislative assembly. Such officers could naturally be expected to behave in the most inappropriate ways. By contrast, government officials authorized and paid by colonial assemblies and selected from the people would pose no similar threat. They would not be "Swarms of Officers," but simply accountable local officials doing the jobs with which they were entrusted.

JUDICIAL POWER

The first charge to deal with the judiciary asserts that the King had "obstructed the Administration of Justice, by refusing his Assent to Laws for establishing Judiciary Powers." Here, as in earlier charges, the Declaration is not complaining about too much government but about too little government. Failure to establish functioning courts is literally an obstruction of justice.[43] But the mere existence of courts is not sufficient; instead, the Declaration lays out a clear vision for the roles of judges and juries in a properly structured judiciary.

Judges

The Declaration complains that the King "has made Judges depen-dent on his Will alone, for the Tenure of their Offices, and the Amount and Payment of their Salaries." This charge is a mirror image of the military charge. Whereas the King is denounced for making the mil-itary "independent" of the civil power, he is denounced for making judges "dependent" on royal power.

For most of English history, common law judges could be fired by the king for any reason, and judges who courted royal displeasure, such as Sir Edward Coke in 1616, quickly found themselves booted to the curb. A significant reform came in 1701, when royal judges were granted tenure during "good behavior," meaning they could not be removed by the king. Only Parliament, through its impeachment power, could remove a judge from office. However, the judge's com-mission was deemed to expire at the end of a reign, which allowed new kings to appoint new judges. This loophole was closed in 1760, when judges were granted effective life tenure regardless of a change of monarch.[44]

These protections, however, did not apply to judges in the col-onies. In 1761, the British government announced that all colonial judges would hold office only at the pleasure of the king.[45] As historian Bernard Bailyn noted, "everywhere there was bitterness at the decree and fear of its implications."[46] There was a very real risk that judges would become entirely tools of the monarch, subject to dismissal in any case in which they ruled against royal interests.

And it wasn't just security of tenure, it was also about salaries. Colonial judges had typically been paid by appropriations from colo-nial legislatures. Yet in the late 1760s, a powerful rumor began circu-lating that salaries would soon be paid directly by the Crown, cutting out any involvement by local elected officials.[47] One of the most thor-ough denunciations of this potential practice came in 1773 from the Massachusetts House, which declared that the "independence, as well as the uprightness of the Judges of the land, is essential to the impartial administration of justice, and one of the best securities of the rights, liberty, and property of the people." Paying judicial salaries through the Crown rather than colonial legislatures was "unconstitutional ...

[and] directly the reverse of the constitution, and appointment of the Judges in Great Britain." Any judge who accepted a royal salary, the House concluded, "will discover to the world, that he has not a due sense of the importance of an impartial administration of justice, that he is an enemy to the constitution, and has it in his heart to promote the establishment of an arbitrary government in this province."[48]

To be clear, the American complaint wasn't entirely about judicial independence in the abstract, but the specific problem of judicial dependence on the Crown. Many early state constitutions accordingly placed the judicial appointment power in the legislature, with no role for the state's executive.[49] The unacceptable outcome was a judiciary staffed by subservient royal officials, unconnected to the people at large.

Juries

The use of juries to decide criminal and civil cases was the most distinctive feature of the English common law. By the eighteenth century, juries held a revered position in English and American legal thought.[50] In his famous *Commentaries on the Laws of England*, Sir William Blackstone wrote, "trial by jury ever has been, and I trust ever will be, looked upon as the glory of the English law.... [I]t is the most transcendent privilege which any subject can enjoy, or wish for, that he cannot be affected either in his property, his liberty, or his person, but by the unanimous consent of twelve of his neighbours and equals."[51] Trial by jury, Blackstone argued, must remain "sacred and inviolate."[52]

Colonial Americans were especially sensitive to any potential restrictions on jury trial. In the late 1760s, Parliament had encouraged the king to employ a statute from the reign of Henry VIII that allowed treasons committed outside the realm of England to be tried in England itself. The obvious target was American dissenters, who would then be deprived of their ability to defend themselves before a local jury. The possible use of this statute provoked condemnation throughout the colonies and was regularly denounced as an unconstitutional violation of the right to jury trial.[53] Equally problematic were extensions of the jurisdiction of admiralty courts, which sat without juries, and the restoration of French civil law in the greatly expanded province of Quebec. Although the Quebec Act retained English law for criminal matters, it effectively eliminated jury trial in most civil cases.[54]

The Declaration and Resolves of the First Continental Congress in October 1774 had repeatedly emphasized the importance of juries. The Congress resolved that "the respective colonies are entitled to the common law of England, and more especially to the great and inestimable privilege of being tried by their peers of the vicinage." It denounced various British statutes for "extend[ing] the power of the admiralty courts beyond their ancient limits" and "depriv[ing] the American subject of trial by jury." Another statute was attacked for "depriv[ing] the American subject of a constitutional trial by jury of the vicinage." The Quebec Act was condemned for "abolishing the equitable system of English laws, and erecting a tyranny there."[55] Similarly, the 1775 Declaration of the Causes and Necessity of Taking Up Arms criticized parliamentary statutes for "depriving us of the accustomed and inestimable privilege of trial by jury."[56]

Four of the charges in the Declaration of Independence relate directly or indirectly to jury trial. The most explicit, of course, is the charge condemning the King and Parliament "for depriving us, in many Cases, of the Benefits of Trial by Jury." It's not just the deprivation of jury trial, but the deprivation of the "Benefits of Trial by Jury." That is, not only are the rights of accused persons or civil litigants at stake, but the rights of the community at large to decide criminal and civil disputes. As the democratic branch of the judicial department, juries were a powerful check on judges.[57] Legal historian John Phillip Reid noted that, for eighteenth-century Americans, "trial by jury was an essential element in their definition of restrained government. Juries checked official power by ensuring that government was less arbitrary."[58] Or, as Alexis de Toqueville would later observe, "The jury ... puts the real control of affairs into the hands of the ruled, or some of them, rather than into those of the rulers." "The jury system as understood in America seems to me as direct and extreme a consequence of the dogma of the sovereignty of the people as universal suffrage. They are both equally powerful means of making the majority prevail."[59]

Three other charges address juries implicitly. The Declaration condemns the King and Parliament for "transporting us beyond

Seas to be tried for pretended Offences," a reference to the proposed use of the treason statute of Henry VIII to try Americans in Great Britain. Here, the Declaration was admittedly getting a bit ahead of itself. As Pauline Maier pointed out, "Even the most assiduous efforts have, however, identified no colonists of the revolutionaries' generation who were actually transported 'beyond seas to be tried for pretended offenses.'"[60] But, as one might say, it's the thought that counts, and the underlying problem here was clear: trial in Britain deprived American colonists of the right to a local jury, an affront both to the person accused and to the larger community, which would no longer have a voice in the trial.

The next charge denounces the King and Parliament for "abolishing the free System of English Laws in a neighbouring Province," a reference to the Quebec Act of 1774 and its extension of French civil law into the territory west of the Appalachian Mountains. By abolishing English law, the British government had also abolished jury trials, creating an "arbitrary Government" and a form of "absolute Rule."

Finally, in an earlier charge, the Declaration complains that the British government had protected British troops "by a mock Trial, from Punishment for any Murders which they should commit on the Inhabitants of these States." This is a reference to the Administration of Justice Act of 1774, which allowed British officials who were charged with murder in the colonies to be tried in England. This, of course, eliminated any role for local juries, reducing the trials to a mockery.

All of these charges highlight the absolute centrality of the jury to a well-functioning and properly structured court system. It is not just a nice thing to have, a special privilege for persons accused of crime – it is the essential means by which the community at large participates in the judicial system, lending its voice and approval to every potential deprivation of life, liberty, and property.

~~~

We can now see just how far off so many commenters on the Declaration have been. Harry V. Jaffa, for example, thought that the Declaration conveyed an "openness, or vagueness, concerning the desirable kind of government." The only requirement was that it be "nondespotic."[61] Scott Gerber concluded, "The Declaration of Independence is *neutral* about the form of government the people institute to secure their natural rights. The Declaration recognizes any form as legitimate, provided it secures natural rights and is created by popular consent."[62]

This is simply false. The Declaration offers specific guidance on the form of government. At minimum, an adequate government must include these structural features: (1) a broad commitment to the rule of law and a recognition that no official is above the law; (2) representative legislatures, elected by and responsible to the people, who will have the power of consenting to taxation; (3) a military subordinate to civilian authorities; (4) limitations on an executive's veto power; (5) an executive that is bound to follow the law; (6) executive officials accountable to the people; (7) a judiciary that is independent of the executive; and (8) an inviolable role for juries. This basic outline is fully consistent with the state constitutions that were drafted after 1776 and with the federal constitution of 1787.

All of these structural features help ensure a well-functioning democracy and the people's fundamental right to self-government.[63] A week before he died, Thomas Jefferson emphasized this aspect of the Declaration, writing "may [the Declaration of Independence] be to the world, what I believe it will be ... the Signal of arousing men to burst the chains, under which Monkish ignorance and superstition had persuaded them to bind themselves, and to assume the blessings & security of self-government."[64]

PART IV

Liberty and Equality

To this point, this book has spent very little time addressing what many people would consider the most important words in the Declaration of Independence: "We hold these Truths to be self-evident, that all Men are created equal, that they are endowed by their Creator with certain unalienable Rights, that among these are Life, Liberty, and the Pursuit of Happiness." These words arguably inscribe liberty and equality as the central tenets of the American creed. As President Lincoln would proclaim at Gettysburg, the nation was "conceived in liberty and dedicated to the proposition that all men are created equal."

In 1776, however, it was far from clear that these were the most critical words in the document.[1] The Declaration's primary purpose was not to declare universal truths, but to declare independence and to assert the sovereignty of the United States as a new member of the world community.[2] To do so, it needed to make a clear argument, one in which the charges against the King would play the critical role. The charges had to establish that the King was a tyrant and that the Americans were justified in overthrowing his rule. Accordingly, British critics devoted most of their attention to refuting the charges, and very little to countering the more general statements in the second paragraph.

Over time, the charges against the King have faded into obscurity, and hardly anyone could credibly claim that their modern recitation gets the patriotic juices flowing. By contrast, the statement about self-evident truths carries the imprimatur of timeless wisdom and is, by far, the most remembered, cherished, and debated portion of the Declaration. As historian David Armitage put it, "When peace had been restored with Britain, and the precise incidents that lay behind the grievances had been forgotten, all of substance that remained to be revered was the second paragraph."[3]

Unfortunately, the second paragraph, despite its solemnity and beauty, is abstract and easily subject to wildly differing interpretations, a malleability that has been there since the very beginning. It is quite likely that many of the Declaration's drafters did not consider its language to be inconsistent with race-based slavery, although many other readers in the 1770s concluded that it was. If even people in the late eighteenth century disagreed about the paragraph's meaning, it is hardly surprising that later generations have as well, appealing to the document for a whole range of propositions, from women's equality and civil rights to opposition to minimum wage laws and opposition to abortion. Politicians and courts of all ideological persuasions convinced themselves that the Declaration of Independence's commitment to liberty and equality directly supported their preferred policy positions. The document has become in effect a national Rorschach test – one sees in the Declaration what one is already primed to see.

Such a wide variety of views suggests that courts should approach this language with caution. A Rorschach test is not a good template for government. Unlike the charges against the King, which provide more definite guidance, courts invoking the liberty and equality language of the Declaration are likely to do so in an opportunistic fashion, to support propositions to which they are already committed for other reasons. When courts rely on the Declaration's language about liberty and equality, they should do so carefully and with full awareness of these provisions' highly checkered history in American jurisprudence.

9   DEBATING AMERICAN SCRIPTURE

Our nation's greatest political leaders have frequently turned to the Declaration (or, to be more precise, the Declaration's second paragraph) as a source of inspiration. Abraham Lincoln was perhaps the most notable and consistent enthusiast, treating the Declaration of Independence as his political bible. In a February 1861 speech at Independence Hall, Lincoln stated, "I have never had a feeling politically that did not spring from the sentiments embodied in the Declaration of Independence."[1] Eighty years later, President Franklin Roosevelt asserted that "it is altogether fitting that we should rededicate ourselves to defend and perpetuate those inalienable rights which found true expression in the immortal Declaration. Those words never had a deeper or more solemn meaning for America than they have in this hour of anxiety and peril."[2] And in his 1963 "I Have a Dream" speech, Martin Luther King, Jr., referred to the "magnificent words of the Constitution and the Declaration of Independence" and called on America to "live out the true meaning of its creed: We hold these truths to be self-evident, that all men are created equal."

King's use of the term "creed" suggests that the Declaration had obtained an almost mythical, quasi-religious status. Historian Pauline Maier would later coin the term "American Scripture" to describe the Declaration's place in American civic life. The cultural centrality of the Declaration, of course, is undeniable. Even more than the Constitution, it is the primary text of the American political experience, rivalled perhaps only by the Gettysburg Address, which is itself a celebration and extension of the Declaration. But if the Declaration is a form of scripture, it is nonetheless subject to the same fierce disagreements that plague all canonical texts. Abraham Lincoln was acutely aware of this problem, noting in his Second Inaugural Address that the Union and the Confederacy "read the same Bible and pray to the same God and each invokes His aid against the other."

When Lincoln, Roosevelt, and King were invoking the Declaration of Independence to support their political agendas, so were their political adversaries. The Southern secessionists liberally quoted from the Declaration's second paragraph, claiming a right to self-determination rooted in the consent of the governed.[3] Alf Landon, Roosevelt's 1936 Republican opponent, criticized the New Deal extensively in his convention acceptance speech, arguing for a return to "the basic principles upon which our Nation is founded ... 'the life, liberty and pursuit of happiness' of the great Declaration."[4] And the ultra-right-wing John Birch Society, which opposed the *Brown* decision and the civil rights movement, proudly states that it "endorses the timeless principles of the Declaration of Independence which proclaimed that our personal rights come from God, not from government."[5]

These disagreements are not minor quibbles – secession, the New Deal, and civil rights are among the most fundamental issues of American society and government, yet all sides of these debates have invoked the Declaration of Independence for rhetorical support. It is easy to suppose that one side must be right, that there was one clear understanding of the Declaration in 1776, and that with a little more historical digging we can figure it all out. But disputes over the Declaration's second paragraph have been with us from the very beginning. In 1776, people were already arguing about the relationship between the Declaration of Independence and American slavery. The text, if not yet canonical, was clearly disputed.

Similar debates have persisted long after slavery's demise, not just in the political realm, but in court, where judges have been no more successful than politicians in finding consensus on the document's meaning. Endless disagreements have highlighted how little interpreters have in common, other than a belief that their understanding of the Declaration must be the correct one.

SLAVERY

The central paradox of American history is that the seemingly universal language of liberty and equality in the Declaration of Independence was authored by men who enslaved their fellow human beings.[6] Thomas Jefferson, of course, is the most notable, owning hundreds of enslaved persons and fathering a number of children with his deceased wife's enslaved teenage half-sister Sally Hemings.[7] But Jefferson was far from the only one. Although the exact figures are contested, it appears that a majority of the signers of the Declaration of Independence owned slaves at some point in their lives.[8] Richard Henry Lee, author of the congressional resolution for independence, may have been one of the most obtuse; according to one account, he enlisted his slaves to partic- ipate in a 1765 protest denouncing the Stamp Act as a form of slavery (curiously, Lee had applied to be a Stamp Act agent himself).[9] Signer Benjamin Rush of Pennsylvania had published an antislavery tract in 1773, arguing that one "must look upon all Mankind as equal," but his outspokenness on the issue was far from typical.[10]

One way to resolve the paradox is to claim that the Declaration, properly understood, doesn't condemn race-based slavery at all. The most well-known exponent of this idea was Chief Justice Roger Taney. In the infamous 1857 *Dred Scott* case Taney concluded that Black Americans – unlike all other people on earth – were not, and never could be, citizens of the United States and that Congress had no power to ban slavery in the territories. But Taney also admired the Declaration of Independence – four years later he would admon- ish the Lincoln Administration over its suspension of habeas corpus, claiming the "constitution of the United States is founded upon the principles of government set forth and maintained in the Declaration of Independence," one of which was civilian control of the military.[11]

Taney thus needed to jump through considerable hoops to explain how his opinion in *Dred Scott* was consistent with the Declaration. He noted the apparent tension with the document's statements about liberty and equality, observing that those provisions "would seem to embrace the whole human family, and if they were used in a similar instrument at this day would be so understood." But, he concluded, "it is too clear for dispute, that the enslaved African race were not intended to be included, and formed no part of the people who framed and adopted this declaration; for if the language, as understood in that day, would embrace them, the conduct of the distinguished men who framed the Declaration of Independence would have been utterly and flagrantly inconsistent with the principles they asserted; and instead of the sympathy of mankind, to which they so confidently appealed, they would have deserved and received universal rebuke and reprobation."[12]

But Taney could not conceive of his beloved framers as hypocrites, since they "were great men – high in literary acquirements – high in their sense of honor, and incapable of asserting principles inconsistent with those on which they were acting." Therefore, the only possible interpretation of their language was that "it would not in any part of the civilized world be supposed to embrace the negro race, which, by common consent, had been excluded from civilized Governments and the family of nations, and doomed to slavery."[13]

Although Taney's opinion in *Dred Scott* is generally regarded as the single worst opinion in the history of the United States Supreme Court, his argument merits consideration. Indeed, some modern critical race scholars have suggested that Taney's candid acknowledgment of white supremacy, though deplorable, was nonetheless an accurate assessment of how American law actually functioned at the time.[14] The simple fact is that numerous slaveholders willingly signed the Declaration of Independence without any sense that they had committed themselves to an antislavery manifesto. The Declaration also denounces the continent's Native peoples as "merciless Indian Savages, whose known Rule of Warfare, is an undistinguished Destruction, of all Ages, Sexes and Conditions," which is not exactly a ringing endorsement of racial egalitarianism. Historian Robert Parkinson has argued that the leaders of the Revolution deliberately stoked fears of slave rebellions and attacks by Native peoples to stir enthusiasm for the war.[15] Moreover, with the notable exception of James Wilson, it appears that none of the most prominent political figures of the Founding era subsequently quoted or relied on the Declaration's claim that all men are created equal.[16]

Significantly, Jefferson's original draft of the Declaration contained language unequivocally condemning slavery – language that the Continental Congress removed. The draft stated, "He has waged cruel War against human Nature itself, violating its most sacred Rights of Life and Liberty in the Persons of a distant People who never offended him, captivating and carrying them into Slavery in another Hemisphere, or to incur miserable Death, in their Transportation thither." It denounced the King for vetoing "every legislative Attempt to prohibit or to restrain an execrable Commerce, determined to keep open a Market where Men should be bought and sold." Finally, it complained that the King was now inciting the enslaved population to rebellion, "thus paying off, former Crimes committed against the Liberties of one People, with Crimes which he urges them to commit against the Lives of another."[17] It was vivid, direct, brimming with moral outrage, and far too much for his fellow delegates to stomach; they reduced it to the bland claim that the King had "incited domestic Insurrections amongst us." Jefferson blamed the excision of the language "reprobating the enslaving of the inhabitants of Africa" on delegates from South Carolina and Georgia, although he noted "our Northern brethren" were also "a little tender" on that subject, for although they "have very few slaves among themselves yet they had been pretty considerable carriers of them to others."[18] But Congress was probably wise to delete these passages; for all their moral clarity, blaming the King for slavery regimes that the American colonists had supported and profited from for generations would only add credence to the charge of hypocrisy.[19] The deliberate exclusion of the only explicitly antislavery language in the draft document, however, supports the view that the drafters were not intentionally writing an antislavery manifesto.

Several modern scholars have agreed with Taney's ultimate conclusion. Fred Kaplan argues that "Jefferson and his colleagues did not mean that 'all men are created equal' in the modern sense." Rather, he meant that "all white Englishmen and Europeans were born with the right to life, liberty, and the pursuit of happiness."[20] John Phillip Reid suggested that the "equality boast in the Declaration of Independence ... meant not that individuals were equal, but that the American people were entitled to an equality of rights with the British."[21] Two others conclude, "Our best guess is that the clause simply asserts the proposition that all peoples who identify themselves as one – that is, those who identify themselves as a society, nation, or state for action in history – are equal to others who have likewise identified themselves."[22]

Law professor Kermit Roosevelt III has recently offered the most extended defense of this position. Roosevelt argues that modern American ideals of equality are more appropriately traced to the Reconstruction Amendments than to the Founders. As he sees it, we consistently misread the Declaration's equality language by viewing it through the prism of later events. It had nothing to do with the equality of individuals within a society; it merely rejected the divine right of kings. No one was born entitled to rule others.[23] Moreover, in Roosevelt's view, the Declaration does not condemn slavery even implicitly; the Declaration speaks only of equality within a hypothetical state of nature. Once a political community is formed, the members are free to treat outsiders, which by definition includes enslaved persons, as badly as they want.[24]

Roosevelt makes a powerful argument for why the Declaration of Independence doesn't mean what it literally seems to mean. There was no contradiction between slavery and "equality," because the signers of the document were not endorsing anything like "equality" in a modern sense. Under this view, the drafters weren't hypocrites at all; the problem is with modern readers, who fail to understand the Declaration's use of "equality" in its original eighteenth-century context.

Although this argument has considerable force, I am ultimately unpersuaded. The simple historical reality is that numerous other Americans (and Britons) immediately saw the tension between the lofty language of the Declaration of Independence and the reality of race-based slavery. It's not a matter of applying twenty-first or even nineteenth-century morality – people living at the time identified the same contradiction in pretty much the same way that we do.[25]

In Britain, no one expressed this sentiment more pithily than Samuel Johnson, who, in his 1775 response to the Declaration and Resolves of the First Continental Congress, asked, "how is it that we hear the loudest yelps for liberty among the drivers of negroes?"[26] Critics of the Declaration of Independence were quick to sound the same theme. Thomas Hutchinson's attack on the Declaration, published in London in 1776, acidly remarked that he wished "to ask the Delegates of Maryland, Virginia, and the Carolinas, how their Constituents justify the depriving more than an hundred thousand Africans of their rights to liberty, and *the pursuit of happiness.*"[27] John Lind's response, subsidized and widely distributed by the British ministry, was even more pointed. He noted that the Declaration's charge that the King had "incited domestic Insurrections amongst us" was a reference to Lord Dunmore's proclamation of freedom to enslaved persons who reached the British lines. Lind argued,

> Is it for *them* to say, that it is tyranny to bid a slave to be free? to bid him to take courage, to rise and assist in reducing his tyrants to a due obedience to *law*? to hold out as a motive to him, that the load that crushed his limbs should be lightened; that the whip which harrowed upon his back shall be broken, that he shall be raised to the rank of freeman and a citizen? It is their boast that they have taken up arms in support of these their own *self-evident truths* – "that all men are *equal*" – "that all men are endowed with *unalienable* rights of life, *liberty*, and the *pursuit of happiness.*" Is it for *them* to complain *of the offer of freedom* held out to these wretched beings? of the offer of reinstating them in that *equality*, which, in this very paper, is declared to be the *gift of God to all*; in those *unalienable rights*, with which, in this very paper, God is declared to have *endowed* mankind?[28]

In 1776, Hutchinson and Lind were making precisely the argument that Taney would later deem historically unthinkable, pointing out the obvious discrepancy between the lofty language of the Declaration of Independence and the reality of American slavery.

Perceptive Americans understood this point as well. In October 1776, William Gordon published a lengthy letter in Boston's *Independent Chronicle*, quoting the Declaration's second paragraph and arguing, "If these, Gentlemen, are our genuine sentiments, and we are not provoking the Deity by acting hypocritically to serve a turn, let us apply earnestly and heartily to the extirpation of slavery from among ourselves." The alternative, Gordon warned, was to "contradict our own professions and act incongruously."[29] Similarly, Lemuel Haynes, a Black New Englander, prepared an antislavery manuscript in 1776. At the head of the manuscript, Haynes placed the opening of the Declaration of Independence's second paragraph.[30]

In 1778, the New Jersey legislature objected to a provision in the draft Articles of Confederation that sought to apportion requisitions for land forces based on the number of white inhabitants in each state. The legislature archly noted, "In the Act of Independence we find the following Declaration: 'We hold these Truths to be self-evident, that all Men are created equal; that they are endowed by their Creator with certain unalienable Rights, among which are Life, Liberty, and the Pursuit of Happiness;' of this Doctrine it is not a very remote Consequence that all the Inhabitants of every Society, be the Colour of their Complexion what it may, are bound to promote the Interest thereof, according to their respective Abilities: They ought therefore to be brought into the Account on this Occasion."[31] The implication was clear: treating members of society differently on the basis of race was inconsistent with the broad premises of the Declaration of Independence. And this was hardly a fringe or marginal voice – it was the New Jersey legislature addressing the Continental Congress.

Antislavery advocates quickly seized on the liberating potential of the Declaration of Independence. In 1778, Philadelphia abolitionist Anthony Benezet published a pamphlet arguing that slavery contradicted the second paragraph of the Declaration of Independence. "Nothing," he argued, could "more clearly and positively militate against the slavery of the Negroes."[32] A few years later David Cooper noted that it was "time to demonstrate ... that America was in earnest ... [when she] ... insisted, that *all mankind* came from the hand of their Creator *equally free*." Citing the second paragraph of the Declaration of Independence, Cooper observed, "If these solemn *truths* uttered at such an awful crisis, are *self-evident*: unless we can show that the African race not *men*, words can hardly express the amazement which naturally arises on reflecting, that the very people who make these pompous declarations are slave-holders, and, by their legislative conduct, tell us, that these blessings were only meant to be the *rights* of *whitemen* not of *all men*." "We need not turn over the libraries of Europe," he continued, "for authorities to prove that blacks are born equally free with whites; it is declared and recorded as the sense of America" in the Declaration of Independence.[33] In congressional debates in 1789, Representative Josiah Parker of Virginia argued for eliminating slavery, noting, "The inconsistency in our principles, with which we are justly charged, should be done away, that we may show, by our actions, the pure beneficence of the doctrine we hold out to the world in our Declaration of Independence."[34] In 1790, Representative Elias Boudinot, who had previously served as the president of the Continental Congress, argued that slavery and slave trafficking were "contrary to the genius of our Government, and the principles of the Revolution. ... [B]y the Declaration of Independence, in 1776, Congress declare: 'We hold these truths to be self-evident: that all men are created equal; that they are endowed by their Creator with certain unalienable rights; that among these are life, liberty, and the pursuit of happiness.' This, then, is the language of America in the day of distress."[35]

These arguments reached a receptive audience in court. In the early 1780s, Massachusetts courts considered the issue of slavery under the state constitution. An opinion by Chief Justice William Cushing concluded that slavery was inconsistent with the state constitution's proclamation that "all men are born free and equal" and that "every subject is entitled to liberty." Although the language was not identical to that in the Declaration of Independence, it was very close. Cushing found that slavery was "effectively abolished as it can be by the granting of rights and privileges wholly incompatible and repugnant to its existence."[36]

In 1791, the African-American astronomer and mathematician Benjamin Banneker wrote to Thomas Jefferson, the sitting United States Secretary of State. Banneker pointedly noted the inconsistency between the Declaration and slavery:

> This Sir, was a time in which you clearly saw into the injustice of a State of Slavery, and in which you had just apprehensions of the horrors of its condition, it was not Sir, that your abhorrence thereof was so excited, that you publickly held forth this true and invaluable doctrine, which is worthy to be recorded and remember'd in all Succeeding ages. "We hold these truths to be Self evident, that all men are created equal, and that they are endowed by their creator with certain unalienable rights, that among these are life, liberty, and the pursuit of happyness."

Banneker asked Jefferson how he could be "guilty of that most criminal act, which you professedly detested in others, with respect to yourselves."[37]

By the 1790s, invocations of the Declaration of Independence had become commonplace in antislavery propaganda, and these invocations would increase in intensity during the first half of the nineteenth century.[38] In an 1819 speech, Justice Joseph Story, for example, argued that slavery was inconsistent with the "tenor of the Declaration of Independence."[39] Denmark Vesey, who allegedly plotted a slave rebellion, regularly quoted the Declaration in support of freedom.[40] In the famous *Amistad* case, John Quincy Adams repeatedly gestured to the copy of the Declaration of Independence hanging in the courtroom, and argued, "The moment you come, to the Declaration of Independence, that every man has a right to life and liberty, an inalienable right, this case is decided."[41] When an African-American newspaper in Ohio launched in 1843, it introduced itself with significant quotes from the Declaration.[42]

One of the more noteworthy invocations of the Declaration to oppose slavery came in the 1819 trial of the Maryland abolitionist preacher Jacob Gruber on a charge of inciting a slave rebellion. Gruber's attorney argued, "A hard necessity, indeed, compels us to endure the evil of slavery for a time.... Yet while it continues, it is a blot on our national character.... [U]ntil the time shall come when we can point without a blush, to the language held in the declaration of independence, every friend of humanity will seek to lighten the galling chain of slavery, and better, to the utmost of his power, the wretched condition of the slave."[43] The argument itself is less striking than the identity of the attorney who delivered it – the future Chief Justice of the United States, Roger B. Taney.[44]

By the mid-nineteenth century, southern apologists for slavery came to dismiss the Declaration's equality language as an obvious falsehood, as it was so clearly inconsistent with the practice of slavery.[45] In 1826, the fiftieth anniversary of the Declaration, Senator John Randolph of Virginia declared in a congressional debate that he could not agree to the proposition that all men are born free and equal "for the best of all reasons, because it is not true." The notion, he said was a "falsehood, and a most pernicious falsehood, even though I find it in the Declaration of Independence."[46] Senator John Calhoun of South Carolina argued in 1848 that "there is not a word of truth in the whole proposition, as expressed and generally understood." The phrase, he concluded, had been "inserted into our Declaration of Independence without any necessity."[47] We are now learning, he warned, of "the danger of admitting so great an error to have a place in our declaration of independence."[48]

Other politicians, seeking a more moderate path, did not condemn the Declaration as false, but sought to read it narrowly, in the manner of Chief Justice Taney. Stephen Douglas, for example, argued, "No man can vindicate the character, motives, and conduct of the signers of the Declaration of Independence, except upon the hypothesis that they referred to the white race alone, and not to the African, when they declared all men to have been created equal – that they were speaking of British subjects on this continent being equal to British subjects born and residing in Great Britain."[49] (Abraham Lincoln felt that Douglas's view reduced the Declaration to "mere rubbish – old wadding left to rot on the battle-field after victory is won," a document "shorn of its vitality, and practical value; and left without the *germ* or even the *suggestion* of the individual rights of man in it.")[50]

As these accounts demonstrate, the relationship between the Declaration of Independence and American slavery has always been bitterly contested.[51] Under very narrow readings, the document doesn't speak to race-based slavery at all. But under broader readings, the Declaration states ideals that were clearly inconsistent with slavery. There is probably no definitive answer to this controversy, but at least this much is clear: the drafters created and signed a document that was fully capable of being read in an antislavery manner. They debated nearly every word of the document, and they could have easily written something more specific, something less capable of being invoked by opponents of slavery. But they did not. They chose to employ idealistic, universal language, and, in some ways, they have to own it. They knowingly risked the possibility that the language would be understood, as it almost immediately was, as inconsistent with race-based slavery. Noting the incongruity between their professed principles and their actual behavior is hardly anachronistic. Thomas Hutchinson, John Lind, William Gordon, and Lemuel Haynes all made that point in 1776 – they all understand the Declaration as expressing a broader commitment to human liberty and equality.

THE CHECKERED HISTORY OF LIBERTY
AND EQUALITY IN COURT

The debates over slavery suggested the Declaration of Independence was a powerful rhetorical weapon in political argument. Everyone wanted the Declaration on "their side" of deeply contested issues. Not surprisingly, the Declaration's references to liberty and equality would come to be invoked in court, in bitter disputes over constitutional meaning. Here, too, advocates of every conceivable position have cited the Declaration to support their causes. Like the Bible, it can be read in multiple ways, or as Antonio memorably put it in *The Merchant of Venice*, "The devil can cite Scripture for his purpose." The language of liberty and equality has become a national Rorschach test; one sees in that language what one is already inclined to see. When both sides of a dispute are citing the Declaration, no one's mind is likely to be changed. Indeed, it is hard to identify a case where the Declaration's invocation of liberty and equality made a determinative difference in the outcome; more typically, those phrases serve as rhetorical decoration for positions reached on other grounds.

Prior to the Civil War, the most extensive consideration of the Declaration of Independence in a Supreme Court opinion was Chief Justice Taney's analysis of the equality provision in the *Dred Scott* case. Curiously, the dissenting justices did not counter with strong antislavery readings of the Declaration. Justice Benjamin Curtis observed "it would not be just to them, nor true in itself, to allege that they intended to say that the Creator of all men had endowed the white race, exclusively, with the great natural rights which the Declaration of Independence asserts," but concluded that the Declaration was not directly relevant, since the real issue was legal status of free Blacks under state law at the time of the adoption of the Constitution.[52] Justice John McLean's dissent ignored the Declaration entirely.[53] It was left to Abraham Lincoln to offer the most forceful condemnation of Taney's view of the Declaration. Lincoln argued that Taney did "obvious violence to the plain unmistakable meaning of the Declaration," such that if the Declaration's framers were to "rise from their graves, they could not at all recognize it."[54]

The Declaration did not fare much better in court in the years following the Civil War. Consider the fate of the Fourteenth Amendment, added to the Constitution in 1868, and designed to ensure equality for Black Americans by requiring states to respect the "privileges and immunities of citizens of the United States," to follow "due process of law," and to guarantee the "equal protection of the laws." During the so-called *Lochner* era (roughly the late-nineteenth century to 1937), courts turned a blind eye to Jim Crow segregation, but were receptive to challenges by business interests hostile to governmental regulation. The era was named for *Lochner v. New York*, a 1905 decision of the United States Supreme Court invalidating a maximum-hours law for bakers.[55]

Lochner-era judges who detested governmental regulation loved to quote the liberty and equality language of the Declaration. In 1873, the Supreme Court decided its first case under the Fourteenth Amendment. As a public health measure, the state of Louisiana had restricted butchering in the New Orleans area to a racially integrated slaughterhouse. Although the Court upheld the law on a 5–4 vote, Justice Stephen Field, writing for the four dissenters, claimed that the Fourteenth Amendment "was intended to give practical effect to the declaration of 1776 of inalienable rights, rights which are the gift of the Creator, which the law does not confer, but only recognizes."[56] In an 1884 case involving the same Louisiana law, Justice Joseph Bradley argued in a concurring opinion that Louisiana had no right to establish a monopoly in the butchering profession, claiming, "The right to follow any of the common occupations of life is an inalienable right, it was formulated as such under the phrase 'pursuit of happiness' in the declaration of independence...."[57] Justice Field reiterated his earlier opinion, noting, "These inherent rights have never been more happily expressed than in the declaration of independence, that new evangel of liberty to the people."[58] The Declaration's guarantee of "pursuit of happiness" included the "right to pursue any lawful business or vocation, in any manner not inconsistent with the equal rights of others, which may increase their prosperity or develop their faculties, so as to give to them their highest enjoyment."[59]

Justice David Brewer (Justice Field's nephew) expanded upon these views in an 1891 address at Yale Law School. Brewer argued that the "cornerstone of the foundation upon which the constitution was built, and upon which it rests today, was and is the Declaration of

Independence."[60] Under the Declaration, the "acquisition, possession, and enjoyment of property are matters which human government cannot forbid."[61] He went on to criticize excessive taxation and the use of eminent domain and the police powers.[62] Brewer's hostility to governmental power was unrelenting. In an 1898 opinion, for example, he argued that New York's inheritance tax was unconstitutional, claiming, "Equality in right, in protection, and in burden is the thought which has run through the life of this nation, and its constitutional enactments, from the Declaration of Independence to the present hour."[63]

Field's and Brewer's individual (and highly individualistic) views on the Declaration soon commanded a majority of the Supreme Court. In 1897, the Supreme Court struck down a Texas law that allowed for the recovery of attorneys' fees in certain suits against railway companies, observing that the Declaration is the "thought and spirit" of the Constitution and that it is "always safe to read the constitution in the spirit of the Declaration of Independence."[64] A few years later, the Court quoted this observation about the Declaration when striking down a Kansas statute regulating large stockyards.[65] In another 1897 case, the Supreme Court explicitly adopted Justice Bradley's 1884 position that the Declaration protected the right to follow any of the common occupations of life.[66]

Lower courts followed the Supreme Court in relying on the Declaration to invalidate various business regulations. The Supreme Court of Illinois cited the Declaration to strike down regulations of the horseshoeing profession, and the Supreme Court of North Dakota cited it to strike down a licensing requirement for professional photographers.[67] In 1937, the United States Court of Appeals for the Ninth Circuit held that the National Labor Relations Board could not use its powers to protect unionized employees, because "the word 'liberty' as used in the Fifth Amendment to the Constitution and in the Declaration of Independence included the right to freely contract."[68]

Judges during the *Lochner* era showed little hesitation in striking down minimum-wage laws, maximum-hours laws, and various other labor protections on the ground that such laws interfered with a "liberty of contract" that was grounded in part on the Declaration of Independence. Beginning in 1937, the Supreme Court began to decisively reject these arguments, and the *Lochner*-era decisions are now reviled across partisan lines.[69] Traditional conservatives view them as improper judicial interference with the decisions of the elected branches of government, and liberals view them as favoring corporate and business interests over the rights of workers. And the fact that the Declaration of Independence played such a large role in those decisions has led many to be skeptical of invoking the Declaration in court.[70]

Following the *Lochner* era, the Declaration continued to be invoked on all sides of the political spectrum. On the liberal side, for example, in 1963 the US Supreme Court invalidated a Georgia voting system that overweighted rural residents. The Court noted, "The conception of political equality from the Declaration of Independence, to Lincoln's Gettysburg Address, to the Fifteenth, Seventeenth, and Nineteenth Amendments can mean only one thing – one person, one vote."[71] On the conservative side, New York's highest court upheld a state-written prayer in public schools in 1961, noting that the prayer "includes an acknowledgment of the existence of a Supreme Being just as does the Declaration of Independence."[72] In 1969, a Michigan appellate court invoked the Declaration to uphold bans on obscenity, concluding, "[O]ur federal Constitution ... was built upon the morals of the Declaration of Independence. Our founding fathers accepted a moral code that recognized the harm that is brought about in the minds and hearts of men by being exposed to obscene publications."[73] And on the far political fringes, the 1970s and 1980s saw a number of tax protestors unsuccessfully argue in court that the federal income tax laws violated the Declaration of Independence.[74]

More recently, the Declaration appeared on both sides of the same-sex marriage debate. A federal court in Virginia, for example, found that prohibitions on same-sex marriage were inconsistent with the Declaration's guarantee of equality.[75] But when the US Supreme Court recognized a constitutional right to same-sex marriage in the *Obergefell* decision in 2015, Justices Antonin Scalia and Clarence Thomas dissented, citing the Declaration of Independence. Justice Scalia complained, "This practice of constitutional revision by an unelected committee of nine, always accompanied (as it is today) by extravagant praise of liberty, robs the People of the most important liberty they asserted in the Declaration of Independence and won in the Revolution of 1776: the freedom to govern themselves."[76] Justice Thomas felt that the majority had rejected "the idea – captured in our Declaration of Independence – that human dignity is innate and suggests instead that it comes from government."[77] The infamous Roy Moore of Alabama later authored an opinion claiming, "as the Declaration of Independence states, a human being is bound to recognize that the rights to life, liberty, and the pursuit of happiness are endowed by God. Those rights are not subject to a redefinition that rejects the natural order God has created."[78] *Obergefell*, Moore argued, contradicted the laws of nature invoked in the Declaration of Independence.[79] One of the Declaration's most fervent academic proponents, Harry V. Jaffa, had taken a similar view, concluding that the Declaration does not protect "sodomy and lesbianism," because these "are unnatural acts and, being unnatural, the very negation of anything that could be called a right according to nature."[80] (He also rejected the view that the Declaration's equality language required a one-person/one-vote rule for legislative districts, a view he described as "absolutely incoherent.")[81]

Some of the more recent judicial invocations of the Declaration of Independence border on the bizarre. Wisconsin Supreme Court Justice Rebecca Grassl Bradley, for example, quoted a large portion of the Declaration's second paragraph (in a section entitled "First Principles") in a dispute about whether Wisconsin statutory law prohibited charging patients for copies of electronic health records.[82] A West Virginia Supreme Court justice concluded that the state had no power to regulate drunken use of an all-terrain vehicle on private land, and argued that, under the Declaration of Independence, "the legitimate end of government is to protect the private realm where citizens may freely embrace their natural rights."[83] A Texas Supreme Court justice, in a case about restrictions on eyebrow-threading businesses, claimed, "The might of the majority, whatever the vote count, cannot trample individuals' rights recognized in both our federal and state Constitutions, not to mention in our nation's first law, the Declaration."[84] A January 6 defendant even claimed that occupying the Capitol was exercising a right given "in the 2nd paragraph of the Declaration of Independence."[85]

The fundamental problem is that for many of our country's most difficult and divisive issues, the Declaration of Independence can be plausibly cited by both sides. Justice Clarence Thomas, for example, invokes the Declaration of Independence more than any other modern justice, most notably to criticize affirmative action programs. In his view affirmative action "can only weaken the principle of equality embodied in the Declaration of Independence."[86] Paternalism in affirmative action programs, he has argued, "is at war with the principle of inherent equality" in the Declaration of Independence "that underlies and infuses our Constitution."[37] Similarly, concurring in the Court's 2023 decision striking down college affirmative action programs, he proclaimed, "We must adhere to the promise of equality under the law declared by the Declaration of Independence and codified by the Fourteenth Amendment."[88] For Thomas, the Declaration's commitment to equality means that the law must be color-blind. By contrast, Justice Ketanji Brown Jackson has noted the significant racial disparities "with respect to the health, wealth, and well-being of American citizens." "Every moment these gaps persist," she argued, "is a moment in which this great country falls short of actualizing one of its foundational principles – the 'self-evident' truth that all of us are created equal."[89] In her view, race-based affirmative action furthers the Declaration's commitment to equality. It is safe to say that both Justices Thomas and Jackson genuinely believe that the Declaration is on their side, and that neither will ever be persuaded by the other.[90]

Debate over abortion rights similarly finds proponents and opponents talking past each other. For many Americans, the Declaration's guarantee of liberty means the right to make basic decisions about one's own body and its recognition of equality means that women should not be forced to endure reproductive consequences that men do not.[91] For opponents of abortion, fetuses have a right to life guaranteed by the Declaration of Independence and equality means that fetuses should have the same rights as all other persons.[92] As with affirmative action, both sides will fervently cite the Declaration, fully confident that the document is on their side.

~~~

Although one scholar has argued that "the Declaration of Independence charges an independent judiciary to protect the innate rights of life, liberty, and the pursuit of happiness against tyrannical majorities," the history recounted above should lend a note of caution.[93] It is one thing to endorse the ideals of the Declaration of Independence; it is an entirely different matter to flesh out precisely how those ideals should apply to modern controversies. These ideals were contested even in 1776, and they have continued to be contested ever since. They are in effect a national Rorschach test, revealing ourselves both at our best and at our worst. And it doesn't seem particularly appealing to be governed by a Rorschach test.

To be clear, I am not arguing that courts should decline to enforce norms of liberty and equality. These norms are explicitly rooted in the Bill of Rights and the Fourteenth Amendment, among other provisions, where they have generated a significant body of decided cases.[94] But constitutional decisions about liberty and equality should be rooted in those provisions, not in a free-floating invocation of the Declaration of Independence. The Declaration has historically been enlisted to serve the shabbiest of causes, as well as the most noble, and there is little reason to think that modern judges will perform much more impressively than their predecessors.

CONCLUSION

Early in his second term, President Donald Trump unveiled a copy of the Declaration of Independence, which he had placed behind protective curtains in the Oval Office.[1] Like Trump's other alterations to the office, this addition seems to be largely driven by appearances. For him, the document is primarily an interesting physical artifact; its substantive content does not appear to have penetrated his consciousness. When asked about it in a May 2025 interview, Trump seemed to confuse the Declaration with an anniversary card, stating that it was "a declaration of unity and love and respect and it means a lot and it's something very special to our country."[2] A few months later, in a rambling claim that President Obama should be prosecuted for treason, Trump digressed to discuss the Oval Office décor: "We have the Declaration of Independence now, in the room, which wasn't here. I guess people didn't feel too good about putting it here, but I do."[3]

Outside the Oval Office, controversy was swirling over many of Trump's actions, including the erroneous removal of a man to an El Salvadoran prison; DOGE units rampaging through the federal government, cancelling contracts and firing federal workers seemingly at random; the abrupt unilateral imposition of tariffs; the use of the military for domestic law enforcement; and the seeming disregard for long-established legal practices and norms.

Perceptive observers soon noted that many of Trump's actions are reminiscent of those for which George III was criticized in the Declaration of Independence.[4] Consider, for example, these passages, in light of Trump's behavior:

He has [utterly neglected to attend to] ... Laws of immediate and
pressing Importance....

He has endeavoured to prevent the Population of these States;
for that Purpose obstructing the Laws for the Naturalization of
Foreigners; refusing to pass others to encourage their Migrations
hither....

He has affected to render the Military independent of and superior
to the Civil Power....

For cutting off our Trade with all Parts of the World:

For imposing Taxes on us without our Consent....

For transporting us beyond Seas to be tried for pretended Offences

The similarity is uncanny.

Trump's violations of the norms of the Declaration of Independence
are perhaps the most egregious in recent memory, but inconsistency
with the document's ideals is regrettably not unique to President
Trump. The simple reality is that for years, courts and American
political culture have failed, in many respects, to live up to the values
articulated in the Declaration of Independence. And those failures are
rooted in persistent but erroneous myths about what the Declaration
actually means. Just as any building depends on a properly constructed
foundation, any understanding of our national life requires an accurate
assessment of our founding. A poorly built foundation can give us no
faith in the integrity of whatever is constructed above.

The most pernicious myth – and the most harmful to our national
identity – is the myth that the Declaration created thirteen entirely independent nations. Consider, for example, the statement, "After independence, the States considered themselves fully sovereign nations."[5]
As this book has shown, there is little historical support for the notion
that the states ever individually exercised all the powers of sovereignty,
and it was decisively rejected by justices of the Supreme Court in the
1790s (who presumably knew something about the Revolution that
they had just gone through). But that statement was confidently uttered
by Justice Clarence Thomas, writing for a majority of the Supreme
Court in the 2019 *Hyatt* decision, which held that states have immunity from civil suits brought in the courts of other states. The majority
may have reached the correct result in *Hyatt*, but one can have little

confidence in its reasoning, because it starts out from such a deeply flawed historical premise. So too with a host of other recent federalism decisions that have assumed the centrality of states in our constitutional order, including decisions holding states immune from suits for money damages for violations of federal law.[6] They may be justifiable on other grounds, but they cannot be supported as logical deductions from an initial premise of complete state sovereignty. Only when we understand that the states have never existed outside of union with the other states can we begin to properly assess the respective roles of the nation and the states in our constitutional structure.

The perniciousness of the thirteen-independent nation view extends beyond court decisions that present a distorted view of the Founding – it goes to the heart of our national identity. If the United States did not become a nation on July 4, 1776, when did it? The thirteen-nation theorists have never offered a compelling answer to this question. And for good reason – no other date is as remotely plausible, or at all consistent with the historical tradition of celebrating the Fourth of July as the national birthday, a tradition that dates back to the late eighteenth century itself. The United States, as a nation, came into being simultaneously with the British colonies becoming states. We don't remember the term "United Colonies" as much as we should, but for Americans in 1776, it was very clear what had happened – the United Colonies had become the United States. And with the Declaration of Independence, the United States announced itself as *One Nation*.

Our culture has similarly distorted the Declaration by treating it as largely an airy statement about individual rights, devoid of any meaningful insight into the conduct or structure of government. Yet, when the Declaration is read in its entirety, when we attend carefully to *why* the Americans were declaring independence, we can see that the Declaration's deepest commitment is to constitutional government and the rule of law, and to the fundamental principle that no one, not even a king, is above the law. Charge after charge insists that the King not only showed horrific judgment, but that he acted *unlawfully*. The Americans declared independence because, from their perspective, the British had repeatedly failed to follow the law.

This point is often lost in depictions of the American Revolution that focus primarily on economic or social explanations. Historian

Steven Sarson has noted that it is "strange that few historians have taken the Declaration of Independence seriously as an account of the causes of the American Revolution."[7] But the Declaration of Independence is the most explicit statement of the reasons for revolution, and it deserves our close attention. When we examine the charges against the King, we see a profoundly legalistic document, one that repeatedly condemns the British for engaging in lawless, unconstitutional actions. Not surprisingly, the Americans committed their new nation to be a nation *Under Law*, one in which unconstitutional behavior would be constrained through the rule of law. There were varying views on how to achieve this ideal, but few revolutionary Americans would have disagreed that it was an ideal worth fighting and dying for.

The commitment to the rule of law was intimately related to an understanding of the structures that would most effectively advance constitutional self-government. Read carefully, the Declaration's charges against the King contain numerous insights about the form of government. Courts have often intuitively understood this, treating the charges as a sort of "negative constitution," a manual of what *not* to do. Practices so deplorable as to justify an armed rebellion stand as hallmarks of unacceptable behavior, and it is implausible to assume that any later constitutional document chose to embrace them. These indispensable structural commitments include representative assemblies and jury trials.

We have not always lived up to these ideals, and a particularly egregious modern violation of the Declaration of Independence occurs through aggressive gerrymandering of legislative districts. In Ohio, for example, a state in which Republicans are approximately 56% of the voters, Republicans nonetheless control 66% of the state's congressional seats, 67% of seats in the state house of representatives, and 79% of the seats in the state senate.[8] In these cases, the legislature has literally ceased to be "representative." It has instead become hijacked by one political party for its own purposes; representatives are selecting their voters, not the other way around. In a famous decision requiring state legislative districts to be drawn on the basis of population, Chief Justice Earl Warren memorably noted, "Legislators represent people, not trees or acres. Legislators are elected by voters, not farms or cities or economic interests.... [T]he right to elect legislators in a free and unimpaired fashion is a bedrock of our political system."[9] Although the United States Supreme Court has concluded that there is no judicial remedy for partisan gerrymandering, the inconsistency with the Declaration of Independence's commitment to representation is glaring.[10]

Our nation's political discourse has also been marred by frequent invocations of the claim that government is somehow the enemy, that it needs to be pared down as much as possible, and that only a miniscule federal government is consistent with the Founders' vision for America. Anything but a night-watchman state is a modern perversion that must be eliminated. This distorted vision reverberates from President Ronald Reagan's claim in his First Inaugural Address that "government is not the solution to our problem; government is the problem" to the indiscriminate assault on federal agencies by President Trump's DOGE unit. But this is simply not the vision of the Declaration of Independence, which complains first and foremost about the British failure to provide functional and competent government. The document envisions an energetic government, staffed by intelligent, well-trained people who will work together to promote the public good. People who embrace this vision do not randomly fire career civil servants, do not place multi-million-dollar decisions in the hands of teenagers and people without any substantive experience in government, do not place unqualified quacks in positions of significant authority, and do not seek to dismantle entire governmental departments because of ideological disagreements with some of their decisions. Such incompetent government is precisely the kind that the Declaration condemns most vociferously.

~~~

Can the Declaration still speak to us in any meaningful way 250 years later? After all, the world has changed dramatically since 1776, with technologies and even values that would have been unimaginable to the Declaration's drafters. And just because a principle is articulated in the Declaration of Independence isn't necessarily a sufficient reason for following it now. As Justice Oliver Wendell Holmes memorably put it, "It is revolting to have no better reason for a rule of law than that so it was laid down in the time of Henry IV."[11]

But the Declaration proclaims values of which we can be deservedly proud. Constitutionalism, representative government, the rule of law, and respect for human liberty and equality distinguish functional societies from dictatorships and oligarchies. We have not always fully adhered to these values, and as of this writing they are increasingly under attack. Whether we have a country in 250 years from now (and, if so, what kind of country it will be) will depend in part on the choices that we make now. Nothing can be taken for granted. America is, as it has always been, a work in progress, a continuing experiment in self-government, and an ongoing struggle to ensure that we remain One Nation Under Law.

APPENDIX

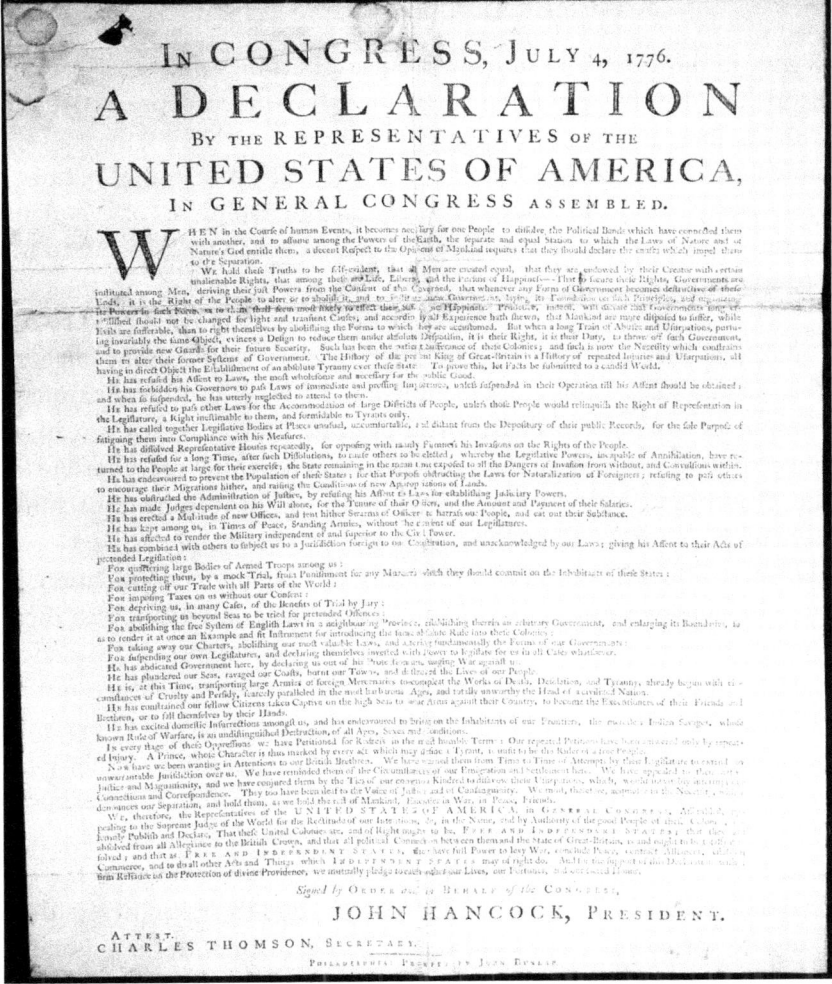

Figure A.1 The Dunlap Broadside, printed on the night of July 4, 1776, by Philadelphia printer John Dunlap.

THE DUNLAP BROADSIDE – THE FIRST PRINTING
OF THE DECLARATION OF INDEPENDENCE

In CONGRESS, July 4, 1776.

A DECLARATION

By the REPRESENTATIVES of the

UNITED STATES OF AMERICA,

In GENERAL CONGRESS Assembled.

When in the Course of human Events, it becomes necessary for one People to dissolve the Political Bands which have connected them with another, and to assume among the Powers of the Earth, the separate and equal Station to which the Laws of Nature and of Nature's God entitle them, a decent Respect to the Opinions of Mankind requires that they should declare the causes which impel them to the Separation.

We hold these Truths to be self-evident, that all Men are created equal, that they are endowed by their Creator with certain unalienable Rights, that among these are Life, Liberty, and the Pursuit of Happiness – That to secure these Rights, Governments are instituted among Men, deriving their just Powers from the Consent of the Governed, that whenever any Form of Government becomes destructive of these Ends, it is the Right of the People to alter or to abolish it, and to institute new Government, laying its Foundation on such Principles, and organizing its Powers in such Form, as to them shall seem most likely to effect their Safety and Happiness. Prudence, indeed, will dictate that Governments long established should not be changed for light and transient Causes; and accordingly all Experience hath shewn, that Mankind are more disposed to suffer, while Evils are sufferable, than to right themselves by abolishing the Forms to which they are accustomed. But when a long Train of Abuses and Usurpations, pursuing invariably the same Object, evinces a Design to reduce them under absolute Despotism, it is their Right, it is their Duty, to throw off such Government, and to provide new Guards for their future Security. Such has been the patient Sufferance of these Colonies; and such is now the Necessity which constrains them to alter their former Systems of Government. The History of the present King of Great-Britain is a History of repeated Injuries and Usurpations, all having in direct Object the Establishment of an absolute Tyranny over these States. To prove this, let Facts be submitted to a candid World.

HE has refused his Assent to Laws, the most wholesome and necessary for the public Good.

HE has forbidden his Governors to pass Laws of immediate ar.d pressing Importance, unless suspended in their Operation till his Assent should be obtained; and when so suspended, he has utterly neglected to attend to them.

HE has refused to pass other Laws for the Accommodation of large Districts of People, unless those People would relinquish the Right of Representation in the Legislature, a Right inestimable to them, and formidable to Tyrants only.

HE has called together Legislative Bodies at Places unusual, uncomfortable, and distant from the Depository of their public Records, for the sole Purpose of fatiguing them into Compliance with his Measures.

HE has dissolved Representative Houses repeatedly, for opposing with manly Firmness his Invasions on the Rights of the People.

HE has refused for a long Time, after such Dissolutions, to cause others to be elected; whereby the Legislative Powers, incapable of Annihilation, have returned to the People at large for their exercise; the State remaining in the mean time exposed to all the Dangers of Invasion from without, and Convulsions within.

HE has endeavoured to prevent the Population of these States; for that Purpose obstructing the Laws for Naturalization of Foreigners; refusing to pass others to encourage their Migrations hither, and raising the Conditions of new Appropriations of Lands.

HE has obstructed the Administration of Justice, by refusing his Assent to Laws for establishing Judiciary Powers.

HE has made Judges dependent on his Will alone, for the Tenure of their Offices, and the Amount and Payment of their Salaries.

HE has erected a Multitude of new Offices, and sent hither Swarms of Officers to harass our People, and eat out their Substance.

HE has kept among us, in Times of Peace, Standing Armies, without the consent of our Legislatures.

He has affected to render the Military independent of and superior to the Civil Power.

He has combined with others to subject us to a Jurisdiction foreign to our Constitution, and unacknowledged by our Laws; giving his Assent to their Acts of pretended Legislation:

For quartering large Bodies of Armed Troops among us:

For protecting them, by a mock Trial, from Punishment for any Murders which they should commit on the Inhabitants of these States:

For cutting off our Trade with all Parts of the World:

For imposing Taxes on us without our Consent:

For depriving us, in many Cases, of the Benefits of Trial by Jury:

For transporting us beyond Seas to be tried for pretended Offences:

For abolishing the free System of English Laws in a neighbouring Province, establishing therein an arbitrary Government, and enlarging its Boundaries, so as to render it at once an Example and fit Instrument for introducing the same absolute Rule into these Colonies:

For taking away our Charters, abolishing our most valuable Laws, and altering fundamentally the Forms of our Governments:

For suspending our own Legislatures, and declaring themselves invested with Power to legislate for us in all Cases whatsoever:

He has abdicated Government here, by declaring us out of his Protection and waging War against us.

He has plundered our Seas, ravaged our Coasts, burnt our Towns, and destroyed the Lives of our People.

He is, at this Time, transporting large Armies of foreign Mercenaries to compleat the Works of Death, Destruction, and Tyranny, already begun with circumstances of Cruelty and Perfidy, scarcely paralleled in the most barbarous Ages, and totally unworthy the Head of a civilized Nation.

He has constrained our fellow Citizens taken Captive on the high Seas to bear Arms against their Country, to become the Executioners of their Friends and Brethren, or to fall themselves by their Hands.

He has excited domestic Insurrections amongst us, and has endeavoured to bring on the Inhabitants of our Frontiers, the merciless Indian Savages, whose known Rule of Warfare, is an undistinguished Destruction, of all Ages, Sexes, and Conditions.

In every stage of these Oppressions we have Petitioned for Redress in the most humble Terms: Our repeated Petitions have been answered only by repeated Injury. A Prince, whose Character is thus marked by every act which may define a Tyrant, is unfit to be the Ruler of a free People.

NOR have we been wanting in Attentions to our British Brethren. We have warned them from Time to Time of Attempts by their Legislature to extend an unwarrantable Jurisdiction over us. We have reminded them of the Circumstances of our Emigration and Settlement here. We have appealed to their native Justice and Magnanimity, and we have conjured them by the Ties of our common Kindred to disavow these Usurpations, which, would inevitably interrupt our Connections and Correspondence. They too have been deaf to the Voice of Justice and of Consanguinity. We must, therefore, acquiesce in the Necessity, which denounces our Separation, and hold them, as we hold the rest of Mankind, Enemies in War, in Peace, Friends.

WE, therefore, the Representatives of the UNITED STATES OF AMERICA, in GENERAL CONGRESS, Assembled, appealing to the Supreme Judge of the World for the Rectitude of our Intentions, do, in the Name, and by Authority of the good People of these Colonies, solemnly Publish and Declare, That these United Colonies are, and of Right ought to be, FREE AND INDEPENDENT STATES; that they are absolved from all Allegiance to the British Crown, and that all political Connection between them and the State of Great-Britain, is and ought to be totally dissolved; and that as FREE AND INDEPENDENT STATES, they have full Power to levy War, conclude Peace, contract Alliances, establish Commerce, and to do all other Acts and Things which INDEPENDENT STATES may of right do. And for the support of this Declaration, with a firm Reliance on the Protection of Divine Providence, we mutually pledge to each other our Lives, our Fortunes, and our sacred Honor.

Signed by ORDER *and in* BEHALF *of the* CONGRESS,
JOHN HANCOCK, PRESIDENT.

ATTEST.
CHARLES THOMSON, SECRETARY.

PHILADELPHIA: PRINTED BY JOHN DUNLAP.

NOTES

Introduction

1. Remarks by President Trump at Signing of an Executive Order on the White House Hispanic Prosperity Initiative, July 9, 2020, 2020 WL 3867483 (White House).

2. Remarks by Vice President Harris at a Campaign Event, May 14, 2024, www.whitehouse.gov/briefing-room/speeches-remarks/2024/05/14/remarks-by-vice-president-harris-at-a-campaign-event-2/.

3. David Montgomery, "Belief in American Ideals? Generations of American Ancestors? What Americans Say Makes Someone American," July 23, 2025, https://today.yougov.com/politics/articles/52636-what-makes-someone-american-heritage-constitution-declaration.

4. Charles Warren, "Fourth of July Myths," *William and Mary Quarterly* 2, no. 3 (July 1945): 237.

5. Garry Wills, *Inventing America: Jefferson's Declaration of Independence* (New York: Vintage, 1979), xvi.

6. In a 2016 opinion, Justice Stephen Breyer admitted that the question was befuddling: "The original 13 states, once dependents of Britain, became independent entities perhaps at the time of the Declaration of Independence, perhaps at the signing of the Treaty of Paris, perhaps with the creation of the Articles of Confederation. (I need not be precise.)" Puerto Rico v. Sanchez Valle, 579 U.S. 59, 81 (2016) (Breyer, J., dissenting).

7. Max Farrand, *The Records of the Federal Convention of 1787* (New Haven, CT: Yale University Press, 1911). 1: 324.

8. Ronald Reagan, Inaugural Address 1981, www.reaganlibrary.gov/archives/speech/inaugural-address-1981.

9. Franchise Tax Board of California v. Hyatt, 587 U.S. 230, 237 (2019).

10. See, for example, Seminole Tribe v. Florida, 517 U.S. 44 (1996) (holding that Congress cannot waive states' sovereign immunity under its Article I powers);

Shelby County v. Holder, 570 U.S. 529 (2013) (invalidating the pre-clearance coverage provisions of the Voting Rights Act).
11. See Chapter 5.

Part I The Document

1. Roger Ebert, Clueless caper just fool's gold, Nov. 18, 2004, www.rogerebert .com/reviews/national-treasure-2004.

Chapter 1 Where Is the Declaration of Independence?

1. Sheep Welfare – Understanding Sheep Behavior – RSPCA, www.rspca.org .uk/adviceandwelfare/farm/sheep.
2. Wood's address is stated as, "In Fifth Street, a Little below Walnut Street," in a January 9, 1772, advertisement in the *Pennsylvania Gazette*.
3. The process of parchment production is described in Sean Paul Doherty and Stuart Henderson, "Production of Parchment Legal Deeds in England, 1690–1830," *Historical Research* 95, no. 270 (Nov. 2022): 575–77, 584.
4. *Pennsylvania Packet*, Dec. 23, 1771; *Pennsylvania Gazette*, Jan. 9, 1772.
5. *Pennsylvania Gazette*, Jan. 25, 1775 (advertisement of William Woodhouse, offering "the best largest English Parchment, each skin sufficient for two deeds, by the roll or skin"). English parchment was not advertised in the *Gazette* again until January 10, 1778, when Philadelphia was under British occupation. *Pennsylvania Gazette*, Jan. 10, 1778.
6. *Pennsylvania Gazette*, Jan. 9, 1772.
7. Ibid., March 3, 1779. Wood's parchment was available through the printer John Dunlap, who would print the first copy of the Declaration of Independence. *Pennsylvania Gazette*, Sept. 7, 1774.
8. Chris Coelho, *Timothy Matlack: Scribe of the Declaration of Independence* (Jefferson, NC: McFarland, 2013), 28–33. Only three names separate Wood's name from Matlack's in the 1774 provincial tax records for the City of Philadelphia. Proximity in tax records is not conclusive evidence of proximity in physical location, but it seems likely that the men were neighbors in the Dock Ward. "Provincial Tax, City of Philadelphia – 1774," in *Pennsylvania Archives (3d Ser.)*, ed. William Henry Egle (Harrisburg: Commonwealth of Pennsylvania, 1897), 14: 223, 229. Their businesses were also nearby. Matlack's brewery was on Sixth Street near the State House, about a block from Wood's parchment shop. Coelho, *Timothy Matlack*, 29.
9. Coelho, *Timothy Matlack*, 17.
10. An expert at the Library of Congress noted that it was "not even an excellent sheet of parchment to begin with; apparently it was a home-made

(colonial-made) piece of parchment found fairly quickly in the markets of Philadelphia." Verner Clapp, "The Declaration of Independence: A Case Study in Preservation," *Special Libraries* 62, no. 12 (Dec. 1971): 503.

11. James Worsham and Victoria Blue, Museum Receives Millionth Visitor of the Year, National Archives News, Aug. 19, 2019. It is possible that Wood's parchment was also used for the copy of the United States Constitution that is currently on display at the National Archives. Wood was still making parchment in 1787, and was celebrated for his accomplishments as a parchment maker in 1788. *Pennsylvania Gazette*, Sept. 10, 1788.

12. Sarah Fiddyment et al., "So You Want To Do Biocodicology? A Field Guide to the Biological Analysis of Parchment," *Heritage Science* 7 (2019): 35. As of 2024, the National Archives had not performed any such analysis. Jessie Kravitz, Historian, National Archives, email message to author, May 21, 2024.

13. *JCC*, 5: 516 (July 4, 1776).

14. Julian P. Boyd, *The Declaration of Independence: The Evolution of the Text* (Washington, DC: Library of Congress, rev. ed. 1999), 36.

15. Frederick R. Goff, *The John Dunlap Broadside: The First Printing of the Declaration of Independence* (Washington, DC: Library of Congress, 1976), 8. Many of those corrections involved removing extraneous quotation marks. Jay Fliegelman suggested that these were leftover marks from Jefferson's handwritten copy, marks that indicated where Jefferson should pause when reading the document aloud. Jay Fliegelman, *Declaring Independence: Jefferson, Natural Language, & the Culture of Performance* (Stanford, CA: Stanford University Press, 1993), 4–15.

16. Goff, *John Dunlap Broadside*, 7.

17. Ibid., 9.

18. Ibid., 11.

19. Frederick R. Goff, "A Contemporary Broadside Printing of the Declaration," *Quarterly Journal of Current Acquisitions* 15 (Nov. 1947): 12. Litigation over ownership of one of these copies reached the Supreme Court of Virginia in 2009. State of Maine v. Adams, 672 S.E.2d 862, 864 (Va. 2009). On the distribution of the Declaration throughout the United States and the world, see Emily Sneff, *When the Declaration of Independence Was News* (New York: Oxford University Press, 2026).

20. *JCC*, 5: 590–91 (July 19, 1776).

21. Coelho, *Timothy Matlack*, 55.

22. *JCC*, 5: 626 (Aug. 2, 1776).

23. Tony P. Wrenn, "The Honest Man – Matthew Thornton of New Hampshire," *Pioneer America* 1, no. 2 (1969): 30, 31.

24. John Adams to Caesar Augustus Rodney, April 30, 1823, *Founders Online*, National Archives, https://founders.archives.gov/documents/Adams/99-02-02-7810.

25. In a 1986 article, law professor Wilfred J. Ritz argued that the parchment copy in the National Archives was signed by the delegates on July 4, that the July 19 order referred only to a change of the document's title, and that the August 2 entry in the congressional journals refers only to the handful of members who had failed to sign by that date. Wilfred J. Ritz, "The Authentication of the Engrossed Declaration of Independence on July 4, 1776," *Law & History Review* 4, no. 1 (1986): 179–204. The argument is strained in the extreme, and to my knowledge, no serious historian has found it persuasive. On July 9, 1776, for example, John Adams wrote to Samuel Chase (who was absent from Congress on July 4 and who wanted to mark his assent to the document), noting, "As soon as an American Seal is prepared, I conjecture the Declaration will be Subscribed by all the Members, which will give you the opportunity you wish for, of transmitting your Name, among the Votaries of Independence." John Adams to Samuel Chase, July 9, 1776, *LDC*, 4: 414. On the actual dates of signing, see, for example, Pauline Maier, *American Scripture: Making the Declaration of Independence* (New York: Vintage, 1997), 150–53; Garry Wills, *Inventing America: Jefferson's Declaration of Independence* (New York: Vintage, 1979), 341–44; Edmund Cody Burnett, *The Continental Congress* (New York: Norton, 1941), 195–96.

26. *JCC*, 7: 48 (Jan. 18, 1777); Maier, *American Scripture*, 153. On later editions of the Declaration, see John Bidwell, *The Declaration in Script and Print: A Visual History of America's Founding Document* (University Park, PA: Pennsylvania State University Press, 2024).

27. David W. Dunlap, "A Patriotic Tribute, a Time-Honored Tradition," *New York Times*, June 23, 2024, A3.

28. Maier, *American Scripture*, 159. For an example of a 1776 British printing of the Declaration based on the Dunlap Broadside, see Emily Sneff, "Hanging Up Hancock, Declaration Stories, Oct. 1, 2025, www.declarationstories.org/stories/hanging-up-hancock.

29. Maier, *American Scripture*, 159–60.

30. Boyd, *Declaration of Independence*, 26.

31. Thomas Starr, "Separated at Birth: Text and Context in the Declaration of Independence," *Proceedings of the American Antiquarian Society* 110 (April 2000): 199.

32. Caroline Archer-Parré and Malcolm Dick, Introduction to *Pen, Print, and Communication in the Eighteenth Century*, ed. Caroline Archer-Parré and Malcolm Dick (Liverpool: Liverpool University Press, 2020), 2.

33. Bernard Bailyn, *The Ideological Origins of the American Revolution*, enl. ed. (Cambridge, MA: Harvard University Press, 1992), 2.

34. Robert G. Parkinson, *Thirteen Clocks: How Race United the Colonies and Made the Declaration of Independence* (Chapel Hill, NC: University of North Carolina Press, 2021), 5.

35. For a particularly egregious misunderstanding of this point, see Michael Warner, *The Letters of the Republic: Publication and the Public Sphere in Eighteenth-Century America* (Cambridge, MA: Harvard University Press, 1990), 107–08 ("[W]hereas the signed copy of the Declaration continues to be a national fetish, from which printed copies can only be derived imitations, the Constitution found its ideal form in every printed copy, beginning, though not specially, with its initial publication, in the place of the weekly news copy of the *Pennsylvania Packet*."). In reality, the Declaration and Constitution were printed and circulated in a very similar manner.

36. Marjorie Taylor Greene, "The average age of the signers of the Declaration of Independence....," X, July 5, 2024, 7:24 am, https://x.com/RepMTG/status/1809231806215884830.

37. Determining the precise text of legal documents is far from straightforward. The parchment text of the Constitution enshrined in the National Archives is likely not the governing text, either; rather, it is the printed text that was sent to the states for ratification. Akhil Reed Amar, *America's Unwritten Constitution: The Precedents and Principles We Live By* (New York: Basic Books, 2012), 64–68. Even determining the text of federal statutes is far more difficult than it would seem. See, for example, Jesse M. Cross, "Where Is Statutory Law?," *Cornell Law Review* 108 (2023): 1041–116.

38. Eli Merritt, *Disunion among Ourselves: The Perilous Politics of the American Revolution* (Columbia, MO: University of Missouri Press, 2023), 276.

39. A sermon celebrating the Declaration, for example, was published in 1777 with the Dunlap Broadside caption and "UNITED STATES of AMERICA" on the title page. Peter Whitney, *American Independence Vindicated, A SERMON Delivered September 12, 1776. At a LECTURE Appointed for Publishing the DECLARATION of INDEPENDENCE Passed July 4, 1776. By the REPRESENTATIVES of the UNITED STATES of AMERICA in GENERAL CONGRESS ASSEMBLED* (Boston: E. Draper, 1777).

40. See, for example, *The Declaration of Independence: Origins and Impact*, ed. Scott Douglas Gerber (Washington, DC: CQ Press, 2002), xv–xvii. In 1781, the Continental Congress ordered a printed edition of state constitutions, the Articles of Confederation, the treaties with France, and the Declaration of Independence. This edition inexplicably combined the caption of the Dunlap Broadside with the signatures of the ceremonial parchment. *The Constitutions of the Several Independent States of America* (Philadelphia: Francis Bailey, 1781), 187, 191. Later volumes by private publishers sometimes continued this conflation. See, for example, *The Constitutions of the Sixteen States which Compose the Confederated Republic of America* (Boston: Manning & Loring, 1797), 5–12. None of these editions, however, include "united States."

41. List of extant Dunlap Broadsides, https://en.wikipedia.org/wiki/Physical_history_of_the_United_States_Declaration_of_Independence. Reproductions

of twenty-one broadsides can be found in Goff, *John Dunlap Broadside*, 20–61.

42. As this book was going to press, I learned that the Dunlap Broadside on display in the Archives Rotunda is a facsimile of an original that is stored elsewhere in the Archives.

Chapter 2 Who Wrote the Declaration of Independence?

1. See generally Susan Sorek, *The Emperors' Needles* (Exeter, UK: Bristol Phoenix Press, 2010).
2. National Park Service, Washington Monument – History and Culture, www.nps.gov/wamo/learn/historyculture/index.htm.
3. Thomas Jefferson, Design for Tombstone and Inscription, before 4 July 1826, 4 July 1826, *Founders Online*, National Archives, https://founders.archives.gov/documents/Jefferson/98-01-02-6185.
4. John Hamilton Works, Jr., Thomas Jefferson's Original Graveyard Monument at the University of Missouri, www.tjheritage.org/thomas-jeffersons-originial-graveyard-monument-university-of-missouri.
5. Flores v. Colvin, 2015 WL 12551998, at *6 (S.D. Tex. 2015).
6. US Citizenship and Immigration Services, Civics (History and Government) Questions for the Naturalization Test, rev. 01/19, available at www.uscis.gov/sites/default/files/document/questions-and-answers/100q.pdf.
7. For another approach to this question, see Akhil Reed Amar, *The Words That Made Us: America's Constitutional Conversation, 1760–1840* (New York: Basic Books, 2021), 127–28.
8. *JCC*, 5: 425 (June 7, 1776).
9. *JCC*, 5: 428–29 (June 10, 1776); Pauline Maier, *American Scripture: Making the Declaration of Independence* (New York: Vintage, 1997), 42.
10. *JCC*, 5: 431 (June 11, 1776).
11. Accounts of this process from many decades later almost certainly suffer from flawed historical memories. For an overview, see Robert E. McGlone, "Deciphering Memory: John Adams and the Declaration of Independence," *Journal of American History* 85, no. 2 (Sept. 1998): 411–38.
12. See generally Maier, *American Scripture*, 99–105.
13. John Adams, *Diary and Autobiography of John Adams*, ed. L.H. Butterfield (Cambridge, MA: Harvard University Press, 1962), 3: 336.
14. Maier, *American Scripture*, 102.
15. Ibid., 101.
16. Thomas Jefferson to James Madison, August 30, 1823, *Founders Online*, National Archives, https://founders.archives.gov/documents/Jefferson/98-01-02-3728.
17. *JCC*, 1: 63–64 (Oct. 14, 1774).

18. Fred Kaplan, *His Masterly Pen: A Biography of Jefferson the Writer* (New York: HarperCollins, 2022), 133.

19. John Wilkes, Debate in the Commons on the Address of Thanks, October 31, 1776, in *American Archives: Fifth Series*, ed. Peter Force (Washington, DC: 1853), 3: 983, 987.

20. Ibid., 125.

21. Thomas Jefferson to James Madison, August 30, 1823, *Founders Online*, National Archives, https://founders.archives.gov/documents/Jefferson/98-01-02-3728.

22. Ibid.

23. Thomas Jefferson to Henry Lee, May 8, 1825, *Founders Online*, National Archives, https://founders.archives.gov/documents/Jefferson/98-01-02-5212.

24. Cf. Maier, *American Scripture*, 135 ("The sentiments Jefferson eloquently expressed were, in short, absolutely conventional among Americans of his time.").

25. Julian P. Boyd, *The Declaration of Independence: The Evolution of the Text* (Washington, DC: Library of Congress, rev. ed. 1999), 16.

26. Robert Dodsley, *The Preceptor: Containing a General Course of Education* (London: J. Dodsley, 1769), 2: 331. John Adams's copy of this book can be viewed at https://archive.org/details/preceptorcontain02dods/page/n5/mode/2up. See also Thomas E. Ricks, *First Principles: What America's Founders Learned from the Greeks and Romans and How That Shaped Our Country* (New York: Harper Perennial, 2020), 52–55.

27. Boyd, *Declaration of Independence*, 17.

28. Maier, *American Scripture*, xvii.

29. Adams, *Diary and Autobiography*, 3: 336–37.

30. Thomas Jefferson to James Madison, August 30, 1823, *Founders Online*, National Archives, https://founders.archives.gov/documents/Jefferson/98-01-02-3728.

31. Thomas Jefferson to Benjamin Franklin, [June 21, 1776?], in *The Papers of Benjamin Franklin*, ed. William B. Willcox (New Haven, CT: Yale University Press, 1982), 22: 485–86.

32. Maier, *American Scripture*, 98.

33. Ibid., 150.

34. Thomas Jefferson, Anecdotes of Benjamin Franklin, c. Dec. 4, 1818, in *The Papers of Thomas Jefferson, Retirement Series*, ed. J. Jefferson Looney (Princeton: Princeton University Press, 2016), 13: 462–65.

35. Maier, *American Scripture*, 149–50; Stephen E. Lucas, "Justifying America: The Declaration of Independence as a Rhetorical Document," in *American Rhetoric: Context and Criticism*, ed. Thomas W. Benson (Carbondale, IL: Southern Illinois University Press, 1989), 72.

36. Jefferson, Anecdotes of Benjamin Franklin, 463–64.

37. Lucas, "Justifying America," 72.

38. Maier, *American Scripture*, 99.

39. Ibid., 150.

40. Danielle Allen, *Our Declaration: A Reading of the Declaration of Independence in Defense of Equality* (New York: Liveright, 2014), 47, 81.

41. Garry Wills, *Inventing America: Jefferson's Declaration of Independence* (New York: Vintage, 1978), ix.

42. Ibid., 180.

43. Ibid., 239.

44. Ibid., 174.

45. Thomas Jefferson to Thomas Mann Randolph, Jr., May 30, 1790, in *The Papers of Thomas Jefferson*, ed. Julian P. Boyd (Princeton: Princeton University Press, 1961), 16: 448–50.

46. Ronald Hamowy, "Jefferson and the Scottish Enlightenment: A Critique of Garry Wills's Inventing America: Jefferson's Declaration of Independence," *William & Mary Quarterly* 36 (Oct. 1979): 503, 508.

47. Ibid., 514.

48. Thomas Jefferson to Henry Lee, May 8, 1825, *Founders Online*, National Archives, https://founders.archives.gov/documents/Jefferson/98-01-02-5212.

49. For recent defenses of Locke's influence on the Declaration, see Steven Sarson, *The Course of Human Events: The Declaration of Independence and the Historical Origins of the United States* (Charlottesville, VA: University of Virginia Press, 2025), 19–31; S. Adam Seagrave, "European Antecedents to the Declaration of Independence," in *The Cambridge Companion to the Declaration of Independence*, ed. Michael Zuckert and Mark A. Graber (New York: Cambridge University Press, 2026), 4–18.

50. Allen Jayne, *Jefferson's Declaration of Independence: Origins, Philosophy and Theology* (Lexington, KY: University Press of Kentucky, 1998), 6–7.

51. Ibid., 81.

52. Alan Dershowitz, *America Declares Independence* (Hoboken, NJ: John Wiley & Sons, 2003), 14–62.

53. A Kansas appellate judge, for example, argued that "Jefferson, the primary author of the Declaration of Independence, is frequently described as something of a deist, acknowledging a supreme being, but embracing no particular religion. So the references in the Declaration of Independence do not plainly point to Christian or Biblical teachings as interpretive tools." Hodes & Nauser, MDs, P.A. v. Schmidt, 368 P.3d 667, 693 (Kan. Ct. App. 2016) (Atcheson, J., concurring). The absence of overtly Christian teachings is plain in the Declaration itself; one does not need to point to Jefferson's deism to interpret whatever religious meaning it may hold.

54. For a similar view, see John Phillip Reid, "The Irrelevance of the Declaration," in *Law in the American Revolution and the Revolution in Law*, ed. Hendrik Hartog (New York: New York University Press, 1981), 83 ("Jefferson's

perceptions of David Hume and Jean Jacques Burlamaqui are relevant to the meaning of the document only to the extent his congressional colleagues knew of these perceptions and endorsed them with their votes.").

55. Robert M.S. McDonald, "Thomas Jefferson's Changing Reputation as Author of the Declaration of Independence: The First Fifty Years," *Journal of the Early Republic* 19, no. 2 (Summer 1999): 171–72.

56. For assessments of Morris's importance, see Jonathan Gienapp, "Representing the Nation: Gouverneur Morris's Nationalist Constitutionalism," *Georgetown Journal of Law & Public Policy* 21, no. 1 (Winter 2023): 67–102; Melanie Randolph Miller, "A Great Statesman: Reclaiming Gouverneur Morris," *Georgetown Journal of Law & Public Policy* 21, no. 1 (Winter 2023): 103–30.

57. Wills, *Inventing America*, 340.

58. Ibid., 90.

59. Maier, *American Scripture*, 45.

60. Ibid.

61. The Answer of the Congress to the King's proclamation, *JCC*, 3: 409 (Dec. 6, 1775).

62. Lucas, "Justifying America," 109.

63. The classic historical work on this problem is Edmund Morgan, *Inventing the People: The Rise of Popular Sovereignty in England and America* (New York: W.W. Norton, 1988). Cf. Sanford Levinson, "'Popular Sovereignty' and the Declaration of Independence," in *Cambridge Companion to the Declaration of Independence*, 90–108.

64. David Armitage, *The Declaration of Independence: A Global History* (Cambridge, MA: Harvard University Press, 2007), 30.

65. Wills, *Inventing America*, 333.

66. Maier, *American Scripture*, 131.

67. [Thomas Hutchinson], *Strictures upon the Declaration of the Congress at Philadelphia* (London: 1776), 31.

68. Hans L. Eicholz, *Harmonizing Sentiments: The Declaration of Independence and the Jeffersonian Idea of Self-Government* (New York: Peter Lang, 2001), 105.

69. Cf. Boyd, *Declaration of Independence*, 15 ("In a broad sense, the author of the Declaration was the American people.").

70. William Henry Drayton, *A Charge, on the Rise of the American Empire* (Charleston, SC: David Bruce, 1776), 10.

71. Gouverneur Morris to the Earl of Carlisle, Sept. 19, 1778, *To Secure the Blessings of Liberty: Selected Writings of Gouverneur Morris*, ed. J. Jackson Barlow (Indianapolis, IN: Liberty Fund, 2012), 41.

72. Thomas Jefferson to John W. Campbell, Sept. 3, 1809, *Founders Online*, National Archives, https://founders.archives.gov/documents/Jefferson/03-01-02-0390.

73. I am unpersuaded by Garry Wills's argument that Jefferson was referring to his initial draft of the Declaration on his tombstone, as opposed to the document adopted by Congress. Wills, *Inventing America*, 308. Why would Jefferson use the phrase "the American Declaration of Independence" as a surreptitious reference to his initial draft?

Chapter 3   Is the Declaration of Independence Law?

1. Garry Wills, *Inventing America: Jefferson's Declaration of Independence* (New York: Vintage, 1978), xxv.
2. Frederick Schauer, "Why the Declaration of Independence Is Not Law – And Why It Could Be," *Southern California Law Review* 89, no. 3 (March 2016): 628.
3. Mark Graber, "The Declaration of Independence and Contemporary Constitutional Pedagogy," *Southern California Law Review* 89, no. 3 (March 2016): 512.
4. Darrell A.H. Miller, "Continuity and the Declaration of Independence," *Southern California Law Review* 89, no. 3 (March 2016): 602.
5. Willi Paul Adams, *The First American Constitutions: Republican Ideology and the Making of the State Constitutions in the Revolutionary Era*, exp. ed. (Lanham MD: Rowan & Littlefield, 2001), 2.
6. Quoted in Lewis E. Lerhman, "On Jaffa, Lincoln, Marshall, and Original Intent," in *Original Intent and the Framers of the Constitution: A Disputed Question*, ed. Harry V. Jaffa, Bruce Ledewitz, Robert L. Stone, and George Anastaplo (Washington, DC: Regnery Gateway, 1994), 5.
7. Troxel v. Granville, 530 U.S. 57, 91 (2000) (Scalia, J., dissenting).
8. Ibid.
9. Schifanelli v. U.S. Government, 865 F.2d 1259 (Table), 1988 WL 138496, at *1 (4th Cir. 1988).
10. Rywelski v. Biden, 2024 1905670, at *2 (10th Cir. 2024).
11. Derden v. McNeel, 978 F.2d 1453, 1456 n.4 (5th Cir. 1992).
12. Rywelski v. Biden, 2023 WL 4440656, at *2 (N.D. Okla. 2023).
13. Morgan v. County of Hawaii, 2016 WL 1254222, at *24 (D. Haw. 2016).
14. Planned Parenthood Great Northwest v. Idaho, 522 P.3d 1132, 1168 (Idaho 2022); cf. Jones v. DeSantis, 410 F.Supp.3d 1284, 1300 (N.D. Fla. 2019) ("The Declaration of Independence is aspirational [and] not the law.").
15. Elias v. Chisolm, 2020 WL 10051520, at *8 n.2 (C.D. Cal. 2020).
16. Coffey v. U.S., 939 F.Supp. 185, 191 (E.D.N.Y. 1996).
17. Statewide Grievance Comm. v. Presnick, 559 A.2d 220, 226 (Conn. App. Ct. 1989).
18. Demos v. Kincheloe, 563 F.Supp. 30, 31 (E.D. Wash. 1982).
19. Hurt v. Social Security Admin., 544 F.3d 308, 309 (D.C. Cir. 2008).
20. Collins v. Nutter, 2105 WL 500170, at *1 (E.D. Pa. 2015).

21. Bey v. Nissan Motors Acceptance Corp., 1992 WL 174730, at *1 (E.D. Pa. 1992).
22. Nixon v. Rose, 631 F.Supp. 794, 796 (N.D. Ind. 1985).
23. Meyer v. United States, 1987 WL 4750, at *1 (N.D. Ill. 1987).
24. Rywelski v. Biden, 2024 WL 1905670, at *1 (10th Cir. 2024).
25. Hughes v. Opel, 2024 WL 1443329, at *2–3 (D. Maryland 2024).
26. Vasquez v. City of New York – Office of the Mayor, 2024 WL 1348702, at *1–2 (E.D.N.Y. 2024).
27. Olson v. Missoula Field Office, 2023 WL 999918, at *5 (D. Montana 2023).
28. Recinos v. Washington State Nursing Comm'n, 2023 WL 6850201, at *2 (W.D. Wash. 2023).
29. Kengne v. Georgia Power Co., 2002 WL 17492257, at *6 (N.D. Ga. 2022).
30. Rizer v. County of Bastrop, Texas, 2018 WL 7350680, at *1–2 (W.D. Tex. 2018).
31. McKinney v. Blumenthal, 1979 WL 1342, at *1 (N.D. Ga. 1979).
32. Robinson v. Consumer Financial Protection Bureau, 689 Fed.Appx. 151, 151 (3d Cir. 2017).
33. Zamora v. Jones, 2015 WL 2018186, at *2 (E.D. Cal. 2015).
34. McClees v. Urban Financial Group, 2013 WL 6501743, at *1 (D.N.J. 2013).
35. Kowall v. United States, 53 F.R.D. 211, 214 n.2 (W.D. Mich. 1971).
36. Ibid.
37. Byrn v. New York City Health & Hospitals Corp., 286 N.E.2d 887, 893 (N.Y. 1972) (Burke, J., dissenting).
38. Ibid.
39. Perez v. Lippold, 198 P.2d. 17, 30 (Cal. 1948) (Carter, J., concurring).
40. Ibid., 32.
41. DS and RS v. Dept. of Public Assistance and Social Services, 607 P.2d 911, 919 (Wyo. 1980).
42. Fidelity & Cas. Co. of New York v. Union Sav. Bank Co., 163 N.E. 221, 222 (Ohio Ct. App. 1928).
43. Curry v. District of Columbia, 14 App.D.C. 423, 440 (D.C. 1899).
44. State v. Cutshall, 15 S.E. 26, 263 (N.C. 1892) (affirming the dismissal of an indictment for an out-of-state bigamous marriage).
45. Litchfield v. State, 126 P. 707, 713 (Okla. Crim. App. 1912).
46. Interest of A.M., 630 S.W.2d 25, 25 (Tex. 2019) (Blacklock, J., concurring).
47. Marks v. Hudson, 2018 WL 11469616, at *2 (S.D. Tex. 2018), rev'd Marks v. Hudson, 933 F.3d 481 (5th Cir. 2019).
48. People v. Zetterlund, 127 N.E.3d 21, 29, n.1 (Ill. App. Ct. 2018) (McDade, J., concurring). For additional instances of judicial reference to the Declaration with respect to unwritten rights, see Chapter 9.
49. Gulf, C. & S.F. Ry. Co. v. Ellis, 165 U.S. 150, 160 (1897); see also Bute v. Illinois, 333 U.S. 640, 651 (1948) ("The Constitution was conceived in large part in the spirit of the Declaration of Independence.").

50. In Interest of H.S., 550 S.W.3d 151, 178 (Tex. 2018) (Blacklock, J., dissenting).
51. Bell v. Maryland, 378 U.S. 226, 286 (1964) (Goldberg, J., concurring). In an article published while he was chairman of the Equal Employment Opportunity Commission, Clarence Thomas argued that the Constitution should be seen as the "fulfillment of the ideals of the Declaration of Independence." Clarence Thomas, "Toward a 'Plain Reading' of the Constitution – The Declaration of Independence in Constitutional Interpretation," *Howard Law Journal* 30, no. 4 (1987): 985.
52. Mark Tushnet, *Taking the Constitution Away from the Courts* (Princeton, NJ: Princeton University Press, 1999), 9–17.
53. Ibid., 14, 116.
54. Scott Douglas Gerber, *To Secure These Rights: The Declaration of Independence and Constitutional Interpretation* (New York: NYU Press, 1995), 3. For criticism of Gerber's view, see Lee J. Strang, "Originalism, The Declaration of Independence, and the Constitution: A Unique Role in Constitutional Interpretation?," *Penn State Law Review* 111 (2006): 449–57.
55. Charles L. Black, Jr., *A New Birth of Freedom: Human Rights, Named and Unnamed* (New York: Grosset/Putnam 1997), 8.
56. Robert D. McFadden, "Harry V. Jaffa, Conservative Scholar and Goldwater Muse, Dies at 96," *New York Times*, Jan. 12, 2015.
57. Harry V. Jaffa, "What Were the 'Original Intentions' of the Framers of the Constitution?," in *Original Intent and the Framers of the Constitution*, 23.
58. Harry V. Jaffa, *How to Think about the American Revolution: A Bicentennial Cerebration* (Durham, NC: Carolina Academic Press, 1978), x.
59. Harry V. Jaffa, *Crisis of the House Divided* (New York: Doubleday, 1959), 379; Jaffa, "What were the 'Original Intentions,'" 27.
60. Patrick M. O'Neil, "The Declaration as Ur-Constitution: The Bizarre Jurisprudential Philosophy of Professor Harry V. Jaffa," *Akron Law Review* 29, no. 2 (1995): 252.
61. Stuart Banner, *The Decline of Natural Law: How American Lawyers Once Used Natural Law and Why They Stopped* (New York: Oxford University Press, 2021), 1.
62. R.H. Helmholz, *Natural Law in Court: A History of Legal Theory in Practice* (Cambridge, MA: Harvard University Press, 2015), 131.
63. Banner, *Decline of Natural Law*, 19.
64. See generally ibid.
65. Ibid., 8.
66. See, for example, Carl L. Becker, *The Declaration of Independence: A Study in the History of Political Ideas* (New York: Vintage, 1922), 74–79.
67. America's Historical Imprints, https://infoweb.newsbank.com/apps/readex/?p=EAIX.

68. I. Bernard Cohen, *Science and the Founding Fathers: Science in the Political Thought of Jefferson, Franklin, Adams, and Madison* (New York: Norton, 1995), 113–21.

69. Lucas, "Justifying America," 82.

70. John Phillip Reid, "The Irrelevance of the Declaration," in *Law in the American Revolution and the Revolution in Law*, ed. Hendrik Hartog (New York: New York University Press, 1981), 87–88.

71. Ibid., 48.

72. Ibid., 48–62. For an argument that natural rights and natural law arguments increased after 1772, see Michael D. Hattem, *Past and Prologue: Politics and Memory in the American Revolution* (New Haven: Yale University Press, 2020), 127–34. Similarly, Steven Sarson has suggested that natural law arguments were important throughout the dispute with Great Britain. Steven Sarson, *The Course of Human Events: The Declaration of Independence and the Historical Origins of the United States* (Charlottesville, VA: University of Virginia Press, 2025), 31–41.

73. John Phillip Reid, *Constitutional History of the American Revolution: The Authority of Rights* (Madison, WI: University of Wisconsin Press, 1986), 92.

74. Lehrman, "On Jaffa," 5.

75. Jaffa, *How to Think about the American Revolution*, 46.

76. Timothy Sandefur, *The Conscience of the Constitution: The Declaration of Independence and the Right to Liberty* (Washington, DC: Cato Institute, 2014), 14–15.

77. Patel v. Texas Dep't of Licensing and Regulation, 469 S.W.3d 69, 120, n.200 (Tex. 2015) (Willett, J., concurring); see also Ex parte State ex rel. Alabama Policy Institute, 200 So.3d 495, 568 n.3 (Ala. 2015) (Moore, C.J., concurring) (noting that the Declaration was part of the "official codification of the … laws of the United States"); Walter Berns, *Taking the Constitution Seriously* (New York: Simon & Schuster, 1987), 23 (noting that the 1970 edition of the United States Code treats the Declaration as an "organic law" of the United States).

78. Act of June 30, 1926, ch. 712, 44 Stat. 777.

79. United States House of Representatives, Office of the Law Revision Counsel, "Detailed Guide to the United States Code and Features," https://uscode .house.gov/detailed_guide.xhtml.

80. On the history of compilations of federal statutes, see Ralph H. Dwan and Ernest R. Feidler, "The Federal Statutes – Their History and Use," *Minnesota Law Review* 22, no. 7 (June 1938): 1008–29; Erwin C. Surrency, "The Publication of Federal Laws: A Short History," *Law Library Journal* 79, no. 3 (Summer 1987): 469–84.

81. Act of March 3, 1795, 1 Stat. 443. In 1780, the Continental Congress authorized a volume that would include the Declaration, the Articles of

Confederation, the treaties with France, and the various state constitutions. *JCC*, 18: 1217 (Dec. 29, 1780).

82. *The Laws of the United States of America*, vol. 1 (Philadelphia: Richard Folwell, 1796).

83. Act of April 18, 1814, 3 Stat. 129.

84. Act of March 3, 1845, 5 Stat. 798–800.

85. Richard Peters, ed., *The Public Statutes at Large of the United States of America*, vol. 1 (Boston: Little and Brown, 1845), 1–20. On Peters's earlier career as a reporter of Supreme Court decisions, see Craig Joyce, "The Rise of the Supreme Court Reporter: An Institutional Perspective on Marshall Court Ascendancy," *Michigan Law Review* 83, no. 5 (1985): 1291–1391.

86. For a somewhat different perspective, see Frank I. Michelman, "The Ghost of the Declaration Present: The Legal Force of the Declaration of Independence Regarding Acts of Congress," *Southern California Law Review* 89, no. 3 (March 2016): 575–600.

87. For a discussion of the Declaration's use in a handful of constitutional cases, see Charles H. Cosgrove, "The Declaration of Independence in Constitutional History: A Selective Interpretation and Analysis," *University of Richmond Law Review* 32, no. 1 (Jan. 1998): 107–64; Mark David Hall, "The Declaration of Independence in the Supreme Court," in *The Declaration of Independence: Origins and Impact*, ed. Scott Douglas Gerber (Washington, DC: CQ Press, 2002), 142–60; Graber, "Declaration of Independence and Constitutional Pedagogy," 513–32.

88. For example, Md. Const. of 1776, pmbl.; N.C. Const. of 1776, pmbl.; Pa. Const. of 1776, pmbl.; S.C. Const. of 1778, pmbl., Vt. Const. of 177, pmbl.

89. N.Y. Const. of 1777, pmbl.

90. State v. Superior Ct. of King Co., 189 P. 1016, 1022 (Wash. 1920).

91. Gwathmey v. North Carolina, 464 S.E.2d 674, 679 (N.C. 1995); see also Cooper v. Runnels, 291 P.2d 657, 659 (Wash. 1955) (same).

92. Incline Energy, LLC v. Penna Group, LLC, 787 F.Supp.2d 1140, 1142 n.2 (D. Nevada 2011).

93. Fla. Stat. § 2.01.

94. Liverpool & Great Western Steam Co. v. Phenix Ins. Co., 129 U.S. 397, 445 (1889).

95. U.S. v. Leche, 44 F.Supp. 765, 766 (E.D. La. 1942); see also United Copper Securities Co. v. Amalgamated Copper Co., 232 F. 574, 577 (2d Cir. 1916).

96. Harcourt v. Gaillard, 25 U.S. 523, 527 (1827).

97. Mitchell v. Einstein, 105 A.D. 413, 418 (N.Y. App. Div. 1905); see also Saunders v. N.Y. Central & H.R.R. Co., 30 Abb. N. Cas 88, 99 (N.Y. 1893).

98. Seneca Nation of Indians v. Christy, 27 N.E. 275, 278 (N.Y. 1891).

99. Case of Pea Patch Island, 30 F. Cas. 1123, 1154 (Arbitration Court 1848) (No. 18,311).

100. Phillips v. Delaware, 330 A.2d 136, 141 (Del. 1974).
101. Ibid.
102. New Jersey v. Delaware, 291 U.S. 361, 370 (1934).
103. Howard v. Ingersoll, 54 U.S. 381, 398 (1851).
104. Inglis v. Trustees of Sailor's Snug Harbour, 28 U.S. (3 Pet.) 99, 121 (1830).
105. For example, Trimbles v. Harrison, 40 Ky. 140, 143 (Ky. 1840) ("The declaration of independence of 1776, was a renunciation of allegiance to Great Britain, by all the inhabitants of the United Colonies, who did not elect to except themselves from the renunciation."); State ex rel. Phelps v. Jackson, 65 A. 657 (Vt. 1907) ("though born a British subject, his continued residence in this country after the Declaration of Independence, giving allegiance to the new government, establishes his American citizenship").
106. Chanet v. Villeponteaux, 3 McCord 29, 30 (S.C. Ct. App. L. & Equity 1825); see also Lynch v. Clarke, 1 Sand. Ch. 583, 681 (N.Y. Ch. 1844) ("In our decisions, the time fixed for the application of the rule, is the Declaration of Independence.").
107. Inglis, 121.
108. Carlton F.W. Larson, *The Trials of Allegiance: Treason, Juries, and the American Revolution* (New York: Oxford University Press, 2019), 42–57.
109. *JCC*, 4: 475 (June 24, 1776).
110. Joseph Hawley to Elbridge Gerry, July 17, 1776, in *The American Tory*, ed. Morton Borden and Penn Borden (Englewood Cliffs, NJ: Prentice-Hall 1972), 73.
111. John Adams to John Winthrop, June 23, 1776, *Founders Online*, National Archives, https://founders.archives.gov/documents/Adams/06-04-02-0134.
112. Larson, *Trials of Allegiance*, 69–73.
113. David Ramsay, *History of the American Revolution* (Philadelphia: R. Aitken & Son, 1789), 340.
114. Act of Mar. 21, 1864, ch. 36, § 4, 13 Stat. 30, 31 (Nevada); Act of Mar. 21, 1864, ch. 37, § 4, 13 Stat. 32, 33 (Colorado); Act of Feb. 22, 1889, ch. 180, § 4, 25 Stat. 676, 677 (North Dakota, South Dakota, Montana & Washington); Act of July 16, 1894, ch. 138, § 3, 28 Stat. 107, 108 (Utah); Act of June 16, 1906, ch. 3335, Pub. L. No. 234, § 3, 34 Stat. 267, 269 (Oklahoma); Act of June 20, 1910, ch. 310, § 2, 36 Stat. 557, 558 (Arizona & New Mexico); Act of July 7, 1958, Pub. L. No. 85-508, § 3, 72 Stat. 339, 339 (Alaska); Act of Mar. 18, 1959, Pub. L. No. 86-3, § 3, 73 Stat. 4, 5 (Hawaii). Wyoming and Idaho were admitted without Enabling Acts.
115. Lawrence N. Park, "Admission of States and the Declaration of Independence," *Temple Law Quarterly* 33, no. 4 (Summer 1960): 410–16.
116. 38 Cong. Globe 788 (1864) (statement of Sen. Davis).
117. Atwater v. Hassett, 111 P. 802, 813 (Okla. 1910).
118. Coyle v. Smith, 221 U.S. 559, 570 (1911).
119. Ibid., 577.

120. Beck v. Neville, 540 P.3d 906, 914 (Ariz. 2024).
121. Ibid., 921 (Timmer, V.C.J., concurring in part and in the result).
122. Larson v. Seattle Popular Monorail Authority, 131 P.3d 892 (Wash. 2006) (Johnson, J., dissenting).
123. Colorado Anti-Discrimination Comm'n v. Case, 380 P.2d 34, 44 (Colo. 1962) (Frantz, J., specially concurring); see also Vogts v. Guerrette, 351 P.2d 851, 864 (Colo. 1960) (Frantz, J., dissenting) (arguing that the Enabling Act is "fundamental and paramount law" and that judges must defer to the "Declaration of Independence, the Enabling Act, and the Constitution").
124. John C. Eastman, "The Declaration of Independence as Viewed from the States," in *The Declaration of Independence: Origins and Impact*, ed. Scott Douglas Gerber (Washington, DC: CQ Press, 2002), 96.
125. For overviews and analyses of these provisions, see Steven G. Calabresi and Sofia M. Vickery, "On Liberty and the Fourteenth Amendment: The Original Understanding of the Lockean Natural Rights Guarantees," *Texas Law Review* 93 (2015): 1299–1443; Joseph R. Grodin, "Rediscovering the State Constitutional Right to Happiness and Safety," *Hastings Constitutional Law Quarterly* 25 (Fall 1997): 1–34.
126. Iowa const., art I, sec. 1.
127. Hodes & Nauser, MDs, P.A. v. Schmidt, 440 P.3d 461 (Kan. 2019).
128. Gacke v. Pork Xtra, L.L.C., 684 N.W.2d 168, 176 (Iowa 2004) (quoting State v. Osborne, 154 N.W. 294, 300 (Iowa 1915)).
129. MKB Management Corp. v. Burdick, 855 N.W.2d 31, 61–62 (N.D. 2014); State v. Cromwell, 9 N.W.2d 914, 918 (N.D. 1943).
130. Morris v. Brandenburg, 376 P.3d 836, 855 (N.M. 2016).
131. State v. Williams, 728 N.E.2d 342, 354 (Ohio 2000).
132. Erlinger v. United States, 2024 WL 3074427, at *5 (2024).
133. Securities and Exchange Comm'n v. Jarkesy, 2024 WL 3187811, at *7 (2024) (citing the Declaration's reference to jury trials).
134. Case of Williams, 29 F. Cas. 1330, 1333 (C.C.D. Conn. 1799) (No. 17,708). Similar arguments can be found in political debate as early as 1783, when an author in a Philadelphia newspaper wrote, "Let it be remembered, that one of the reasons assigned by Congress for the declaration of independence was, 'the King of Great Britain has made judges dependent on his will alone for the tenure of their offices, and the amount and payment of their salaries.'" *Pennsylvania Gazette*, March 26, 1783.
135. United States v. Rahimi, 602 U.S. 680, 781 (2024) (Kavanaugh, J., concurring).
136. United States v. Zubaydah, 595 U.S. 195, 250 (2022) (Gorsuch, J., concurring).
137. Youngstown Sheet & Tube Co. v. Sawyer, 343 U.S. 579, 641 (1952) (Jackson, J., concurring).

138. For decisions invoking multiple charges, see Duncan v. Louisiana, 391 U.S. 145, 152 (1968); U.S. ex rel. Toth v. Quarles, 350 U.S. 11, 16 n. 9 (1955).

139. Smith v. United States, 599 U.S. 236, 247 (2023); see also Sessions v. Dimaya, 584 U.S. 148, 175 (2018) (Gorsuch, J., concurring in part); United States v. Ghanem, 993 F.3d 1113, 1128 (9th Cir. 2021); Calderon v. Sessions, 330 F.Supp.3d 944, 953 n.6 (S.D.N.Y. 2018); State v. Rimmer, 877 N.W.2d 652, 665 (Iowa 2016); U.S. v. Auernheimer, 748 F.3d 525, 532 (3d Cir. 2014); U.S. v. Muhammad, 502 F.3d 646, 651 (7th Cir. 2007); U.S. v. Cabrales, 524 U.S. 1, 6 (1998); U.S. v. Busic, 549 F.2d 252, 253 (2d Cir. 1977).

140. Stern v. Marshall, 564 U.S. 462, 483–84 (2011); see also U.S. v. Hatter, 532 U.S. 557, 569 (2001).

141. Kisor v. Wilkie, 588 U.S. 558 (2019) (Gorsuch, J., concurring); Oil States Energy Services, LLC, v. Greene's Energy Group, LLC, 584 U.S. 325, 346 (2018) (Gorsuch, J., dissenting); Consumer Financial Protection Bureau v. All American Check Cashing, Inc., 33 F.4th 218, 227 (5th Cir. 2022) (Jones, J., concurring); In re Abdul-Aziz Ali, 558 F.Supp.3d 1167, 1175 n.13 (Ct. of Mil. Comm'n Review 2021); In re Renewable Energy Corp., 792 F.3d 1274, 1277–78 (10th Cir. 2015); Wellness Intern. Network, Ltd. v. Sharif, 575 U.S. 665, 689 (2015) (Roberts, C.J., dissenting); DePascale v. New Jersey, 47 A.3d 690, 696 (N.J. 2012); Lee v. State Bd. of Pension Trustees, 739 A.2d 336, 341 (Del. 1999); In re Clay, 35 F.3d 190, 191 (5th Cir. 1994); U.S. v. Will, 449 U.S. 200, 219 (1980); Pillsbury Co. v. F.T.C., 354 F.2d 952, 963 (5th Cir. 1966); O'Malley v. Woodrough, 307 U.S. 277, 284 (1939); O'Donoghue v. U.S., 289 U.S. 516, 531 (1933); Smith v. Normant, 13 Tenn. 271, 273 (Tenn. 1833).

142. State v. $2,345 in United States Currency, 220 N.E.2d 542, 550 (Ind. 2023); Jarkesy v. Securities and Exchange Comm'n, 34 F.4th 446, 451 n.2 (5th Cir. 2022); Lee v. United States, 825 F.3d 311, 314 (6th Cir. 2016); Allstate New Jersey Ins. Co. v. Lajara, 117 A.3d 1221, 1227 (N.J. 2015); Neder v. U.S., 527 U.S. 1, 30–31 (1999) (Scalia, J., concurring in part and dissenting in part); Jones v. U.S., 526 U.S. 227, 246 (1999); Adams v. U.S. ex rel. McCann, 317 U.S. 269, 276 (1942); McKeon v. Central Stamping Co., 264 F.385, 387 (3d Cir. 1920); Maxwell v. Dow, 176 U.S. 581, 609 (1900) (Harlan, J., dissenting); State v. Cutshall, 15 S.E. 261, 262 (N.C. 1892); U.S. v. New Bedford Bridge, 27 F.Cas 91, 114 (C.C.D. Mass. 1847) (No. 15,867); Bains v. The James and Catherine, 2 F.Cas. 410, 414 (C.C.D. Pa. 1832).

143. Gladon v. Greater Cleveland Reg'l Transit Auth., 662 N.E.2d 287, 308–11 (Ohio 1996) (Douglas, J., dissenting). In 1971 case, Justice Hugo Black suggested that the preclearance provisions of the 1965 Voting Rights Act offended at least four of the Declaration's charges against the king. Perkins v. Matthews, 400 U.S. 379, 407 n.7 (1971) (Black, J., dissenting). In an earlier case, he cited two of the charges to object to preclearance. South Carolina v. Katzenbach, 383 U.S. 301, 359 n.2 (1966) (Black, J., concurring and dissenting).

144. Doe2 v. Shanahan, 917 F.3d 694, 730 (D.C. Cir. 2019) (Williams, J., concurring); U.S. v. Dreyer, 804 F.3d 1266, 1282 (9th Cir. 2015) (Berzon, J., concurring); Al-Marri v. Pucciarelli, 534 F.3d 213, 251 (4th Cir. 2008) (Motz, J, concurring in the judgment); Silveira v. Lockyer, 312 F.3d 1052, 1076–77 (9th Cir. 2002); Reid v. Covert, 354 U.S. 1, 29 (1957); Ex parte Merryman, 17 F.Cas. 144, 152 n.3 (C.C.D. Md. 1861).

145. Atkinson v. Garland, 70 F.4th 1018, 1031–32 (7th Cir. 2023) (Wood, J., dissenting); Abbott v. Biden, 70 F.4th 817, 836 (5th Cir. 2023).

146. Atkinson v. Gurich, 248 P.3d 356, 360 n.22 (Okla. 2011); Solorio v. U.S., 483 U.S. 435, 459 (Marshall, J., dissenting).

147. Harris v. City of Houston, 151 F.3d 186, 191 (5th Cir. 1998) (DeMoss, J., dissenting); Bonaparte v. Nelson, 285 P.100, 115 (Okla. 1929) (Andrews, J., dissenting); Stein v. City of Mobile, 24 Ala. 591, 600 (Ala. 1854).

148. In re Desbois, 2 Mart (o.s.) 185, 194–95 (La. 1812).

149. Larrabee v. Del Toto, 45 F.4th 81, 103 (D.C. Cir. 2022) (Tatel, J., concurring in part and dissenting in part).

150. J&J Const. Co. v. Bricklayers and Allied Craftsmen, Local 1, 664 N.W.2d 728, 739 (Mich. 2003) (Young, J., concurring); Cooper v. Hindley, 126 P. 916, 919 (Wash. 1912).

151. Rossito-Canty v. Cuomo, 86 F.Supp.3d 175, 185 (E.D.N.Y. 2015). Although not directly linked to the charges against the King, a handful of opinions have emphasized the Declaration's commitment to self-government and popular consent. For example, Arizona State Legislature v. Arizona Independent Redistricting Comm'n, 576 U.S. 787, 820 (2015); Harper v. Hall, 868 S.E.2d 499, 546 (N.C. 2022); Rucho v. Common Cause, 588 U.S. 684, 726 (2019) (Kagan, J., dissenting).

152. John Adams to Abigail Adams, July 3, 1776, *Founders Online*, National Archives, https://founders.archives.gov/documents/Adams/04-02-02-0016.

153. *Pennsylvania Evening Post*, July 2, 1776. A nearly identical statement appeared in the *Pennsylvania Gazette*, July 3, 1776.

Part II Creating an American Nation

1. Beth Nguyen, "I Grew Up Not Knowing My Birthday," www.theatlantic .com/family/archive/2023/07/my-two-birthdays/674561/ (July 4, 2023).

2. Willmoore Kendall and George W. Carey, *The Basic Symbols of the American Political Tradition* (Baton Rouge, LA: Louisiana State University Press, 1970), 90.

3. Ibid., 89.

4. Garry Wills, *Inventing America: Jefferson's Declaration of Independence* (New York: Vintage, 1978), 332.

5. Joel Richard Paul, *Indivisible: Daniel Webster and the Birth of American Nationalism* (New York: Riverhead, 2022), 3.

6. Ibid., xiii.

7. Anthony J. Bellia Jr. and Bradford R. Clark, "The International Law Origins of American Federalism," *Columbia Law Review* 120 (May 2020): 838, 841. For a refutation, see David S. Schwartz, "The International Law Origins of Compact Theory: A Critique of Bellia and Clark on Federalism," *Journal of American Constitutional History* 1 (Fall 2023): 629–68. For the authors' response, see Anthony J. Bellia, Jr. and Bradford R. Clark, "Constitutional Federalism and the Nature of the Union," *William & Mary Law Review* 66, no. 2 (2024): 281–393.

8. Steven K. Green, *Inventing a Christian America: The Myth of the Religious Founding* (New York: Oxford University Pres, 2015); see also Kermit Roosevelt III, *The Nation That Never Was: Reconstructing America's Story* (Chicago: University of Chicago Press, 2022), 116 ("Before the Constitution, the states were essentially sovereign nations.").

9. Franchise Tax Board of California v. Hyatt, 587 U.S. 230, 237 (2019).

10. Board of Regents of University of Wisconsin System v. Phoenix Intern. Software, Inc., 653 F.3d 448, 471 (7th Cir. 2011).

11. In 1787, Alexander Hamilton described the United States, both under the Articles and under the proposed new Constitution, as a "confederate republic," in which the "extent, modifications and objects of the Federal authority are mere matters of discretion." Alexander Hamilton, "The Federalist No. 9," in *The Federalist Papers*, ed. Garry Wills (New York: Bantam, 1982).

12. On the continuing internal sovereignty of American Indian nations, see Seth Davis, Eric Biber, and Elena Kampf, "Persisting Sovereignties," *University of Pennsylvania Law Review* 170 (2022): 549–636.

13. Shumet Amare Zekele, "Self-determination, Secession, and Indigeneity in Ethiopia's Federation," *Social Sciences & Humanities Open* 7 (2023): 100415.

14. As early as 1774, the resolves of the First Continental Congress were being described as the "American Constitution." Mary Beth Norton, *1774: The Long Year of Revolution* (New York: Vintage, 2020), 274.

15. Jonathan Gienapp, *The Second Creation: Fixing the American Constitution in the Founding Era* (Cambridge, MA: Harvard University Press, 2018), 27, 30.

16. I differ here from scholars who have claimed that the Declaration was or is a constitution. See, for example, J.M. Balkin, "The Declaration and the Promise of a Democratic Culture," *Widener Law Symposium J.* 4 (Spring 1999): 168. The Declaration lacks many of the features of a written constitution and its purpose was to declare independence, not to constitute a government. It is more accurate to regard the period between the Declaration and the formal adoption of the Articles as one governed by an unwritten constitution.

17. Respublica v. Chapman, 1 U.S. (1 Dall.) 53, 56 (Pa. 1781).

18. Bellia and Clark, "International Law Origins," 846.
19. For scholarship advancing nationalist views of the founding, see Craig Green, "Beyond States: A Constitutional History of Territory, Statehood, and Nation-Building," *University of Chicago Law Review* 90, no. 3 (2023): 813–908; Craig Green, "United/States: A Revolutionary History of American Statehood," *Michigan Law Review* 119, no.1 (2020): 1–69; John Mikhail, "A Tale of Two Sweeping Clauses," *Harvard Journal of Law & Public Policy* 42 (2018): 29–42; Eric M. Freedman, "Why Constitutional Lawyers and Historians Should Take a Fresh Look at the Emergence of the Constitution from the Confederation Period: The Case of the Drafting of the Articles of Confederation," *Tennessee Law Review* 60, no. 4 (Summer 1993): 783–840; Eric M. Freedman, "The United States and the Articles of Confederation: Drifting toward Anarchy or Inching toward Commonwealth?," *Yale Law Journal* 88, no. 1 (Nov. 1978): 142–66; Richard B. Morris, "The Forging of the Union Reconsidered: A Historical Refutation of State Sovereignty over Seabeds," *Columbia Law Review* 74, no. 6 (Oct. 1974): 1056–93.

Chapter 4 Text

1. *Massachusetts Spy*, May 31, 1775.
2. Continental Congress, Commission to George Washington, June 19, 1775, *The Papers of George Washington, Revolutionary War Series*, ed. Philander D. Chase (Charlottesville, VA: University Press of Virginia, 1985), 1: 6–8.
3. The Declaration as Adopted by Congress, July 6, 1775, *The Papers of Thomas Jefferson*, ed. Julian P. Boyd (Princeton, NJ: Princeton University Press, 1950), 1: 213–19.
4. *Massachusetts Spy*, July 12, 1775.
5. *Pennsylvania Ledger*, Aug. 5, 1775.
6. For example, *Pennsylvania Gazette*, Feb. 28, 1776 (congressional directions to the committees of the "United Colonies" and the conventions of the "United Colonies").
7. George Washington to John Hancock, March 19, 1776, *The Papers of George Washington: Revolutionary War Series* (Charlottesville: University Press of Virginia, 1988), 3: 489–91.
8. George Washington, "Whereas the Ministerial Army ...," *N.Y. Gazette*, April 8, 1776.
9. *JCC*, 4: 215, 217 (March 20, 1776).
10. *Proceedings of the Provincial Conference of Committees, of the province of Pennsylvania* (Philadelphia: W. & T. Bradford, 1776), 30.
11. Joseph Ward to John Adams, June 20, 1776, *The Adams Papers*, ed. Robert J. Taylor (Cambridge, MA: Harvard University Press, 1979), 4: 320–21.

12. Resolutions of the Virginia Convention Calling for Independence, May 15, 1776, *The Papers of Thomas Jefferson*, ed. Julian P. Boyd (Princeton: Princeton University Press, 1950), 1: 290–91.

13. Cf. Walter Berns, *Taking the Constitution Seriously* (New York: Simon & Schuster, 1987), 79 ("Were these ties, personal as well as collective, broken when allegiance to George III was announced?").

14. Alexander Hamilton, Brief in Rutgers v. Waddington (1784), *The Law Practice of Alexander Hamilton: Documents and Commentary*, ed. Julius Goebel, Jr. (New York: Columbia University Press, 1964), 1: 349 (emphasis added).

15. See, for example, The Oxford English Dictionary Online (noting as a first definition "persons unspecified as regards number, class, or identity"), www .oed.com/dictionary/people_n?tab=meaning_and_use#31137290.

16. Cf. Eliga H. Gould, *Among the Powers of the Earth: The American Revolution and the Making of a New World Empire* (Cambridge, MA: Harvard University Press, 2012), 10 ("Americans in 1776 could and did refer to themselves as a single people, and they were sufficiently well-versed in the classics to know that this usage was an English synonym for the Latinate 'nation.'").

17. Samuel Johnson, *A Dictionary of the English Language* (London: W. Strahan, 1755), 2: 333.

18. See, for example, the claim that British troops were protected from punishment for murders committed "on the Inhabitants of these States," which would include persons not fully part of the political community, such as children or foreigners temporarily resident in the United States. The other reference is to the "merciless Indian Savages," described as the "Inhabitants of our Frontiers," and not considered part of the American political community.

19. The Constitution distinguishes the term "people," which is always used in a political sense, from the term "persons," which is applied more broadly. The Preamble famously states, "We, the People of the United States … do ordain and establish this Constitution for the United States of America." It is the "people," and only the "people," who can perform the political act of constituting a new government. Article One provides that members of the House of Representatives will be elected by the "People of the several States." By contrast, when referring to particular individuals, the Constitution refers to "Persons," such as members of Congress (the "Names of Persons" voting for and against measures are to be entered "on the Journal") and candidates for the presidency (electors shall vote for "two Persons" and shall make a "List of all the Persons voted for"). Most notoriously, the Constitution originally based representation in the House of Representatives on "the whole Number of free Persons" plus "three fifth of all other Persons," a euphemism for the enslaved population.

20. *Her Majesties Most Gracious Speech to Both Houses of Parliament, on Thursday, the Sixth Day of March, 1706* (London: Charles Bill, 1706/7), 4.

21. *Boston News-Letter*, March 22, 1708.

22. *A Speech in the Parliament of Scotland* (London: Andrew Bell, 1706), 5.
23. Daniel Williams, *A Thanks-giving Sermon, Occasioned by the Union of England and Scotland* (London: J. Humfreys, [1707?]), 5.
24. Charles Bean, *A Sermon Preach'd before the University of Oxford, on the First of May, 1707* (London: Tim Goodwin, 1707), 12.
25. *A Form of Prayer and Thanksgiving* ([Edinburgh], 1707), 6.
26. *Newport Mercury*, August 1, 1774.
27. Pauline Maier, *American Scripture: Making the Declaration of Independence* (New York: Vintage, 1997), 147.
28. For the signatures as they actually appear on the parchment copy, see Carl L. Becker, *The Declaration of Independence: A Study in the History of Political Ideas* (1922, repr., New York: Vintage, 1942), 192–93.
29. In Congress, July 4, 1776 (Baltimore: Mary Katherine Goddard, 1777).
30. This fascinating document, now called the "Sussex Declaration," has been persuasively attributed to James Wilson and the 1780s by scholars Danielle Allen and Emily Sneff. The scribe appears to have transcribed the signers' names directly from the original ceremonial parchment and did not rely on later printed versions. Danielle Allen and Emily Sneff, "The Sussex Declaration: Dating the Parchment Manuscript of the Declaration of Independence Held at the West Sussex Record Office (Chichester, UK)," *Papers of the Bibliographical Society of America* 112 no. 3 (2018): 357–403; Danielle Allen and Emily Sneff, "Golden Letters: James Wilson, the Declaration of Independence, and the Sussex Declaration," *Georgetown Journal of Law and Public Policy* 17 (2019): 193–230.
31. Benjamin Franklin to Noah Webster, Dec. 26, 1789, available at https://franklinpapers.org/framedVolumes.jsp?vol=46&page=378.
32. In four places the Dunlap Broadside fails to capitalize a noun: the word "causes" in the preamble, the word "consent" in the charges, and the words "stage" and "act" in the conclusion to the charges. "Causes," "Consent," and "Act" are capitalized elsewhere in the document, so these lapses are likely inadvertent oversights by the printer, who may have construed these words as verbs.
33. A reproduction of the resolution is in Julian P. Boyd, *The Declaration of Independence: The Evolution of the Text* (Washington, DC: Library of Congress, rev. ed. 1999), 52.
34. *Pennsylvania Ledger*, July 13, 1776; *Providence Gazette*, July 13, 1776; *Connecticut Courant*, July 15, 1776; *Connecticut Journal*, July 17, 1776; *Continental Journal* (Boston), July 18, 1776.
35. *New York Gazette*, July 15, 1776.
36. *Pennsylvania Evening Post*, July 6, 1776; *Pennsylvania Packet*, July 8, 1776; *Pennsylvania Journal* (July 10, 1776); *Constitutional Gazette* (New York), July 10, 1776; *Maryland Journal*, July 10, 1776; *New York Journal*, July 11, 1776; *Pennsylvania Gazette*, July 12, 1776; *Connecticut Gazette*, July 12, 1776; *Providence Gazette*, July 13, 1776; *Norwich Packet*, July 15, 1776; *American*

Gazette (Salem), July 16, 1776; *Massachusetts Spy*, July 17, 1776; *New-England Chronicle*, July 18, 1776; *Newport Mercury*, July 18, 1776; *Freeman's Journal* (New Hampshire), July 20, 1776; *Virginia Gazette* (Dixon & Hunter), July 20, 1776; *Virginia Gazette* (Purdie), July 26, 1776.

37. *Maryland Gazette*, July 11, 1776.

38. *Pennsylvania Evening Post*, July 6, 1776; *Pennsylvania Gazette*, July 10, 1776; *Pennsylvania Journal*, July 10, 1776; *Maryland Journal*, July 10, 1776; *New York Journal*, July 11, 1776; *Pennsylvania Ledger*, July 13, 1776; *Connecticut Courant*, July 15, 1776; *American Gazette*, July 16, 1776; *Connecticut Journal*, July 17, 1776; *Continental Journal* (Boston), July 18, 1776; *Freeman's Journal* (New Hampshire), July 20, 1776; *Virginia Gazette* (Dixon & Hunter), July 20, 1776.

39. *Constitutional Gazette* (New York), July 10, 1776; *New York Gazette*, July 15, 1776; *New-England Chronicle*, July 18, 1776; *Newport Mercury*, July 18, 1776.

40. *Pennsylvania Packet*, July 8, 1776; *Connecticut Gazette*, July 12, 1776; *Norwich Packet*, July 15, 1776; *Massachusetts Spy*, July 17, 1776; *Virginia Gazette* (Purdie), July 26, 1776.

41. *Maryland Gazette*, July 11, 1776.

42. Fliegelman, *Declaring Independence*, 108.

43. Becker, *Declaration of Independence*, 185.

44. The printed versions of the *Journals of the Continental Congress* state that Congress had directed the phrase to read "United States of America." *JCC*, 5: 590–91 (July 19, 1776). The handwritten version of the congressional resolution, possibly in Matlack's hand, is more ambiguous and could be read as "united States of America." Reproduction of Congressional Resolution, July 19, 1776, National Archives Rotunda. It is unclear how much weight should be placed on the written version, however, since it may have been offered orally, and members may have voted without seeing a written resolution.

45. Boyd, *Declaration of Independence*, 60, 63.

46. Ibid., 67, 71.

47. *Pennsylvania Packet*, July 8, 1776; *Pennsylvania Journal*, July 10, 1776; *Pennsylvania Gazette*, July 12, 1776; *New York Journal*, July 11, 1776; *Connecticut Gazette*, July 12, 1776; *Providence Gazette*, July 13, 1776; *Connecticut Courant*, July 15, 1776; *Norwich Packet*, July 15, 1776; *Connecticut Journal*, July 17, 1776; *Massachusetts Spy*, July 17, 1776; *New-England Chronicle*, July 18, 1776; *Continental Journal* (Boston), July 18, 1776; *Freeman's Journal* (New Hampshire), July 20, 1776; *Virginia Gazette* (Purdie), July 26, 1776; *Maryland Gazette*, July 9, 1776.

48. *Pennsylvania Evening Post*, July 6, 1776; *Constitutional Gazette* (New York), July 10, 1776; *New York Gazette*, July 15, 1776; *American Gazette* (Salem), July 16, 1776; *Newport Mercury*, July 18, 1776.

49. *Maryland Gazette*, July 11, 1776; *Pennsylvania Ledger*, July 13, 1776; *Virginia Gazette* (Dixon & Hunter), July 20, 1776. The *Maryland Journal* used

"UNITED STATES OF AMERICA." *Maryland Journal*, July 10, 1776. The *Pennsylvania Journal* used "United STATES of AMERICA." *Pennsylvania Journal*, July 10, 1776. The *American Gazette*'s "UUITED [sic]STATES OF AMERICA" was distinctive. *American Gazette*, July 15, 1776. One feels for the typesetter who managed to botch the country's name so badly, not just in a random document, but in the caption to the Declaration of Independence.

50. *Pennsylvania Evening Post*, July 6, 1776; *Pennsylvania Packet*, July 8, 1776; *Pennsylvania Gazette*, July 10, 1776; *Maryland Journal*, July 10, 1776; *New York Journal*, July 11, 1776; *Connecticut Gazette*, July 12, 1776; *Pennsylvania Ledger*, July 13, 1776; *Providence Gazette*, July 13, 1776; *Connecticut Courant*, July 15, 1776; *Norwich Packet*, July 15, 1776; *Connecticut Journal*, July 17, 1776; *Massachusetts Spy*, July 17, 1776; *Continental Journal* (Boston), July 18, 1776; *New-England Chronicle*, July 18, 1776; *Freeman's Journal* (New Hampshire), July 20, 1776; *Virginia Gazette* (Dixon & Hunter), July 20, 1776; *Virginia Gazette* (Purdie), July 26, 1776; *Maryland Gazette*, July 9, 1776; *American Gazette* (Salem), July 16, 1776.

51. *Constitutional Gazette* (New York), July 10, 1776; *New York Gazette*, July 15, 1776; *Newport Mercury*, July 18, 1776.

52. *Maryland Gazette*, July 11, 1776.

53. In Congress, July 4, 1776 (Baltimore: Mary Katherine Goddard, 1777); *The Constitutions of the Several Independent States of America* (Philadelphia: Francis Bailey, 1781), 187, 190.

54. Gordon S. Wood, *The Creation of the American Republic* (New York: Norton, 1972) (Orig. pub. 1969), 356; cf. Akhil Reed Amar, *America's Constitution: A Biography* (New York: Random House, 2005), 23 (relying on the parchment caption).

55. Forrest McDonald, *States' Rights and the Union: Imperium in Imperio, 1776–1876* (Lawrence, KS: University Press of Kansas, 2000), 10.

Chapter 5 History

1. Pauline Maier, *American Scripture: Making the Declaration of Independence* (New York: Vintage, 1997), 47–96.

2. Meeting of the Town of Malden, Massachusetts, May 27, 1776, in *American Archives (4th Ser.)*, ed. Peter Force (Washington, DC: M. St. Clair Clarke & Peter Force, 1843), 6: 602.

3. Resolution of the Town of Topsfield, Massachusetts, June 21, 1776, in Maier, *American Scripture*, 233–34.

4. Resolution of the Town of Palmer, Massachusetts, June 17, 1776, in *American Archives (4th Ser.)*, 6: 701–02.

5. [Moses Mather], *America's Appeal to the Impartial World* (Hartford, CT: Ebenezer Watson, 1775), 46–47.

6. Joseph Ward to John Adams, Oct. 23, 1775, *Founders Online*, National Archives, https://founders.archives.gov/documents/Adams/06-03-02-012_.

7. "To the worthy OFFICERS and SOLDIERS in the AMERICAN ARMY," *Connecticut Gazette*, Dec. 1, 1775.

8. *New England Chronicle*, Jan. 11, 1776.

9. [Thomas Paine], *Common Sense; with the Whole Appendix* (Philadelphia: Robert Bell, 1776), 51.

10. Ibid., 135.

11. Ibid., 56.

12. Committee of Secret Correspondence, Instructions to Silas Deane, March 2, 1776, *Founders Online*, National Archives, https://founders.archives.gov/documents/Franklin/01-22-02-0222.

13. William Whipple to John Langdon, May 28, 1776, in *American Archives (4th Ser)*, 6: 1023–24.

14. Resolution of New Hampshire, June 15, 1776, in *American Archives (4th Ser.)*, 6: 1030.

15. "The Interest of America, Letter II," *New York Journal*, June 13, 1776. The author continued, "America must consist of a number of confederate Provinces, Cantons, Districts, or whatever they might be called. These must be united in a General Congress."

16. *Pennsylvania Ledger*, April 6, 1776.

17. *Proceedings of the Provincial Conference of Committees, of the province of Pennsylvania* (Philadelphia: W. & T. Bradford, 1776), 25.

18. [Thomas Paine], *Pennsylvania Evening Post*, June 29, 1776. Paine's possible authorship is discussed in Peter Moore, *Life, Liberty, and the Pursuit of Happiness: Britain and the American Dream* (New York: Farrar, Straus and Giroux, 2023), 500, 542–43 n.19.

19. John Adams to Archibald Bulloch, July 1, 1776, *LDC*, 4: 345.

20. John Adams to Abigail Adams, July 3, 1776, *LDC*, 4: 374.

21. Ibid., 4: 376.

22. *JCC*, 5: 517–18 (July 4, 1776).

23. Ezra Stiles, *The Literary Diary of Ezra Stiles, D.D., Ll.D.*, ed. Franklin Bowditch Dexter (New York: Charles Scribner's Sons, 1901), 2: 21.

24. *Pennsylvania Evening Post*, Aug. 15, 1776.

25. Account of Savannah, Georgia, Aug. 10, 1776, in *American Archives (5th Ser.)*, ed. Peter Force (Washington, DC: M. St. Clair Clarke & Peter Force, 1848), 1: 882.

26. William Henry Drayton, *A Charge, on the Rise of the American Empire* (Charleston, SC: David Bruce, 1776), 10.

27. John Witherspoon's Speech in Congress, July 30, 1776, *LDC*, 4: 584.

28. John Adams, Notes of Debates on the Articles of Confederation, Aug. 1, 1776, in *The Adams Papers: Diary and Autobiography of John Adams*, ed. L.H. Butterfield (Cambridge, MA: Harvard University Press, 1962), 2: 247–48.

29. For example, Akhil Reed Amar, "Of Sovereignty and Federalism," *Yale Law Journal* 96 (1987): 1447 ("The very word chosen to describe the central assembly, 'Congress,' suggested its inter-sovereign character."). In 1787, ten years after he left Congress, John Adams described the body as "not a legislative assembly, nor a representative assembly, but only a diplomatic assembly." John Adams, *A Defence of the Constitutions of Government of the United States of America* (London: C. Dilly, 1787), 362–63. Adams offered no support for this bald assertion, and it is inconsistent with how Congress actually functioned. In a 1788 dispute over the confiscation of Loyalist property, Jared Ingersoll, who served in the Continental Congress from 1780 to 1781, explicitly refuted Adams's claim, stating, "the Congress are not, as Mr. Adams has termed them, an Assemblage of Ambassadors; but a sovereign power, and capable of suing like a corporation." Camp v. Lackwood, 1 U.S. (1 Dall.) 393, 398 (Pa. Ct. Common Pleas 1788).

30. Abner L. Braley, "Provisional Government of Massachusetts," in *Commonwealth History of Massachusetts*, ed. Albert Bushnell Hart (New York: States History Co., 1929), 3: 65.

31. Lindley S. Butler, "Provincial Congresses," www.ncpedia.org/provincial-congresses.

32. *Journals of the Provincial Congress, Provincial Convention, Committee of Safety and Council of Safety of the State of New-York* (Albany, NY: Thurlow Weed, 1842), 1: 7–368; 435–513.

33. *Extracts from the Journal of Proceedings of the Provincial Congress of New Jersey* (Burlington, NJ: Isaac Collins, 1775); *Journal of the Votes and Proceedings of the Provincial Congress of New Jersey* (Burlington, NJ: Isaac Collins, 1776).

34. Constitution of New Hampshire (1776), available at https://avalon.law.yale.edu/18th_century/nh09.asp.

35. Constitution of South Carolina (1776), available at https://avalon.law.yale.edu/18th_century/sc01.asp

36. Constitution of New Jersey (1776), available at https://avalon.law.yale.edu/18th_century/nj15.asp.

37. *JCC*, 5: 425 (June 7, 1776).

38. John Adams to Patrick Henry, June 3, 1776, *LDC*, 4: 122.

39. *JCC*, 5: 431, 433 (June 11, 12, 1776).

40. *JCC*, 5: 433 (June 12, 1776).

41. *JCC*, 5: 546 (July 12, 1776). Benjamin Franklin created a draft "Articles of Confederation and Perpetual Union" in 1775, but it was never acted upon directly by the Continental Congress. Eli Merritt, *Disunion among Ourselves: The Perilous Politics of the American Revolution* (Columbia, MO: University of Missouri Press, 2023), 80–83, 95–97; David C. Hendrickson, *Peace Pact: The Lost World of the American Founding* (Lawrence, KS: University Press of Kansas, 2003), 118–21.

42. For an analysis of this draft, see Hendrickson, *Peace Pact*, 127–37.

43. Cf. Robert W. Hoffert, *A Politics of Tensions: The Articles of Confederation and American Political Ideas* (Niwot, CO: University Press of Colorado, 1992), 41 ("There is little doubt that supporters of the Articles took perpetual union as seriously as state sovereignty.").

44. John Witherspoon's Speech in Congress, July 30, 1776, *LDC*, 4: 587.

45. Union of Utrecht, 1579, quoted in Murray Forsyth, *Unions of States: The Theory and Practice of Confederation* (New York: Leicester University Press, Holmes & Meier Publishers, 1981), 32.

46. Ibid., 34. For an argument that the American Declaration was modeled in part on the Dutch declaration of independence, see Stephen E. Lucas, "The Rhetorical Ancestry of the Declaration of Independence," *Rhetoric and Public Affairs* 1, no. 2 (Summer 1998): 159–69.

47. Samuel von Pufendorf, *Of the Law of Nature and Nations*, trans. Basil Kennett (London: J. Walthoe, 1729) (1672), 683.

48. *JCC*, 5: 546–47.

49. *JCC*, 5: 547–49.

50. *JCC*, 5: 550–52.

51. Gouverneur Morris to Sir Henry Clinton, Oct. 20, 1778, in *To Secure the Blessings of Liberty: Selected Writings of Gouverneur Morris*, ed. J. Jackson Barlow (Indianapolis, IN: Liberty Fund, 2012), 50. On Morris's nationalist views, see Jonathan Gienapp, "Representing the Nation: Gouverneur Morris's Nationalist Constitutionalism," *Georgetown Journal of Law & Public Policy* 21, no. 1 (Winter 2023): 67–102.

52. Thomas Jefferson's Notes of Proceedings in Congress, July 12–August 1, 1776, *LDC*, 4: 443.

53. Ibid., 444.

54. Merritt, *Disunion among Ourselves*, 139–42.

55. *JCC*, 5: 674–89 (Aug. 20, 1776); Jack N. Rakove, *The Beginnings of National Politics: An Interpretative History of the Continental Congress* (Baltimore: Johns Hopkins University Press, 1979), 159–60.

56. Merritt, *Disunion among Ourselves*, 147–48.

57. *JCC*, 9: 915–21.

58. John Adams to the Comte de Vergennes, July 21, 1781, *Founders Online*, National Archives, https://founders.archives.gov/documents/Adams/06-11-02-0321.

59. Alexander Hamilton, "A Letter from Phocion to the Considerate Citizens of New York, [1–27 January 1784]," *Founders Online*, National Archives, https://founders.archives.gov/documents/Hamilton/01-03-02-0314.

60. [Benjamin Rush], "To the People of the United States," *New York Packet*, June 15, 1786.

61. James Madison, "The Federalist #40," in *The Federalist Papers*, ed. Garry Wills (New York: Bantam, 1982), 198. These powers also undermine a recent claim that states first surrendered the "sovereign right to exercise

exclusive governmental authority (free from interference from another sovereign) over persons and things within their territory" with the adoption of the Constitution. Anthony J. Bellia, Jr. and Bradford R. Clark, "Constitutional Federalism and the Nature of the Union," *William & Mary Law Review* 66, no. 2 (2024): 294. In all of these ways the Confederation government operated directly on persons and things within individual states.

62. *JCC*, 9: 908–25.
63. William Henry Drayton, *The Speech of the Hon. William Henry Drayton, Esquire, Chief Justice of South-Carolina* (Charleston, SC: David Bruce, 1778), 4–5.
64. Rakove, *Beginnings of National Politics*, xvi.
65. Ibid., 184–85. Cf. Jack N. Rakove, "American Federalism: Was There an Original Understanding," in *The Tenth Amendment and State Sovereignty: Constitutional History and Contemporary Issues*, ed. Mark R. Killenbeck (Lanham, CO: Rowman & Littlefield, 2002), 112 ("[The states] were manifestly not sovereign when it came to other equally important aspects of governance that contemporaries would have associated with the powers of a nation-state.").
66. *JCC*, 9: 932–34 (Nov. 17, 1777).
67. Benjamin H. Irvin, *Clothed in Robes of Sovereignty: The Continental Congress and the People Out of Doors* (New York: Oxford University Press, 2011), 177.
68. George Washington to Jean de Heintz, Jan. 21, 1784, *The Papers of George Washington (Confederation Series)*, ed. W.W. Abbot (Charlottesville, VA: University of Virginia Press, 1992), 1: 67.
69. James Wilson, *Considerations on the Bank of North-America* (Philadelphia: Hall & Sellers, 1785), 3.
70. *JCC*, 9: 908.
71. Thomas Burke to Richard Caswell, April 29, 1777, *LDC*, 6: 672.
72. Hendrickson, *Peace Pact*, 134.
73. Rakove, *Beginnings of National Politics*, 164, 171. For an argument that Burke's amendment was significant, see Aaron M. Coleman, *The American Revolution, State Sovereignty, and the American Constitutional Settlement, 1765–1800* (Lanham, MD: Lexington Books, 2016), 43–46.
74. Gordon S. Wood, *The Creation of the American Republic, 1776–1787* (New York: Norton, 1972) (Orig. pub. 1969), 354; Rakove, *Beginnings of National Politics*, 185.
75. Thomas Burke, Notes on the Articles of Confederation, c. Dec. 18, 1777, *LDC*, 8: 435.
76. *JCC*, 7: 135–36 n.1 (Feb. 20, 1777).
77. *Pennsylvania Gazette*, March 7, 1781.
78. Richard P. McCormick, "Ambiguous Authority: The Ordinances of the Confederation Congress, 1781–1789," *American Journal of Legal History* 41 (1997): 411, 415.

79. Gordon S. Wood, *Empire of Liberty: A History of the Early Republic, 1789–1815* (New York: Oxford University Press, 2009), 7; cf. Eliga H. Gould, *Among the Powers of the Earth: The American Revolution and the Making of a New World Empire* (Cambridge, MA: Harvard University Press, 2012), 10 (under the Articles the "United States was not so much a nation as a perpetual league or treaty between independent states").

80. Akhil Reed Amar, "Of Sovereignty and Federalism," *Yale Law Journal* 96, no. 7 (1987): 1448.

81. Gregory E. Maggs, "A Concise Guide to the Articles of Confederation as a Source for Determining the Original Meaning of the Constitution," *George Washington Law Review* 85 (2017): 403. In his book, *The Words that Made Us*, Akhil Reed Amar compared the Articles to NATO, the EU, and the UN, but also suggested that the Declaration created a "legal nation-state on the world stage." Akhil Reed Amar, *The Words that Made Us: America's Constitutional Conversation, 1760–1840* (New York: Basic Books, 2021), 735 n.33, 123–24.

82. Peter S. Onuf, *The Origins of the Federal Republic: Jurisdictional Controversies in the United States, 1775–1787* (Philadelphia: University of Pennsylvania Press, 1983), 3.

83. Ibid., 7.

84. Jerrilyn Greene Marston, *King and Congress: The Transfer of Political Legitimacy, 1774–1776* (Princeton, NJ: Princeton University Press, 1987), 149, 210, 230.

85. *JCC*, 3: 404 (Dec. 4, 1775).

86. Maier, *American Scripture*, 14; cf. Richard B. Morris, *The Forging of the Union, 1781–1789* (New York: Harper & Row, 1983), 55 ("A review of the evidence makes it clear that a national government was in operation before the formation of the states.").

87. Rakove, *Beginnings of National Politics*, 89. As Rakove further explains, "A reconstruction of the precedents, events, and atmosphere of 1774–76 does not validate a states'-rightist interpretation of the origins of the union. In addition to congressional prerogatives over war and diplomacy, the procedures used to authorize the creation of new governments in 1775–76 clearly demonstrate that sovereign powers were vested in Congress from the start and that the emerging provincial regimes were regarded as subordinate bodies." Ibid., 173–74 ★.

88. Marston, *King and Congress*, 224.

89. Ibid., 227.

90. *JCC*, 33: 458 (Aug. 3, 1787).

91. Edmund Cody Burnett, *The Continental Congress* (New York: Norton, 1941), 502.

92. Cf. Marston, *King and Congress*, 250 (prior to independence "Congress was performing enough of those functions with sufficient success to enable Americans to view it as a legitimate de facto continental government").

93. Morris, *Forging of the Union*, 76.
94. Craig Green, "United/States: A Revolutionary History of American Statehood," *Michigan Law Review* 119, no. 1 (2020): 17–22.
95. Constitution of New Hampshire (1776), available at https://avalon.law.yale.edu/18th_century/nh09.asp.
96. Constitution of South Carolina (1776), available at https://avalon.law.yale.edu/18th_century/sc01.asp.
97. *JCC*, 4: 342 (May 10, 1776).
98. *JCC*, 4: 358 (May 15, 1776).
99. John Adams, *Diary and Autobiography of John Adams*, ed. L. H. Butterfield (Cambridge, MA: Harvard University Press, 1961), 3: 335.
100. Onuf, *Origins of the Federal Republic*, 31–32; cf. Green, "United/States," 26 ("Even documents that are assumed to be state-centric, from a supposedly state-centric historical period, do not reveal state authority as something antecedent or normatively superior to interstate authority. States and the United States were bound together from the start."); see also Morris, *Forging of the Union*, 59.
101. Martin Flaherty, "Peerless History, Meaningless Origins," *Journal of American Constitutional History* 1 (2023): 706.
102. Morris, *Forging the Union*, 60; Curtis Putnam Nettels, "The Origins of the Union and of the States," *Proceedings of the Massachusetts Historical Society* 72 (1957–1960), 76–77.
103. Morris, *Forging the Union*, 63.
104. *JCC*, 5: 768–78 (Sept. 17, 1776).
105. Treaty of Alliance, 1778, https://avalon.law.yale.edu/18th_century/fr1788-2.asp (emphasis added).
106. *Pennsylvania Packet*, Aug. 11, 1778.
107. William Ellery to Nicholas Cooke, *LDC*, 6: 282–83 (Feb. 15, 1777); *JCC*, 7: 121 (Feb. 14, 1777). On this debate, see Rakove, *Beginnings of National Politics*, 165–66.
108. Benjamin Rush's Notes of Debates, *LDC*, 6: 217–18 (Feb. 4, 1777).
109. Ibid.
110. Ibid.
111. Ibid.
112. The leading scholarly account is Henry J. Bourguignon, *The First Federal Court: The Federal Appellate Prize Court of the American Revolution, 1775–1787* (Philadelphia: American Philosophical Society, 1977).
113. *JCC*, 3: 371–75 (Nov. 25, 1775).
114. Bourguignon, *First Federal Court*, 48.
115. Ibid., 78–81.
116. *JCC*, 5: 747 (Sept. 9, 1776).
117. Bourguignon, *First Federal Court*, 81.
118. Ibid., 85; *JCC*, 7: 75 (Jan. 30, 1777).

119. For an overview, see Bourguignon, *First Federal Court*, 101–11.

120. *JCC*, 13: 97, 134–37 (Jan. 21, 1779; Feb. 2, 1779).

121. *JCC*, 13: 281–85 (March 5, 1779).

122. Bourguignon, *First Federal Court*, 91; *JCC*, 16: 61–64 (Jan. 15, 1780). The court was given its formal name in May 1780. *JCC*, 17: 458 (May 24, 1780).

123. Bourguignon, *First Federal Court*, 116.

124. Ibid., 121, 217. On early admiralty jurisdiction under the Constitution, see Kevin Arlyck, *The Nation at Sea: The Federal Courts and American Sovereignty, 1789–1825* (Cambridge: Cambridge University Press, 2025).

125. *JCC*, 15: 1051–52 (Sept. 13, 1779).

126. Ibid., 1058–59.

127. Thomas Burke to General Assembly of North Carolina, Oct. 31, 1779, *LDC*, 14: 119 n. 19.

128. *Pennsylvania Gazette*, Feb. 9, 1780.

129. John Jay to Comte de Vergennes, c. Sept. 11, 1782, *Founders Online*, National Archives, https://founders.archives.gov/documents/Jay/01-03-02-0043.

130. John Adams, "Memorial to their High-Mightinesses, the States-General of the United Provinces of the Low Countries," April 19, 1781, in John Adams, *A Collection of State Papers* (The Hague: 1782), 4, 11.

131. Alexander Hamilton, Brief in Rutgers v. Waddington (1784), *The Law Practice of Alexander Hamilton: Documents and Commentary*, ed. Julius Goebel, Jr. (New York: Columbia University Press, 1964), 1: 374.

132. Ibid.

133. Ibid., 379.

134. Ibid., 374.

135. Alexander Hamilton, Remarks on an Act Granting to Congress Certain Imposts and Duties, Feb. 15, 1787, *Founders Online*, National Archives, https://founders.archives.gov/documents/Hamilton/01-04-02-0030.

136. Ibid.

137. Shawn David McGhee, *No Longer Subjects of the British King: The Political Transformation of Royal Subjects to Republican Citizens, 1774–1776* (Yardley, PA: Westholme, 2024), 93–128; Carlton F.W. Larson, *The Trials of Allegiance: Treason, Juries, and the American Revolution* (New York: Oxford University Press, 2019), 37–41.

138. The General Committee to the Lancaster Committee, Oct. 19, 1775, *Pennsylvania Archives* (2d Ser.), 13: 503–04. On these charges, see Larson, *Trials of Allegiance*, 45–49.

139. Minutes of the Pennsylvania Committee of Safety, Jan. 3, 1776, *Colonial Records of Pennsylvania*, 10: 444–45. On these charges, see Larson, *Trials of Allegiance*, 49–51.

140. Arrest Warrant from a Secret Committee of the New York Provincial Congress, June 21, 1776, *The Papers of George Washington: Revolutionary*

War Series, ed. Philander D. Chase (Charlottesville, VA: University Press of Virginia, 1993), 5: 72–74.

141. Minutes of the Council of Safety, Nov. 22, 1776, & Dec. 22, 1776, *Colonial Records of Pennsylvania*, 11: 12, 59. On these charges, see Larson, *Trials of Allegiance*, 65.

142. Quoted in John Spargo, *David Redding: Queen's Ranger* (Bennington, VT: Bennington Historical Museum and Art Gallery, 1945), 49.

143. *JCC*, 5: 475 (June 24, 1776).

144. Act of Feb. 11, 1777, ch. 740, Pa. Stat., 9: 46.

145. "We the Subscribers," broadside (1775), Early American Imprints no. 14247.

146. Larson, *Trials of Allegiance*, 65.

147. *Pennsylvania Packet*, July 29, 1776.

148. For example, *JCC*, 7: 258 (April 12, 1777); see also Morris, *Forging of the Union*, 74–75.

149. George Washington, Proclamation concerning Persons Swearing British Allegiance, Jan. 25, 1777, *Founders Online*, National Archives, https://found ers.archives.gov/documents/Washington/03-08-02-0160.

150. Max Farrand, *The Records of the Federal Convention of 1787* (New Haven, CT: Yale University Press, 1911), 1: 324.

151. Ibid., 1: 324. For an argument that Wilson read the Declaration directly from a ceremonial parchment that he had commissioned (one that followed the Dunlap Broadside and the original ceremonial parchment in not naming any states), see Danielle Allen and Emily Sneff, "Golden Letters: James Wilson, the Declaration of Independence, and the Sussex Declaration," *Georgetown Journal of Law & Public Policy* 17 (2019): 193–230.

152. Farrand, *Records of the Federal Convention*, 1: 166.

153. Wilson, *Considerations on the Bank of North-America*, 10. For an excellent analysis of Wilson's understanding of the Declaration of Independence as it relates to the Constitution, see William Ewald, "James Wilson and the American Founding," *Georgetown Journal of Law & Public Policy* 17 (2019): 1–21. On Wilson and the Bank of North America, see John Mikhail, "A Tale of Two Sweeping Clauses," *Harvard Journal of Law & Public Policy* 42 (2018): 35–39.

154. Farrand, *Records of the Federal Convention*, 1: 324.

155. Ibid., 1: 323–24.

156. Ibid., 1: 467.

157. James Wilson, Address in the Pennsylvania Convention, Dec. 4, 1787, in *The Documentary History of the Ratification of the Constitution*, ed. Merrill Jensen (Madison, WI: State Historical Society of Wisconsin, 1976), 2: 472.

158. South Carolina House of Representatives Debates, Jan. 18, 1788, in *The Documentary History of the Ratification of the Constitution*, ed. John P. Kaminski et al. (Madison, WI: State Historical Society of Wisconsin, 2016), 27: 145–46.

159. [John Jay], *The Federalist No. 2*, in *The Federalist Papers*, ed. Garry Wills (New York: Bantam, 1982), 7.

160. [James Madison], *The Federalist No. 45*, in ibid., 233

161. James Madison to Thomas Jefferson, Feb. 8, 1825, *Founders Online*, National Archives, https://founders.archives.gov/documents/Madison/04-03-02-0470.

162. [Tench Coxe], "On the Federal Government. No. 1," *Independent Gazetteer*, Sept. 26, 1787.

163. A Jerseyman, "To the Citizens of New Jersey," *Trenton Mercury*, Nov. 6, 1787, in *The Documentary History of the Ratification of the Constitution*, ed. Merrill Jensen (Madison, WI: State Historical Society of Wisconsin, 1978), 3: 146.

164. Ibid., 150.

165. David Ramsay, *The History of the American Revolution* (Philadelphia: R. Aitken & Son, 1789), 1: 357.

166. *Gazette of the United States*, April 16, 1791, in *Documentary History of the First Federal Congress of the United States of America* (Baltimore: Johns Hopkins University Press, 1995), 14: 472.

167. John P. Kaminski, "Rhode Island: Protecting State Interests," in *Ratifying the Constitution*, ed. Michael Allen Gillespie and Michael Lienesch (Lawrence, KS: University Press of Kansas, 1989), 381 (quoting Providence Town Records).

168. James Iredell to Hannah Iredell, Aug. 3, 1788, quoted in Willis P. Whicard, *Justice James Iredell* (Durham, NC: Carolina Academic Press, 2000), 78; see also John Wilson to Samuel Wilson, Aug. 18, 1788, *Documentary History of the Ratification of the Constitution*, 31: 501 ("the state of No. Carolina is out of the Union"); A Citizen of North Carolina, "To the People of North Carolina," Aug. 18, 1788, *Documentary History of the Ratification of the Constitution*, 31: 505 ("We are now not only independent of all other nations in the world, but entirely independent of the other states, except for our share of the debt hitherto incurred, which we are now utterly unable to pay.").

169. Pauline Maier, *Ratification: The People Debate the Constitution, 1787–1788.* (New York: Simon & Schuster, 2010), 313.

170. Act of July 31, 1789, §§ 38–39, 1 Stat. 29, 48.

171. William S. Powell, *North Carolina Through Four Centuries* (Chapel Hill, NC: University of North Carolina Press, 1989), 228.

172. Act of Sept. 16, 1789, § 2, 1 Stat. 69.

173. Act of Feb. 8, 1790, § 7, 1 Stat. 99, 100–01.

174. Maier, *Ratification*, 458.

175. Kaminski, "Rhode Island," 368, 385. The text of the bill was published in the *Connecticut Courant*, May 24, 1790.

176. Maier, *Ratification*, 223.

177. Convention Debates, Aug. 2, 1788, *Documentary History of the Ratification of the Constitution* (Madison WI: Wisconsin Historical Society Press, 2019), 30: 470.

178. Maier, *Ratification*, 423.
179. Thomas Jefferson to Alexander Donald, Feb. 7, 1788, *Founders Online*, National Archives, https://founders.archives.gov/documents/Jefferson/01-12-02-0602.
180. Maier, *Ratification*, 423.
181. Convention Debates, July 31, 1788, *Documentary History of the Ratification of the Constitution*, 30: 442.
182. Convention Debates, Aug. 2, 1788, *Documentary History of the Ratification of the Constitution*, 30: 470.
183. North Carolina Governor and Council, Address to President George Washington, May 10, 1789, *Documentary History of the Ratification of the Constitution*, 31: 643.
184. For other views, although focused more on 1787, see Jud Campbell, "Four Views of the Nature of the Union," *Harvard Journal of Law & Public Policy* 47 (2024): 13–37.
185. New York Trust Co. v. Eisner, 256 U.S. 345, 349 (1921).

Chapter 6 Memory

1. United States v. Jackson, 661 F.Supp.3d 392, 407 (D. Md. 2023); see also Noem v. Halland, 542 F.Supp.3d 898, 907 (D.S.D. 2001) ("The Fourth of July … commemorates the signing of the Declaration of Independence.").
2. Wilson v. Superior Court, 185 Cal.Rptr. 678, 697 (Cal. Ct. App. 1982).
3. Wuebker v. James, 58 N.Y.S.2d 671, 675 (N.Y. Cty. Ct. 1944).
4. For an overview of federalism decisions more generally in the period prior to the Civil War, see Alison L. LaCroix, *The Interbellum Constitution: Union, Commerce, and Slavery in the Age of Federalisms* (New Haven, CT: Yale University Press, 2024).
5. Camp v. Lockwood, 1 U.S. (1 Dall.) 393, 401 (Pa. Ct. Common Pleas 1788).
6. Ibid., 403.
7. Chisholm v. Georgia, 2 U.S. (2 Dall.) 419 (1793).
8. Ibid., 470.
9. Ibid., 474.
10. See Chapter 5.
11. *The Documentary History of the Supreme Court of the United States, 1789–1800*, ed. Maeva Marcus (New York: Columbia University Press, 1998), 6: 394.
12. Penhallow v. Doane's Administrators, 3 U.S. (3 Dall.) 54, 67–68 (1795) (argument of plaintiffs in error). The sole citation for this point was John Adams's 1787 assertion in his *Defence of the Constitutions of the United States*. See Chapter 5, n.29.
13. Ibid., 71.

14. William Tilghman's Notes of Arguments in the Supreme Court, Feb. 10, 1795, in *Documentary History of the Supreme Court*, 6: 454.
15. *Penhallow*, 74–76 (argument of defendants in error).
16. William Paterson's Notes of Arguments in the Supreme Court, Feb. 9, 1795, in *Documentary History of the Supreme Court*, 6: 440.
17. *Documentary History of the Supreme Court*, 6: 394.
18. *Penhallow*, 116 (opinion of Cushing, J.).
19. Ibid., 80–82 (opinion of Paterson, J.).
20. Ibid., 91–96 (opinion of Iredell, J.).
21. Ibid., 111–13 (opinion of Blair, J.).
22. *New Hampshire Gazette*, Feb. 5, 1795, 1.
23. Jeremiah Smith to William Plumer, Feb. 24, 1795, *Documentary History of the Supreme Court*, 6: 486.
24. *New Hampshire Gazette*, May 26, 1795, 3.
25. United States v. Peters, 9 U.S. (5 Cranch) 115, 140 (1809).
26. Ware v. Hylton, 3 U.S. (3 Dall.) 199, 224 (1796) (opinion of Chase, J.).
27. Ibid., 232. A similar dynamic can be found in the oral argument of John Marshall, who contended both that Virginia "was an independent nation" and that "America, in her own tribunals at least, must from the 4th of July 1776, [be] considered as independent a nation as Great Britain." Ibid., 210–11 (argument of John Marshall). Attorney William Lewis argued, "The war was waged against all America, as one nation, or community; and the peace was concluded on the same principles." Ibid., 219 (argument of William Lewis).
28. Ibid.
29. St. George Tucker, *Blackstone's Commentaries: With Notes of Reference to the Constitution and Laws of the Federal Government of the United States; and of the Commonwealth of Virginia* (Philadelphia: William Young Birch & Abraham Small, 1803), app. 54.
30. Trezevant v. Osborn's Estate, 1 Tread. 61, 64 (S.C. Const. Ct. App. 1812) (opinion of Brevard, J.).
31. M'Ilvaine v. Coxe's Lessee, 6 U.S. (2 Cranch) 280, 293 (argument of William Rawle).
32. Kilham v. Ward, 2 Mass. 236, 256 (1806) (argument of Nathan Dane).
33. Nathan Dane, *General Abridgment and Digest of American Law* (Boston: Hilliard, Gray, Little, and Wilkins, 1829), 9: 24 (appendix).
34. United States v. Curtiss-Wright Export Corp., 299 U.S. 304, 311–13 (1936).
35. Ibid., 315–17. Sutherland had articulated very similar ideas as a United States senator in 1909. David M. Levitan, "The Foreign Relations Power: An Analysis of Mr. Justice Sutherland's Theory," *Yale Law Journal* 55, no. 3 (1946), 473–76. A 1960 U.S. District Court decision stated, "When the Colonies achieved their independence, each one took the prerogatives which had belonged to the Crown. ... Such powers and duties were in the people of

the individual states from the Declaration of Independence to the enactment of the Constitution." Anderson v. Gladden, 188 F.Supp. 666, 670 (D. Oregon 1960). This is directly contrary to *Curtiss-Wright*, which the court did not cite.

36. For a thoughtful argument along these lines, see Michael D. Ramsay, "The Myth of Extraconstitutional Foreign Affairs Power, *William & Mary Law Review* 42 (2000): 379–446; see also Charles A. Lofgren, "United States v. Curtiss-Wright Export Corporation: An Historical Reassessment," *Yale Law Journal* 83 (Nov. 1973): 1–32.

37. For a measured defense of *Curtiss-Wright*, see Curtis A. Bradley, "Sovereign Power Constitutionalism," *University of Chicago Law Review* 92, no. 7 (2025): 1807–84.

38. For similar decisions, see State ex rel. Mills v. Dixon, 213 P. 227, 230 (Mont. 1923) ("[A]lthough the states of the Union were called sovereign and independent states under the Declaration of Independence, they were never in their individual capacity strictly so, because they were always, in respect to some of the higher powers of sovereignty, subject to the control of a common authority, and were never separately recognized or known as members of the family of nations."); Maynard v. Newman, 1 Nev. 271, 273 (Nev. 1865) ("The inauguration of resistance, the organization of armies, the declaration of independence, the sending of commissioners abroad to seek foreign aid, were all the acts of Congress – a body of deputies elected or appointed by the separate states or municipalities, but still acting for the whole body of States as one nation or one people. No one of the colonies, so far as we are aware, ever declared its independence of the mother country. That act was the joint act of all."); Oneida Indian Nation of New York v. State of New York, 691 F.2d 1070, 1088 (2d Cir. 1982) ("[B]eginning with the Declaration of Independence and the formation of the Continental Congress the member states had no more power to make war or enter into treaties of peace or alliance than they had had as colonies under the British Crown. The Articles of Confederation appear merely to have confirmed, rather than to have originated, Congress' peace-treating power.").

For a rare judicial decision squarely stating that the Declaration created thirteen independent nations, see George v. Pierce, 148 N.Y.S. 230, 235 (N.Y. Sup. Ct. 1914) ("Upon the adoption of the Declaration of Independence New York became a nation, and, with other sovereign rights, the protectorate over the Onondagas, the fee of their lands, and this right of pre-emption devolved upon it as the successor of the crown."). In 1856, a justice of the Ohio Supreme Court claimed in a dissenting opinion that the United States Supreme Court had no power to review decisions of state courts, a position contrary to decades of precedent. He argued, "Originally each state of the American Union was, in the language of the declaration of independence, 'free and independent,' possessing all the powers and supremacy of a separate and distinct nation of people." Piqua Branch of the State Bank of Ohio v. Knoup, 6 Ohio St. 342, 394 (Ohio 1856) (Bartley, C.J., dissenting).

39. United States v. California, 332 U.S. 19 (1947); United States v. Louisiana, 339 U.S. 699 (1950); United States v. Texas, 339 U.S. 707 (1950); United States v. Maine, 420 U.S. 515 (1975).

40. *California*, 31–34.

41. Andrew Jackson, Proclamation, Dec. 10, 1832, 11 Stat. 773.

42. Ibid., 777.

43. R. Kent Newmyer, *Supreme Court Justice Joseph Story: Statesman of the Old Republic* (Chapel Hill, NC: University of North Carolina Press, 1985), 176.

44. On Story generally, see ibid. On the reception of the *Commentaries*, see ibid., 192–93.

45. Joseph Story, *Commentaries on the Constitution of the United States* (Boston: Hilliard, Gray, 1833), 1: 186.

46. Ibid., 198–99.

47. Ibid., 202.

48. Ibid.

49. Ibid., 203. On Story's nationalist views, see Benjamin Clark, *Contending for American Nationhood: Joseph Story and the Debate over a Federal Common Law* (Lanham, MD: Lexington, 2024), 87–134. See also James Kent, *Commentaries on American Law* (New York: G. Halsted, 1826), 1: 1 ("When the United States ceased to be a part of the British empire, [it] assumed the character of an independent nation.").

50. Robert V. Remini, *Daniel Webster: The Man and His Time* (New York: Norton, 1997), 208.

51. [Joseph Story], "Statemen – Their Rareness and Importance: Daniel Webster," *The New-England Magazine* 7 (Aug. 1834): 103.

52. Daniel Webster, "The Constitution Not a Compact between Sovereign States," in *The Great Speeches and Orations of Daniel Webster*, ed. Edwin P. Whipple (Boston: Little, Brown, 1895), 276–77.

53. James Madison to Daniel Webster, March 15, 1833, *Founders Online*, National Archives, https://founders.archives.gov/documents/Madison/99-02-02-2705.

54. Abraham Lincoln, "Speech in Independence Hall," Feb. 22, 1861, in *The Collected Works of Abraham Lincoln*, ed. Roy P. Basler (New Brunswick, NJ: Rutgers University Press, 1953), 4: 240.

55. Abraham Lincoln, First Inaugural Address, March 4, 1861, in ibid., 4: 253.

56. Abraham Lincoln, Message to Congress in Special Session, July 4, 1861, in ibid., 4: 433–34.

57. Len Travers, *Celebrating the Fourth: Independence Day and the Rites of Nationalism in the Early Republic* (Amherst, MA: University of Massachusetts Press, 1997), 17–20.

58. *Pennsylvania Evening Post*, July 5, 1777.

59. Ibid. On the celebrations in Philadelphia, see Benjamin H. Irvin, *Clothed in Robes of Sovereignty: The Continental Congress and the People Out of Doors* (New York: Oxford University Press, 2011), 142–52.

60. William Williams to Jonathan Trumbull, July 5, 1777, *LDC*, 7: 303.
61. Irvin, *Clothed in Robes of Sovereignty*, 159–61.
62. *Pennsylvania Gazette*, June 13, 1778.
63. Irvin, *Clothed in Robes of Sovereignty*, 163–64.
64. *Columbian Herald*, July 10, 1786.
65. *Providence Gazette*, July 14, 1787.
66. *Pennsylvania Evening Herald*, July 14, 1787.
67. *New York Packet*, July 4, 1788.
68. "The Day!," *Gazette of the United States*, July 4, 1789.
69. David Ramsay, *The History of the American Revolution* (Philadelphia: R. Aitken & Son, 1789), 1: 341, 346.
70. *Massachusetts Centinel*, June 12, 1790.
71. *The Mail; or Claypoole's Daily Advertiser*, July 1, 1791.
72. *Massachusetts Spy*, July 7, 1791.
73. *Gazette of the United States*, July 9, 1791.
74. *Daily Advertiser*, July 7, 1791.
75. "Independence Anniversary," *New-York Journal*, July 4, 1792.
76. *Dunlap's Daily Advertiser*, Aug. 1, 1794.
77. Remini, *Daniel Webster*, 51–52.
78. *Connecticut Journal*, July 9, 1788; *New-York Daily Gazette*, July 2, 1791; *General Advertiser*, July 8, 1793; Travers, *Celebrating the Fourth*, 158, 206.
79. John Quincy Adams, *An Address Delivered at the Request of a Committee of the Citizens of Washington; on the Occasion of Reading the Declaration of Independence, on the Fourth of July, 1821* (Washington, DC: Davis & Force, 1821), 21–22.
80. Ibid., 28.
81. See generally Andrew Burstein, *America's Jubilee* (New York: Vintage, 2001), 255–86.
82. Michael D. Hattem, *The Memory of '76: The Revolution in American History* (New Haven, CT: Yale University Press, 2024), 52.
83. Travers, *Celebrating the Fourth*, 220.
84. Thomas Jefferson to Ellen Wayles Randolph Coolidge, Nov. 14, 1825, *Founders Online*, National Archives, https://founders.archives.gov/documents/Jefferson/98-01-02-5659; Thomas Jefferson to James Madison, August 23, 1823, *Founders Online*, National Archives, https://founders.archives.gov/documents/Jefferson/98-01-02-3728.
85. Thomas Jefferson to James Monroe, Oct. 24, 1823, *Founders Online*, National Archives, https://founders.archives.gov/documents/Jefferson/98-01-02-3827. On Jefferson and nationalism, see Peter S. Onuf, *Jefferson's Empire: The Language of American Nationhood* (Charlottesville, VA: University of Virginia Press, 2000), 76–79, and, especially, Brian Steele, *Thomas Jefferson and American Nationhood* (New York: Cambridge University Press, 2012). Professor Steele notes, "The tired and generally unexamined assertion that

Jefferson meant *Virginia* when he said 'my country,' for example, is not only empirically false – Jefferson's 'country' could mean Virginia, America, or Albemarle County, depending on the context – but it is also analytically useless, telling us little about the way Jefferson's deepest values were an inseparable amalgamation of the cosmopolitan, nationalist, and provincial." Ibid. 3. It is possible, Professor Steele suggests, that Jefferson would have sided with Lincoln and the Union in the Civil War, given that "Jefferson was willing to enforce federal law in the face of opposition by state and local authorities, that he believed the Union was empowered to coerce a seceding state, and that he claimed executive prerogative in cases of national self-preservation or even of national interest." Ibid., 289.

86. John Quincy Adams, *An Oration Addressed to the Citizens of the Town of Quincy, on the Fourth of July, 1831, the Fifty-Fifth Anniversary of the Independence of the United States of America* (Boston: Richardson, Lord and Holbrook 1831), 6–7. For context, see Bernadette Meyler, "Between the States and the Signers: The Politics of the Declaration of Independence before the Civil War," *Southern California Law Review* 89, no. 3 (March 2016): 541–74.

87. Adams, *Oration*, 17–18.

88. Ibid., 20.

89. Ibid., 35. In 1871, Congress enacted a law declaring July 4, 1776, "the birthday of the nation" and providing for a centennial celebration. Act of March 3, 1871, ch. 105, 16 Stat. 470–71.

90. The passage most typically cited is from the English translation of *The Law of Nations* by the Swiss writer Emer de Vattel, originally published in French in 1758. Vattel wrote: "In short, several sovereign and independent states may unite themselves together by a perpetual confederacy, without each in particular ceasing to be a perfect state. They will form together a federal republic: the deliberations in common will offer no violence to the sovereignty of each member, though they may, in certain respects, put some constraint on the exercise of it, in virtue of voluntary engagements. A person does not cease to be free and independent, when he is obliged to fulfil the obligations into which he has very willingly entered. Such were formerly the cities of Greece; such are at present the Seven United Provinces of the Netherlands, and such the members of the Helvetic body." Emer de Vattel, *The Law of Nations; or Principles of the Law of Nature: Applied to the Conduct and Affairs of Nations and Sovereigns* (London: J. Newbery et al., 1760).

This passage, however, must be used with caution. First, it is part of cursory introductory material to Vattel's larger treatise; it is asserted, but not argued in any depth. Second, there is considerable reason to doubt that Vattel was central to the thinking of colonial Americans about confederacies in 1776. A search of America's Historical Imprints database, for example, reveals only one citation to Vattel between 1766 and 1780, and a search of America's Historical Newspapers database reveals only two citations to Vattel between

1772 and 1781; none were about the nature of confederacies. I have located no source from the 1770s directly linking the Declaration or the Articles to this passage in Vattel. The closest is a December 1775 letter from Benjamin Franklin thanking the Frenchman Charles-Guillaume-Frédéric Dumas for a copy of Vattel's treatise. Benjamin Franklin to Charles-Guillaume-Frédéric Dumas, Dec. 9, 1775, *Founders Online*, National Archives, https://founders.archives.gov/documents/Franklin/01-22-02-0172. Franklin stated that members of Congress frequently consulted the treatise for knowledge of the law of nations. Even assuming that the savvy Franklin was not simply flattering his audience, nothing in Franklin's letter suggests that Vattel's statements about confederacies – as opposed to the international conduct of nations – was of particular interest. Similarly, Vattel is mentioned only a handful of times in the *Letters of Delegates to Congress*, and not for any point about confederacies. *LDC*, 26: 741. Moreover, it appears that late eighteenth-century Americans relied on a wide variety of sources for international law principles and did not always agree with Vattel. Brian Richardson, "The Use of Vattel in the American Law of Nations," *American Journal of International Law* 106, no. 3 (July 2012): 547–71. Cornell law professor Brian Richardson notes, "The legal theory buttressing Vattel's law of nations … was never adopted by Founding-era U.S. lawyers. In fact, legal work product during this era articulated a basis for the obligation of the law of nations that is directly opposed to the account given in Vattel's *Droit des gens*." Ibid., 560. There is no reason to assume that Vattel's understanding of confederacies, rather than Pufendorf's, which is quite different, was foremost on the minds of the drafters of the Declaration and the Articles. When Elbridge Gerry sought books on international law for Congress when it was in exile in York, he requested Vattel, Grotius, and Pufendorf. Elbridge Gerry to Thomas Wharton, Nov. 8, 1777, *LDC*, 8: 242. Finally, Vattel's statement about confederacies is in many ways beside the point. It assumes previously completely independent states coming together in some form (the immediately preceding passage is about states that share a common king). But the American colonies were never completely independent states, and so their status must be understood through the actual practice of government rather than through abstract theory. Indeed, taken to the extreme, Vattel's passage seems to suggest that even today the American states might constitute independent nations.

Part III Making Government Work

1. Antonin Scalia, *A Matter of Interpretation* (Princeton, NJ: Princeton University Press, 1997), 134.
2. Saikrishna B. Prakash, "America's Aristocracy," *Yale Law Journal* 109, no. 3 (1999): 553–54.

3. Martin Diamond, "The Revolution of Sober Expectations," in *America's Continuing Revolution: An Act of Conservation* (Washington DC: American Enterprise Institute, 1973–1975), 31–32.
4. Willmoore Kendall and George W. Carey, *The Basic Symbols of the American Political Tradition* (Baton Rouge, LA: Louisiana State University Press, 1970), 83; see also Dan Himmelfarb, "The Constitutional Relevance of the Second Sentence of the Declaration of Independence," *Yale Law Journal* 100, no. 1 (October 1990): 174 ("the Declaration is not concerned with democracy – or, for that matter, with any particular form of government").
5. Pauline Maier, *American Scripture: Making the Declaration of Independence* (New York: Vintage, 1997), 105.
6. John Lind, *An Answer to the Declaration of the American Congress* (London: T Cadell, 1776), 11–12.
7. Ibid., 120. On Lind, see Neil L. York, "Natural Rights Dissected and Rejected: John Lind's Counter to the Declaration of Independence," *Law and History Review* 35, no. 3 (2017): 563–93.
8. [Thomas Hutchinson], *Strictures upon the Declaration of the Congress at Philadelphia* (London: 1776), 10. For a British critique of the second paragraph, see *The Scots Magazine*, Aug. 1776, 433–34. On this critique, see Emily Sneff, "Self-Evident Falsehood," *Declaration Stories*, Sept. 17, 2025, www.declarationstories.org/stories/self-evident-falsehood.
9. Maier, *American Scripture*, 106.
10. Carl L. Becker, *The Declaration of Independence: A Study in the History of Political Ideas* (New York: Vintage, 1922), 23.
11. For an historical overview of the charges, see Hans L. Eicholz, *Harmonizing Sentiments: The Declaration of Independence and the Jeffersonian Idea of Self-Government* (New York: Peter Lang, 2001); Steven Sarson, *The Course of Human Events: The Declaration of Independence and the Historical Origins of the United States* (Charlottesville, VA: University of Virginia Press, 2025), 107–40; Woody Holton, "The Twenty-Six Grievances," in *The Cambridge Companion to the Declaration of Independence*, ed. Michael Zuckert and Mark A. Graber (New York: Cambridge University Press, 2026), 19–34.

Chapter 7 The Importance of Government and Law

1. Ronald Hamowy, "The Declaration of Independence," in *A Companion to the American Revolution*, ed. Jack P. Greene and J. R. Pole (Malden, MA: Blackwell, 2000), 260.
2. Timothy Sandefur, *The Conscience of the Constitution: The Declaration of Independence and the Right to Liberty* (Washington, DC: Cato Institute, 2014), 5.
3. Oxford English Dictionary Online, www.oed.com/dictionary/wholesome_adj?tab=etymology.

4. William Shakespeare, *Hamlet*, Act 1, Scene 1.
5. George Washington, General Orders, Aug. 5, 1776, *Founders Online*, National Archives, https://founders.archives.gov/documents/Washington/03-05-02-0427.
6. Benjamin Franklin, *Cool Thoughts on the Present Situation of Our Public Affairs* (Philadelphia: W. Dunlap, 1764), 21.
7. Richard Thompson to George Washington, Sept. 30, 1773, *Founders Online*, National Archives, https://founders.archives.gov/documents/Washington/02-09-02-0264.
8. Steve Pincus, *The Heart of the Declaration: The Founders' Case for an Activist Government* (New Haven, CT: Yale University Press, 2016), 15, 18.
9. Ibid., 15.
10. Ibid., 66–67.
11. Ibid., 92.
12. Ibid., 109.
13. John Adams to John Winthrop, June 23, 1776, *Founders Online*, National Archives, https://founders.archives.gov/documents/Adams/06-04-02-0134.
14. William J. Novak, "Legislation, Regulation, and Administration in the American Revolution," *Law and History Review* (2025): 5, https://doi.org/10.1017/S0738248025101235.
15. Cf. Max M. Edling, *A Revolution in Favor of Government: Origins of the U.S. Constitution and the Making of the American States* (New York: Oxford University Press, 2003), 7 ("Far from concerning themselves with how to erect barriers to government, the Federalists argued for a national government with the ability to act."); Brian Steele, *Thomas Jefferson and American Nationhood* (New York: Cambridge University Press, 2012), 192 ("We miss Jefferson's rationale [for opposing Federalist policies in the 1790s] if we mistake it for antistatism for its own sake. The point was always to make government as responsive to public will as possible....").
16. Cf. John Phillip Reid, *Constitutional History of the American Revolution: The Authority of Rights* (Madison, WI: University of Wisconsin Press, 1986), 9 ("Colonial whigs might speak of American rights but they were thinking of English rights guaranteed to Americans by the British constitution.").
17. Jack P. Greene, *Understanding the American Revolution: Issues and Actors* (Charlottesville, VA: University of Virginia Press, 1995), 72.
18. Richard Henry Lee, Draft Address to the People of Great Britain, June 27, 1775, *LDC*, 1: 548.
19. Speech of Lord Camden on the American Declaratory Bill, 1766, *The Parliamentary History of England from the Earliest Period to the Year 1803* (London: Hansard, 1813), 16: 178.
20. *Anecdotes of the Life of the Right Hon. William Pitt* (Dublin: William Porter, 1792), 1: 330.

21. House of Commons, Nov. 27, 1775, *American Archives (4th Ser.)*, ed. Peter Force (Washington, DC: M. St. Clair Clarke & Peter Force, 1846), 6: 193.

22. Jonathan Gienapp, *The Second Creation: Fixing the American Constitution in the Founding Era* (Cambridge, MA: Harvard University Press, 2018), 24.

23. Mary Beth Norton, *1774: The Long Year of Revolution* (New York: Vintage, 2020), 125–26.

24. Resolutions of the Continental Congress, Oct. 19, 1765, https://avalon.law .yale.edu/18th_century/resolu65.asp.

25. "Constitutional Catechism," *Rivington's New York Gazetteer*, Dec. 9, 1773.

26. *Virginia Gazette*, Sept. 30, 1775, in *William and Mary Quarterly Historical Magazine* 20 (1912): 147.

27. Extracts from the Proceedings of the Convention of Maryland, Held at the City of Annapolis, May 15, 1776, *American Archives (4th Ser.)*, 6: 462.

28. Palmer, Hampshire County, June 17, 1776, *American Archives (4th Ser.)*, 6: 701.

29. George Washington to John Hancock, July 10, 1776, *Founders Online*, National Archives, https://founders.archives.gov/documents/Washington/ 03-05-02-0188.

30. Account of Savannah, Georgia, Aug. 10, 1776, *American Archives (5th Ser.)*, ed. Peter Force (Washington, DC: M. St. Clair Clarke & Peter Force, 1848), 1: 882.

31. Thomas Gage to Henry Conway, Dec. 21, 1765, in *The Correspondence of General Thomas Gage with the Secretaries of State, 1763–1775*, ed. Clarence Edwin Carter (New Haven, CT: Yale University Press, 1931), 79. On the Revolution and American lawyers, see Peter Charles Hoffer and Williamjames Hull Hoffer, *The Clamor of Lawyers: The American Revolution and Crisis in the Legal Profession* (Ithaca, NY: Cornell University Press, 2018); Erwin C. Surrency, "The Lawyer and the Revolution," *American Journal of Legal History* 8, no. 2 (April 1964): 125–35.

32. *Bracton on the Laws and Customs of England*, trans. Samuel E. Thorne (Cambridge, MA: Harvard University Press, 1977), 2: 33.

33. John Phillip Reid, *Constitutional History of the American Revolution: Authority to Legislate* (Madison, WI: University of Wisconsin Press, 1991), 140–41.

34. For an exploration of this idea, see Larry D. Kramer, *The People Themselves: Popular Constitutionalism and Judicial Review* (New York: Oxford University Press, 2004), 9–34.

35. *Pennsylvania Evening Post*, May 23, 1775.

36. *Pennsylvania Evening Post*, May 27, 1775.

37. Marbury v. Madison, 5 U.S. (1 Cranch) 137, 163 (1803).

38. Reid, *Authority to Legislate*, 144.

39. Ibid., 310.

40. "National School Celebration of Columbus Day," *Youth's Companion* 65, no. 1 (1892): 446. Later versions would add a comma between "one nation" and "indivisible," somewhat severing the tight connection in the original.

41. For an elaboration of this point, see Andrew L. Seidel, *The Founding Myth: Why Christian Nationalism Is Un-American* (New York: Sterling, 2019), 68–90.
42. T. Young, [n.t.], *Boston Evening Post*, Aug. 27, 1770. On Young's authorship, see Matthew Stewart, *Nature's God: The Heretical Origins of the American Republic* (New York: Norton, 2014), 138.
43. Stewart, *Nature's God*, 183.
44. Ibid., 24–35. On the variety of contemporary skeptical approaches in addition to deism, see Steven K. Green, *Inventing a Christian America: The Myth of the Religious Founding* (New York: Oxford University Press, 2015), 134–38.
45. Green, *Inventing a Christian America*, 169.
46. Pauline Maier, *American Scripture: Making the Declaration of Independence* (New York: Vintage, 1997), 148.
47. See, for example, Carl J. Richard, *The Founders and the Classics* (Cambridge, MA: Harvard University Press, 1995), 308.
48. Barten Holyday, *Decimus Junius Juvenalis, and Aulus Persius Flaccus Translated and Illustrated, as Well with Sculpture as Notes* (Oxford: W. Downing, 1673), 4.

Chapter 8 The Structure of Government

1. George Washington to John Augustine Washington, May 31–June 4, 1776, *Founders Online*, National Archives, https://founders.archives.gov/documents/Washington/03-04-02-0333.
2. John Adams to Mercy Otis Warren, Jan. 8, 1776, *Founders Online*, National Archives, https://founders.archives.gov/documents/Adams/06-03-02-0202.
3. A Small Merchant, *Connecticut Courant*, April 8, 1776.
4. "The Interest of America, Letter II," *New York Journal*, June 13, 1776.
5. *JCC*, 1: 68 (Oct. 14, 1774).
6. Granville Sharpe, *A Declaration of the People's Natural Right to a Share in the Legislature, Which Is the Fundamental Principle of the British Constitution of State* (1774; repr., Philadelphia, PA: John Dunlap, 1774).
7. Jack P. Greene, *The Constitutional Origins of the American Revolution* (Cambridge: Cambridge University Press, 2011), 69.
8. Thomas Jefferson, *A Summary View of the Rights of British America* (Williamsburg, VA: Clementina Rind, 1774), 12.
9. Bernard Bailyn, *The Ideological Origins of the American Revolution*, enl. ed. (Cambridge, MA: Harvard University Press, 1992), 173. On representation more generally, see ibid., 161–75; Gordon Wood, *The Creation of the American Republic, 1776–1787* (New York: Norton, 1972) (Orig. pub. 1969), 162–96.
10. *JCC*, 1: 68 (Oct. 14, 1775).
11. Jonathan Gienapp, *Against Constitutional Originalism: A Historical Critique* (New Haven, CT: Yale University Press, 2024), 50.

12. Jonathan Gienapp, "In Search of Nationhood at the Founding," *Fordham Law Review* 89 (2021): 1789. For an argument that the Declaration supports representative assemblies defining individual rights more broadly than would courts, see Alexander Tsesis, "Self-Government and the Declaration of Independence," *Cornell Law Review* 97, no. 4 (May 2012): 693–752.

13. Act Declaring the Illegality of Ship-Money, Aug. 7, 1941, in S.R. Gardiner, *The Constitutional Documents of the Puritan Revolution, 1628–1660* (Oxford: Clarendon Press, 1889), 115–17.

14. For a detailed examination of this issue, see John Phillip Reid, *Constitutional History of the American Revolution: The Authority to Tax* (Madison, WI: University of Wisconsin Press, 1987).

15. "To Lord North," *Norwich Packet*, April 6, 1775.

16. *To the King's Most Excellent Majesty. The Humble Petition of the General Assembly of the Colony of New-York* (New York: 1775), 2.

17. Pauline Maier, *American Scripture: Making the Declaration of Independence* (New York: Vintage, 1997), 110–11.

18. [Thomas Hutchinson], *Strictures upon the Declaration of the Congress at Philadelphia* (London: 1776), 13–14.

19. [John Lind], *An Answer to the Declaration of the American Congress* (London: Thomas Cadell, 1776), 29.

20. Mary Beth Norton, *1774: The Long Year of Revolution* (New York: Vintage, 2020), 104.

21. Kermit Roosevelt III, "Reconstruction as Revolution," *University of Pennsylvania Journal of Constitutional Law* 25, no. 5 (July 2023): 1079.

22. Cf. David F. Epstein, *The Political Theory of the Federalist* (Chicago: University of Chicago Press, 1984), 215 n.5 ("the Declaration of Independence certainly recommends a government at least partly popular, but does not condemn the English government for not being wholly popular").

23. Stephen E. Lucas, "Justifying America: The Declaration of Independence as a Rhetorical Document," in *American Rhetoric: Context and Criticism*, ed. Thomas W. Benson (Carbondale, IL: Southern Illinois University Press, 1989), 110.

24. Eric Nelson, *The Royalist Revolution: Monarchy and the American Founding* (Cambridge, MA: Harvard University Press, 2014), 4–5. On the views of George III prior to 1776, see Brendan McConville, *The King's Three Faces: The Rise and Fall of Royal America, 1688–1776* (Chapel Hill, NC: University of North Carolina Press, 2006).

25. On virtue, see Wood, *The Creation of the American Republic*, 65–70.

26. James Madison, *The Federalist #51*, in *The Federalist Papers*, ed. Garry Wills (New York: Bantam, 1982), 262.

27. Samuel H. Beer, *To Make a Nation: The Rediscovery of American Federalism* (Cambridge, MA: Harvard University Press, 1993), 187–88.

28. John Phillip Reid, *Constitutional History of the American Revolution: The Authority of Law* (Madison, WI: University of Wisconsin Press, 1993), 160.

29. Jerrilyn Greene Marston, *King and Congress: The Transfer of Political Legitimacy, 1774–1776* (Princeton, NJ: Princeton University Press, 1987), 41.

30. Jefferson, *Summary View*, 16.

31. John Gray, *The Right of the British Legislature to Tax the American Colonies Vindicated* (London: Thomas Becket, 1774), 18–19.

32. Nelson, *Royalist Revolution*, 2–3.

33. Reid, *Authority of Law*, 173.

34. Wood, *Creation of the American Republic*, 141.

35. On the veto at the Constitutional Convention, see Michael W. McConnell, *The President Who Would Not Be King* (Princeton, NJ: Princeton University Press, 2020), 122–26.

36. In 1878, a New York judge observed,

> The United States are so largely indebted to immigration for their power, greatness and prosperity that it would be an act of folly to return to the illiberal policy of George III, who, in consequence thereof, stands charged in the declaration of independence with having endeavored to prevent the population of the states by obstructing law for the naturalization of foreigners and by refusing to pass others to encourage their immigration hither.

In the Matter of the Application of Christern, et al., 56 How. Pr. 5, 22 (N.Y. 1878).

37. Jefferson, *Summary View*, 5–6.

38. Marston, *King and Congress*, 134–35.

39. Maier, *American Scripture*, 110.

40. Hutchinson, *Strictures upon the Declaration*, 19.

41. Lind, *Answer to the Declaration*, 50.

42. Lucas, "Justifying America," 99.

43. On the North Carolina dispute underlying this charge, see Ryan C. Williams, "Personal Jurisdiction and the Declaration of Independence," *Duke Law Journal* 75, no. 2 (Nov. 2025): 247–97.

44. John Baker, *An Introduction to English Legal History*, 5th ed. (Oxford: Oxford University Press, 2019), 178–79.

45. Bailyn, *Ideological Origins*, 106.

46. Ibid.

47. Ibid., 107.

48. Resolution of the House of Representatives, Respecting the Salaries of the Justices of the Superior Court, March 3, 1773, *Speeches of the Governors of Massachusetts, from 1765 to 1775* (Boston: Russell and Gardner, 1818), 398–99.

49. Wood, *Creation of the American Republic*, 160.

50. John Phillip Reid, *Constitutional History of the American Revolution: The Authority of Rights* (Madison, WI: University of Wisconsin Press, 1986),

47–59. Reid notes that "we cannot recapture the extreme euphoria of British and colonist alike when they thought of jury trial." Ibid., 47.

51. William Blackstone, *Commentaries on the Laws of England: A Facsimile of the First Edition of 1765–1768* (Chicago: University of Chicago Press, 1979), 3: 379.

52. Ibid., 4: 343.

53. Carlton F.W. Larson, *The Trials of Allegiance: Treason, Juries, and the American Revolution* (New York: Oxford University Press, 2019), 34–37.

54. On the Quebec Act, see Christian R. Burset, *An Empire of Laws: Legal Pluralism in British Colonial Policy* (New Haven, CT: Yale University Press, 2023), 64–83.

55. *JCC*, 1: 63–73 (Oct. 14, 1774).

56. *JCC*, 2: 145 (July 6, 1775).

57. See generally Akhil Reed Amar, *The Bill of Rights: Creation and Reconstruction* (New Haven, CT: Yale University Press, 1998), 81–118; Steven A. Engel, "The Public's Vicinage Right: A Constitutional Argument," *New York University Law Review* 75, no. 6 (Dec. 2000): 1658–719.

58. Reid, *Authority of Rights*, 48.

59. Alexis de Tocqueville, *Democracy in America*, trans. George Lawrence (New York: Harper & Row, 1966), 272–73.

60. Maier, *American Scripture*, 118

61. Harry V. Jaffa, *The Conditions of Freedom: Essays in Political Philosophy* (Baltimore: Johns Hopkins University Press, 1975), 158.

62. Scott Gerber, *To Secure These Rights: The Declaration of Independence and Constitutional Interpretation* (New York: New York University Press, 1995), 55.

63. Cf. Akhil Reed Amar, *The Bill of Rights: Creation and Reconstruction* (New Haven, CT: Yale University Press, 1998), xii (arguing that the Bill of Rights was originally not about "vesting minorities with substantive rights against popular majorities" but about "structural ideas" intended "not to impede popular majorities but to empower them").

64. Thomas Jefferson to Roger Chew Weightman, June 24, 1826, *Founders Online*, National Archives, https://founders.archives.gov/documents/Jefferson/98-01-02-6179.

Part IV Liberty and Equality

1. See, for example, Pauline Maier, "The Strange History of 'All Men Are Created Equal,'" *Washington and Lee Law Review* 56, no. 3 (Summer 1999): 873–88.

2. Cf. Jack M. Balkin and Sanford Levinson, "To Alter or Abolish," *Southern California Law Review* 89, no. 3 (March 2016): 402 ("the language in the

Declaration that actually mattered the most to the most people in history [was] not the language of equality and rights, but the language of collective sovereignty, independence, and nationalist self-assertion"). On the importance of international recognition, see David M. Golove and Daniel J. Hulsebosch, "A Civilized Nation: The Early American Constitution, the Law of Nations, and the Pursuit of International Recognition," *New York University Law Review* 85 (Oct. 2010): 932–1066. See also David Armitage, "The Declaration of Independence and International Law," *The William and Mary Quarterly*, 59, no. 1 (Jan. 2002): 39–64; Peter S. Onuf, "A Declaration of Independence for Diplomatic Historians," *Diplomatic History* 22, no. 1 (Winter 1998): 71–83.

3. David Armitage, *The Declaration of Independence: A Global History* (Cambridge, MA: Harvard University Press, 2007), 93.

Chapter 9 Debating American Scripture

1. Abraham Lincoln, "Speech in Independence Hall," Feb. 22, 1861, in *The Collected Works of Abraham Lincoln*, ed. Roy P. Basler (New Brunswick, NJ: Rutgers University Press, 1953), 4: 240.

2. Fourth of July Declaration by the President, 1941, available at www.national ww2museum.org/war/articles/july-4-1941-fdrs-address-nation.

3. For example, Declaration of the Immediate Causes Which Induce and Justify the Secession of South Carolina from the Federal Union, Dec. 24, 1860, https://avalon.law.yale.edu/19th_century/csa_scarsec.asp; *Speech of Hon. J. P. Benjamin of Louisiana on the Right of Secession* (n.p., [1861]), 2–3.

4. Alf Landon, Address Accepting the Republican Presidential Nomination in Topeka, Kansas, July 23, 1936, www.presidency.ucsb.edu/documents/ address-accepting-the-republican-presidential-nomination-topeka-kansas.

5. The John Birch Society, "Who We Are," https://jbs.org/about/; cf. Robert D. Dilley, *Message for America: A Hand Book for Those Who Will Defend Freedom* (Des Moines, IA: Independence Press, 1962), 193 (arguing that the United Nations Charter is "simply the machinery for a one world socialist dictatorship" that is "in direct contrast to the principles of the Declaration of Independence").

6. See generally Richard Newman, "Slavery and the Declaration: A Re-Interpretation," in *The Cambridge Companion to the Declaration of Independence*, ed. Michael Zuckert and Mark A. Graber (New York: Cambridge University Press, 2026), 109–22.

7. See generally Annette Gordon-Reed, *The Hemingses of Monticello: An American Family* (New York: Norton, 2008).

8. Steven Sarson, *The Course of Human Events: The Declaration of Independence and the Historical Origins of the United States* (Charlottesville, VA: University of Virginia Press, 2025), 181.

9. The procession denounced George Grenville as the "Projector of American Slavery." *Maryland Gazette*, Oct. 17, 1765, 1. In a later account, Lee's bitter

enemy John Mercer claimed that two of Lee's slaves had led the procession. *Virginia Gazette*, Sept. 26, 1766. On Lee's attempt to become a stamp collector, see Oliver Perry Chitwood, *Richard Henry Lee: Statesman of the Revolution* (Morgantown, WV: West Virginia University Library, 1967), 36.

10. [Benjamin Rush], *An Address to the Inhabitants of the British Settlements in America, upon Slave-keeping* (Philadelphia: John Dunlap, 1773), 29. In one of the earliest pamphlets in the dispute with Great Britain, James Otis of Massachusetts had argued that the "Colonists are by the law of nature free born, as indeed all men are, white or black…. Does it follow that is right to enslave a man because he is black?" James Otis, *The Rights of the British Colonies Asserted and Proved* (Boston: [1764]), 43. In 1774, Abigail Adams wrote to John Adams, stating, "I wish most sincerely there was not a Slave in the province." Slavery was an "iniquitous Scheme" and it was hypocritical for colonial Americans to be "daily robbing and plundering from those who have as good a right to freedom as we have." Abigail Adams to John Adams, Sept. 22, 1774, *Founders Online*, National Archives, https://founders.archives.gov/documents/Adams/04-01-02-0107.

11. Ex parte Merryman, 17 F. Cas. 144, 152 n.3 (C.C.D. Md. 1861) (No. 9487).

12. Scott v. Sandford, 60 U.S. (19 How.) 393, 410 (1857).

13. Ibid.

14. See, for example, Gabriel J. Chin, "*Dred Scott* and Asian Americans," *University of Pennsylvania Journal of Constitutional Law* 24 (2022): 633, 638, 675; Kevin R. Johnson, "*Dred Scott* and Asian Americans: Was Chief Justice Taney the First Critical Race Theorist?," *University of Pennsylvania Journal of Constitutional Law* 24 (2022): 751–65.

15. Robert G. Parkinson, *Thirteen Clocks: How Race United the Colonies and Made the Declaration of Independence* (Chapel Hill, NC: University of North Carolina Press, 2021).

16. William Ewald, "James Wilson and the American Founding," *Georgetown Journal of Law & Public Policy* 17 (2019): 13–14, 16.

17. *JCC*, 5: 498.

18. Thomas Jefferson, "Notes of Proceedings in the Continental Congress," *Founders Online*, National Archives, https://founders.archives.gov/documents/Jefferson/01-01-02-0160.

19. Eric Slauter, "The Declaration of Independence and the New Nation," in *The Cambridge Companion to Thomas Jefferson*, ed. Frank Shuffelton (New York: Cambridge University Press, 2008), 21–22.

20. Fred Kaplan, *His Masterly Pen: A Biography of Jefferson the Writer* (New York: HarperCollins, 2022), 129.

21. John Phillip Reid, *Constitutional History of the American Revolution: The Authority of Rights* (Madison, WI: University of Wisconsin Press, 1986), 84.

22. Willmoore Kendall and George W. Carey, *The Basic Symbols of the American Political Tradition* (Baton Rouge, LA: Louisiana State University Press, 1970), 155.

23. Kermit Roosevelt III, *The Nation That Never Was: Reconstructing America's Story* (Chicago: University of Chicago Press, 2022), 40.

24. Ibid., 42–48; see also Kermit Roosevelt III, "A Tale of Two Americas," *University of Pennsylvania Journal of Constitutional Law* 25, no. 24 (2023): 942; Kermit Roosevelt III, "Reconstruction as Revolution," *University of Pennsylvania Journal of Constitutional Law* 25, no. 5 (July 2023): 1074–80. For a somewhat similar argument, see Harry V. Jaffa, *Crisis of the House Divided: An Interpretation of the Issues in the Lincoln-Douglas Debates* (New York: Doubleday, 1959), 379–80 (suggesting that the principles of the Declaration apply only to the members of a political society).

25. In April 1776, the Continental Congress resolved that "no slaves be imported into any of the thirteen United Colonies." *JCC*, 4: 258 (April 6, 1776).

26. Samuel Johnson, *Taxation no Tyranny* (London: Thomas Cadell, 1775), 89.

27. [Thomas Hutchinson], *Strictures upon the Declaration of the Congress at Philadelphia* (London: 1776), 9–10.

28. [John Lind], *An Answer to the Declaration of the American Congress* (London: Thomas Cadell, 1776), 107.

29. William Gordon, "Letter V," *Independent Chronicle*, Oct. 3, 1776. On Gordon, see George William Pilcher, "William Gordon and the History of the American Revolution," *The Historian* 34, no. 3 (May 1972): 447–64.

30. The manuscript is transcribed in Ruth Bogin, "'Liberty Further Extended': A 1776 Antislavery Manuscript by Lemuel Haynes, *William and Mary Quarterly* 40, no. 1 (Jan. 1983): 85–105.

31. Legislative Council and General Assembly of New Jersey to United States Congress, June 15–16, 1778, https://rotunda.upress.virginia.edu/founders/RNCN-01-01-02-0003-0008-0001.

32. [Anthony Benezet], *Serious Considerations on Several Important Subjects* (Philadelphia: Joseph Crukshank, 1778), 28.

33. [David Cooper], *A Serious Address to the Rulers of America, On the Inconsistency of Their Conduct Respecting Slavery* (Trenton, NJ: Isaac Collins, 1783), 4, 12–13.

34. *Annals of Congress* (Washington, DC: Gales & Seaton, 1834), 1: 351.

35. Ibid., 2: 1469.

36. Cushing's opinion and the complicated procedural history of the enslavement cases can be found in John D. Cushing, "The Cushing Court and the Abolition of Slavery in Massachusetts: More Notes on the 'Quock Walker Case,'" *American Journal of Legal History* 5, no. 2 (April 1961): 118–44.

37. Benjamin Banneker to Thomas Jefferson, Aug. 19, 1791, in *The Papers of Thomas Jefferson*, ed. Charles T. Cullen (Princeton, NJ: Princeton University Press, 1986), 22: 49, 51.

38. David Waldstreicher, *In the Midst of Perpetual Fetes: The Making of American Nationalism, 1776–1820* (Chapel Hill, NC: University of North Carolina Press, 1997), 311–23; Alexander Tsesis, *For Liberty and Equality: The Life and Times of the Declaration of Independence* (New York: Oxford University Press, 2012), 61–78, 93–124; 130–47. In a 1797 will, Richard Randolph of Virginia argued that slavery was inconsistent with "declaration[s] of rights" and with the "inherent, inalienable and imprescriptible rights of man, and of very principle of moral and political honesty." Will of Richard Randolph, 1797, quoted in William Cabell Bruce, *John Randolph of Roanoke, 1773–1833* (New York: G.P. Putnam's Sons, 1922), 1: 104.

39. *Salem Gazette*, Dec. 11, 1819, in *Life and Letters of Joseph Story*, ed. William W. Story (London: John Chapman, 1851), 1: 361.

40. Kate Masur, *Until Justice Be Done: America's First Civil Rights Movement, from the Revolution to Reconstruction* (New York: Norton, 2021), 122.

41. *Argument of John Quincy Adams, before the Supreme Court of the United States* (New York: S.W. Benedict, 1841), 8, 88; see also State v. Hoppess, 1 Ohio Dec. Reprint 105, 110 (Ohio 1845) (opinion of Read, J.) ("True, the great principles of natural right asserted in the Declaration of Independence, and lying at the foundation of our institutions, if permitted to operate, would liberate all.").

42. Masur, *Until Justice Be Done*, 199.

43. David Martin, *Trial of the Reverend Jacob Gruber* (Fredericktown, MD: George Kolb, 1819), 43.

44. On Taney's transformation from antislavery advocate to proslavery zealot, see Timothy S. Huebner, "Roger B. Taney and Slavery Issue: Looking beyond – and before – Dred Scott," *Journal of American History* 97, no. 1 (June 2010): 17–38.

45. Stephen Lucas, "The Declaration of Independence in the Rhetoric of American Politics," in *The Changing Conversation in America: Lectures from the Smithsonian*, ed. William F. Eadie and Paul E. Nelson (Thousand Oaks, CA: Sage, 2002), 48–49.

46. *Register of Debates in Congress, Comprising the Leading Debates and Incidents of the First Session of the Nineteenth Congress* (Washington, DC: Gales & Seaton, 1826), 2: 125.

47. John C. Calhoun, "Speech on the Oregon Bill," June 27, 1848, in *Union and Liberty: The Political Philosophy of John C. Calhoun*, ed. Ross M. Lence (Indianapolis, IN: Liberty Fund, 1992), 566.

48. Ibid., 569.

49. Abraham Lincoln, "Speech on the Dred Scott Decision at Springfield, Illinois," in *Speeches and Writings, 1832–1858* (New York: Literary Classics of the United States, 1989), 399.

50. Ibid., 400.

51. For a survey of ten possible readings of the Declaration's equality language, see Akhil Reed Amar, *Born Equal: Remaking America's Constitution, 1840–1920* (New York: Basic Books, 2025), 346–57.

52. *Scott*, 60 U.S. (19 How.), 574–75 (Curtis, J., dissenting).

53. Ibid., 529 (McLean, J., dissenting).

54. Lincoln, "Speech on the Dred Scott Decision," 398, 396.

55. Lochner v. New York, 198 U.S. 45 (1905).

56. The Slaughterhouse Cases, 83 U.S. 35, 44 (1873) (Field, J., dissenting).

57. Butchers' Union Slaughter-House & Live-Stock Landing Co. v. Crescent City Live-Stock Landing & Slaughter-House Co, 111 U.S. 746, 763 (1884) (Bradley, J., concurring).

58. Ibid., at 756 (Field, J., concurring).

59. Ibid., at 757. On Field's use of the Declaration of Independence in judicial opinions, see Adam M. Carrington, *Justice Stephen Field's Cooperative Constitution of Liberty* (Lanham, MD: Lexington Books, 2017), 139–58.

60. D. J. Brewer, "Protection of Private Property from Public Attack," in *Green Bag 2d* 10 (Summer 2007): 496.

61. Ibid., 497.

62. Ibid., 498.

63. Magoun v. Illinois Trust & Savings Bank, 170 U.S. 283, 301 (1898) (Brewer, J., dissenting).

64. Gulf, C. & S.F. Ry. Co. v. Ellis, 165 U.S. 150, 160 (1897).

65. Cotting v. Godard, 183 U.S. 79, 107 (1901).

66. Allgeyer v. Louisiana, 165 U.S. 578, 589 (1897).

67. Bessette v. People, 62 N.E. 215, 218 (Ill. 1901); State v. Cromwell, 9 N.W.2d 914, 918 (N.D. 1943).

68. NLRB v. Mackay Radio & Telegraph Co., 87 F.2d 611, 615 (9th Cir. 1937).

69. For example, West Coast Hotel v. Parrish, 300 U.S. 379 (1937); United States v. Carolene Products Co., 304 U.S. 144 (1938); Williamson v. Lee Optical, Inc., 348 U.S. 483 (1955).

70. Carlton F.W. Larson, "The Declaration of Independence: A 225th Anniversary Re-Interpretation," *Washington Law Review* 76 (July 2001): 708–12.

71. Grey v. Sanders, 372 U.S. 368, 381 (1963).

72. Engel v. Vitale, 176 N.E.2d 174, 180 (N.Y. 1961).

73. Dykema v. Bloss, 169 N.W.2d 367, 374 (Mich. Ct. App. 1969).

74. For example, United States v. Collins, 920 F.2d 619, 623 (10th Cir. 1990) (noting defendant filed a "an 84-page motion to dismiss, lavishly larded with citations to the Declaration of Independence"); Burroughs v. Wallingford, 780 F.2d 502, 503 (5th Cir. 1986) (rejecting argument that tax liens violated the Declaration of Independence's guarantee of "un-a-lien-able" rights); United States v. Schmitz, 542 F.2d 782, 783 (9th Cir. 1976) (rejecting

argument that 1040 forms violated the defendant's "rights and duties under the Declaration of Independence of 1776").

75. Bostic v. Rainey, 2014 WL 10022686, at *1 (E.D. Va. 2014).

76. Obergefell v. Hodges, 576 U.S. 644, 714 (2015) (Scalia, J., dissenting).

77. *Obergefell,* 721 (Thomas, J., dissenting). Commenters have noted the striking similarities between Thomas's arguments about human dignity in *Obergefell* and the lyrics of one of his favorite songs, Whitney Houston's "The Greatest Love of All." Corey Robin, "From Whitney Houston to Obergefell: Clarence Thomas on Human Dignity," *Corey Robin* (blog), June 29, 2015, https://coreyrobin.com/2015/06/29/from-whitney-houston-to-obergefell-clarence-thomas-on-human-dignity/.

78. Ex parte State ex rel. Alabama Policy Institute, 200 So.3d 495, 569 (Ala. 2015) (Moore, C.J., concurring).

79. Ibid., 599.

80. Harry V. Jaffa, "Judicial Conscience and Natural Rights," in *Original Intent and the Framers of the Constitution: A Disputed Question,* ed. Harry V. Jaffa, Bruce Ledewitz, Robert L. Stone, and George Anastaplo (Washington, DC: Regnery Gateway, 1994), 263.

81. Harry V. Jaffa, *The Conditions of Freedom: Essays in Political Philosophy* (Baltimore: Johns Hopkins University Press, 1975), 150, 159.

82. Banuelos v. University of Wisconsin Hospitals and Clinics Authority, 988 N.W.2d 627 (Wis. 2023) (Bradley, J., dissenting).

83. Reed v. Beckett, 795 S.E.2d 509, 514 (W. Va. 2016) (Benjamin, J., dissenting).

84. Patel v. Texas Dep't of Licensing and Regulation, 469 S.W.3d 69, 120 (Tex. 2015) (Willett, J., concurring).

85. United States v. Padilla, 2023 WL 1964214, at *2 (D.D.C. 2023).

86. Grutter v. Bollinger, 539 U.S. 306, 378 (2003) (Thomas, J., concurring in part and dissenting in part).

87. Adarand Constructors v. Pena, 515 U.S. 200, 240 (1995) (Thomas, J., concurring in part and concurring in the judgment).

88. Students for Fair Admission, Inc. v. President and Fellows of Harvard College, 600 U.S. 181, 266 (2023) (Thomas, J., concurring). For other uses of the Declaration in criticizing affirmative action, see Fullilove v. Klutznick, 448 U.S. 448, 531, n.13 (1980) (Stewart, J., dissenting); ibid., at 533 n.1 (Stevens, J., dissenting).

89. *Students for Fair Admissions,* 384 (Jackson, J., dissenting).

90. For an analysis of the use of the Declaration of Independence in the affirmative action context, see Katie R. Eyer, "The Declaration of Independence as Bellwether," *Southern California Law Review* 89, no. 3 (March 2016): 427–56.

91. For example, Hodes & Nauser, MDs, P.A. v. Schmidt, 440 P.3d 461 (Kan. 2019).

92. For example, LePage v. Center for Reproductive Medicine, P.C., 2024 WL 656591, at *10, n.11 (Ala. 2024) (Parker, C.J., concurring specially); Byrn v. New York City Health & Hospitals Corp., 286 N.E.2d 887, 893 (N.Y. 1972) (Burke, J., dissenting); Ronald Reagan, "The Sanctity of Human Life," Jan. 13, 1984, in *American Soul: The Contested Legacy of the Declaration of Independence*, ed. Justin Buckley Dyer (Lanham, MD: Rowan & Littlefield, 2012), 134.

93. Alexander Tsesis, "Self-Government and the Declaration of Independence," *Cornell Law Review* 97, no. 4 (May 2012): 695.

94. There is also substantial support for equality in the Constitution's prohibitions on titles of nobility (which were also included in the Articles of Confederation). Although seldom litigated, these provisions were broadly interpreted in the eighteenth century as significantly restricting state grants of hereditary privilege. Carlton F.W. Larson, "Titles of Nobility, Hereditary Privilege, and the Unconstitutionality of Legacy Preferences in Public School Admissions," *Washington University Law Review* 84, no. 6 (2006): 1375–440.

Conclusion

1. Associated Press, "Trump hangs a copy of Declaration of Independence in Oval Office," March 17, 2025, https://apnews.com/article/trump-declaration-of-independence-oval-office-5b9b9a07ac61ab303d77bcb4f6f252e5.

2. James Bickerton, "Donald Trump Describing Declaration of Independence Goes Viral," *Newsweek*, www.newsweek.com/donald-trump-describing-declaration-independence-goes-viral-2067169.

3. Video of July 22 Oval Office Remarks, available at https://x.com/ReallyAmerican1/status/1947690817319239789.

4. For example, Aaron Rupar and Thor Benson, "The Declaration of Independence's warning for Trump," *Public Notice*, April 18, 2025, www.publicnotice.co/p/joanne-freeman-interview-trump?utm_campaign=post; David Corn and Tim Murphy, "Here Are the Declaration of Independence's Grievances against King George III. Many Apply to Trump," *Mother Jones*, July 3, 2025, www.motherjones.com/politics/2025/07/declaration-of-independences-grievances-against-king-george-iii-many-apply-to-trump/.

5. Franchise Tax Board of California v. Hyatt, 587 U.S. 230, 237 (2019).

6. See, for example, Seminole Tribe v. Florida, 517 U.S. 44, 95 (1996) (Stevens, J., dissenting) ("The recitation in the Declaration of Independence of the wrongs committed by George III made [the proposition that the king could do no wrong] unacceptable on this side of the Atlantic.").

7. Steven Sarson, *The Course of Human Events: The Declaration of Independence and the Historical Origins of the United States* (Charlottesville, VA: University of Virginia Press, 2025), 108.

8. David Dewitt, "Ohio Gerrymandering: A Brief and Awful History of the Very Recent Past," *Ohio Capital Journal*, Oct. 11, 2024.

9. Reynolds v. Sims, 377 U.S. 533, 562 (1964).

10. Rucho v. Common Cause, 588 U.S. 684 (2019). In an earlier case, the Court stated, "The conception of political equality from the Declaration of Independence, to Lincoln's Gettysburg Address, to the Fifteenth, Seventeenth, and Nineteenth Amendments can mean only one thing – one person, one vote." Gray v. Sanders, 372 U.S. 368, 381 (1963).

11. Oliver Wendell Holmes, Jr., "The Path of The Law," *Boston Law School Magazine* 1, no. 4 (1897): 11.

INDEX

For EU product safety concerns, contact us at Calle de José Abascal, 56–1°,
28003 Madrid, Spain or eugpsr@cambridge.org.

www.ingramcontent.com/pod-product-compliance
Ingram Content Group UK Ltd.
Pitfield, Milton Keynes, MK11 3LW, UK
UKHW022126100626
472046UK00013B/2004